The Synthetic Biology Primer

A Plain English Guide to Programming Living Systems for Engineers, Entrepreneurs, and the Curious Professional

C. Louis-Charles PhD

Contents

Introduction

Welcome to a Programmable Field

Something fundamental shifted in biology, and it happened faster than most people realize. For most of human history, biology was a science of observation. You watched organisms, cataloged their behaviors, mapped their chemistry, and tried to understand the machinery that evolution had been refining for 3.8 billion years. That era is over. Biology is now something you design. It is, in a precise and increasingly industrial sense, a programmable system, and the engineers and entrepreneurs who grasped that fact first are already building with it.

Consider three events that illustrate the shift. In January 2020, when the genetic sequence of a novel coronavirus was published online, Moderna's team began designing a vaccine. The first candidate sequence was complete within 48 hours. That speed was possible because the vaccine, in a rigorous engineering sense, was a piece of code executed by human cells. The mRNA instructions told the body's machinery to build a specific protein, generate an immune response, and stand ready. The code was written, tested computationally, and sent to fabrication before most governments had finished drafting emergency response plans.

Second event: Bolt Threads is producing spider silk stronger than steel, not by farming spiders at scale but by taking the gene that instructs a spider to build silk, copying it, and expressing it inside engineered yeast—the yeast ferments in large tanks. The silk protein comes out the other side. A material that nature took millions of years to develop is now made in a bioreactor at the scale a company needs to ship a product.

Third event: in research labs and biotechnology companies, scientists are engineering bacteria to navigate the tumor microenvironment and deliver therapeutic payloads directly to cancer cells, programming immune cells to recognize cancer antigens with molecular specificity no chemotherapy drug can replicate, and designing organisms that degrade industrial pollutants and sequester atmospheric carbon at rates no purely chemical process can match. These are not speculative futures. They are current engineering projects operating at commercial or near-commercial scale in Boston, San Francisco, Singapore, and Shenzhen.

What connects them is a single radical idea: that the genetic code is an information system, that biological parts can be standardized and assembled like components in a circuit, and that the same iterative design-build-test-learn cycle that produced the modern software industry can be applied to living systems. That idea is synthetic biology. And you are reading this at the precise moment when it has moved from theoretical to industrial.

Diagram I.1 - The Synthetic Biology Stack

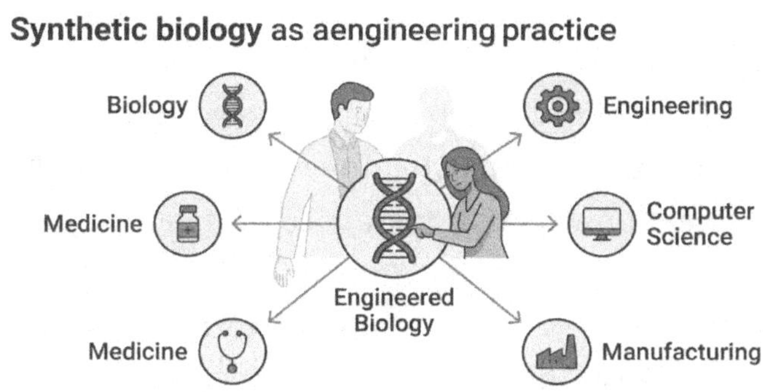

Synthetic biology sits at the intersection of biology, engineering, and computer science. It uses engineering vocabulary: parts, devices, systems, design cycles, and modularity. It uses the physical substrate of biology: DNA, RNA, proteins, and cells. And it uses the informatics logic of computer science: logic gates, feedback loops, optimization, and iteration. When those three disciplines converge, the result is an engineering field unlike any that came before it, one whose raw material is the most sophisticated information-processing system on Earth.

Who This Book Is For

This book was written for you specifically, and you know who you are. You are the software engineer who has spent a career thinking in systems, optimization loops, and abstractions, and who has started to notice that every hard problem in computer science has a biological analog that is older, messier, and more powerful. You have been looking for the right on-ramp to this field. This book is that on-ramp.

You are the biotech entrepreneur sitting across the table from a synthetic biology pitch, realizing you do not yet have the framework to evaluate what they are actually building. The deck mentions CRISPR, metabolic engineering, and a proprietary chassis organism. You can follow the market-size slide. You are less certain about the technical moat. By the time you finish this book, you will know exactly what questions to ask and why those questions matter.

You are the policy professional drafting regulatory guidance on mRNA therapeutics or agricultural biotechnology, and feeling that the briefing documents your agency provides do not give you the technical depth you need to make confident judgments. Science is moving faster than the governance frameworks. This book provides the scientific foundation for good governance.

You are the curious professional in finance, consulting, journalism, or law who has read six articles about CRISPR babies, lab-grown meat, and mRNA vaccines and wants the actual engineering explanation, not the headline. You are not looking for a textbook. You are looking for a clear and substantive account of what is actually being built, how it works, and what it means. That is what this book provides.

Why Most Synthetic Biology Books Fail You

Most books that attempt to explain synthetic biology to a professional audience fall into one of two traps, and this book deliberately avoids both.

The first trap is reduction. The reductive approach treats CRISPR as if it were the whole story of synthetic biology, much like explaining software engineering by focusing only on the text editor. CRISPR is one tool in a much larger engineering toolkit that includes promoters, repressors, ribosome-binding sites, plasmids, BioBrick assembly standards, metabolic pathway engineering, and genetic circuits that implement logical operations within living cells. A reader who learns only about CRISPR has encountered one scalpel in a fully equipped operating theater. This book gives you the whole theater.

The second trap is completeness. The exhaustive approach presents every regulatory network, every metabolic flux pathway, and every molecular mechanism in the academic detail appropriate for a graduate course in bioengineering. It is thorough and largely unreadable by anyone without a relevant PhD. The non-specialist reader exits around page sixty, not because the material is too difficult, but because the presentation is not calibrated for someone who thinks in systems and needs the engineering logic.

This book takes a third path. It explains synthetic biology as an engineering discipline using correct and precise technical vocabulary. When a term appears for the first time, it gets a plain-language explanation in the same sentence or the next one. Then the term stays in use, because the reader who thinks in systems can hold real vocabulary once it is anchored to a clear concept. The analogies earn their place because they reveal something true about the underlying mechanism. An AND gate inside a living cell is not a loose metaphor: it is a description of how two molecular inputs interact to produce or suppress an output, and the logic is mathematically equivalent to the Boolean gate in a processor.

Meet Helix Forge

The narrative anchor throughout this book is Helix Forge, a fictional Boston-based synthetic biology startup founded in 2021 with a mission to make biology as programmable as software. Working across medicine, biomanufacturing, and diagnostics, Helix Forge brings together molecular biologists, bioengineers, and policy experts under one roof. Every chapter opens with a scene from Helix Forge that grounds the science in a real entrepreneurial context. There are four members of the founding team, and each represents one of the readers this book was written for.

Dr. Priya Anand, Co-Founder and Chief Science Officer, is a molecular biologist who spent a decade at MIT's Department of Biological Engineering. Priya brings the deepest scientific expertise on the team and the least patience for hand-waving. She sets the scientific direction, pushes back against analogies that sacrifice accuracy for elegance, and serves as the reader's guarantee that the science in this book is correct. Her instinct is always to ask: but how does it actually work at the molecular level?

Marcus Webb, Co-Founder and CEO, is a software engineer-turned biotech entrepreneur who turned to synthetic biology after realizing that every optimization problem he had solved in tech had a living equivalent. Marcus is the book's primary narrative vehicle and the reader's truest avatar. His "wait, explain that again from first principles" questions drive the book's clearest explanations. His journey from intelligent outsider to informed operator is the arc of the book itself.

Dr. Yuki Tanaka, Head of Genetic Circuit Design, is a bioengineering PhD who spent her postdoctoral years at the Wyss Institute designing genetic logic gates that could sense disease biomarkers and trigger therapeutic responses. Yuki now leads Helix Forge's design team. She can describe a promoter as a power switch and mean it precisely. She represents the beginning engineer who wants to understand technical foundations without drowning in a molecular biology textbook.

Carlos Rivera, Regulatory Affairs and Bioethics Analyst, joined Helix Forge after two years at the FDA's Office of Biotechnology Products. He is the youngest founding member and the most consequential voice when the question changes from "can we?" to "should we?". He represents policy professionals, ethicists, and legal specialists who know that the quality of their judgment depends entirely on the quality of their technical understanding.

Diagram I.2 - The Helix Forge Team

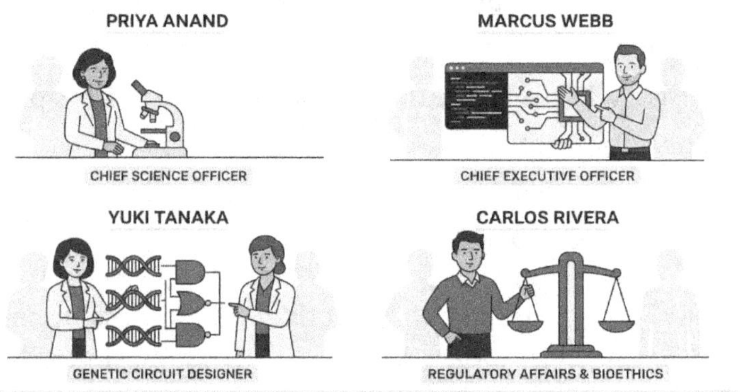

What You Will Be Able To Do

By the time you reach the last page of this book, you will be able to evaluate synthetic biology, its claims, its investments, its regulatory debates, and its research headlines, from a position of genuine understanding rather than informed-sounding guesswork.

You will understand what synthetic biologists mean when they describe a design-build-test-learn cycle: how each iteration produces data that refines the next design, why this resembles software development more than classical bench science, and what it means for the speed of the field when each step becomes faster and cheaper.

You will understand what CRISPR actually is: a bacterial immune system repurposed as a molecular scalpel that can find a specific sequence of DNA in a genome of three billion base pairs and make a precise edit at that location. You will understand how it fits into the broader genetic toolkit, and what comes after it: base editing, which changes individual DNA letters without cutting the double helix; prime editing, which writes new sequences with fewer unintended effects; and CRISPR-based diagnostics that use the same molecular targeting to detect pathogens rather than edit genes.

You will understand how genetic circuits implement logical operations inside living cells. An AND gate produces output only when two molecular inputs are both present. A toggle switch holds one of two stable states until a specific signal flips it to the other state. A repressilator oscillates on a precise timer. These are descriptions of how biological systems process information, and the logic is as precise as anything in a silicon processor.

You will understand the ethical stakes with the clarity that comes from knowing the science. The dual-use problem is not hypothetical. The germline editing debate concerns specific technical capabilities that exist today. Environmental release questions for engineered organisms are active regulatory considerations for field trials happening now. You will be able to engage in these debates with the scientific grounding they require.

And you will see where synthetic biology and artificial intelligence are converging. Machine learning models are designing protein sequences, predicting the behavior of genetic circuits before any biological experiment is run, and optimizing metabolic pathways in silico. When the design phase of the engineering cycle is automated, the pace of the field changes qualitatively. You will understand what that convergence means.

How To Read This Book

This book moves from first principles to applied domains to ethical and strategic implications. You can read it cover to cover, or navigate to chapters most relevant to your immediate needs. Each chapter stands on its own while building on what came before.

Chapter 1, The Living Machine, establishes the foundational vocabulary: what a cell is from an engineering perspective, what DNA does, and how genes work. Start here if you are new to biology. Chapter 2, A Brief and Wild History of Programming Life, traces humanity's evolution from selective breeding to recombinant DNA to the modern era of programmable organisms.

Chapter 3, The Genetic Toolkit, surveys the full set of biological parts and assembly methods: promoters, repressors, ribosome binding sites, plasmids, BioBrick standards, and the registries that catalog them. This chapter puts CRISPR in context. Chapter 4, CRISPR and the Precision Revolution, then explains in detail how CRISPR-

Cas9 works, how base editing and prime editing extend the precision revolution, and what CRISPR-based diagnostics demonstrate about the platform's range.

Chapter 5, Designing Genetic Circuits, explains how logical operations are implemented inside living cells. Chapter 6, Medicine Reimagined, covers mRNA vaccines, CAR-T cell therapies, and engineered bacteria as living medicines. Chapter 7, The Living Factory, explains biomanufacturing and how engineered microbes produce chemicals, materials, and fuels at a commercial scale.

Chapter 8, Engineering What We Eat, covers precision fermentation, cultivated meat, and nitrogen-fixing microbes. Chapter 9, Biology That Listens, explains biosensors and their applications in diagnostics and environmental monitoring. Chapter 10, Biology as Planetary Engineer, addresses bioremediation and biological carbon capture.

Chapter 11, The Ethics of Engineering Life, takes on the hardest questions: dual-use research, germline editing, environmental release, and the governance structures that different jurisdictions have developed in response. Chapter 12, The Road Ahead, synthesizes the book and looks ahead to the convergence of synthetic biology and AI, as well as to what the next decade will look like for engineers, entrepreneurs, and policymakers.

Takeaway

Biology has become a design space. The mechanisms driving this transformation are real, the commercial applications are already generating revenue, and the pace of progress is governed by the same cost curves and iteration dynamics that drive every engineering field that has passed through its foundational phase. The field is not emerging. It has emerged.

This book gives you the understanding you need to operate in it. It does not require a biology degree. It requires the systems-thinking habit of mind you almost certainly already have, applied to a substrate you are about to know deeply. Every concept in these pages was chosen because it earns its place in a complete and honest account of what synthetic biology is, how it works, and what it means.

Priya, Marcus, Yuki, and Carlos are waiting at Helix Forge. The lab is running. There are decisions to make, experiments to design, and arguments to have about what is possible, what is permitted, and what is worth building. The first principles explanation starts on the next page.

The next twelve chapters are not organized as a survey or a history. They are organized as a curriculum for a professional who needs to operate in a field, not pass an exam about it. Each chapter isolates one part of the synthetic biology stack, builds your understanding of that part from the ground up, shows it working in the Helix Forge context, and then names the real companies, real clinical trials, and real products that demonstrate the part in action. By the end, you will have a complete mental model of the field, assembled one layer at a time, the same way a compiler assembles a program.

Understanding synthetic biology also means understanding what it is not. It is not a technology that will replace human judgment with automated biology pipelines any more than software engineering replaced the need for thoughtful system design. Every engineered organism still requires a human researcher to define the biological objective, choose the right chassis, design the genetic parts, interpret the test data, and iterate toward a working system. The tools are becoming faster and more powerful. The need for rigorous human reasoning at every step of the engineering cycle is not diminishing. It is, if anything, increasing, because the design space is now so large that bad decisions can be executed with extraordinary efficiency.

1 The Living Machine

Opening Scenario

Marcus Webb had written software for fifteen years. He had shipped distributed systems that handled millions of concurrent requests and debugged race conditions at three in the morning. He spent four days tracking a memory leak to a single misplaced pointer. He was comfortable with complexity. He was not comfortable with what he saw when he first walked into the Helix Forge lab.

Dr. Priya Anand was waiting at the bench, holding a petri dish up to the window. Inside it, a colony of bacteria glowed faintly yellow in the morning light, alive and luminescent. She let him stare, then lowered the dish. "These bacteria are producing a precursor compound that the pharmaceutical industry has historically manufactured using an oil refinery. We gave them a new genetic program. They run it every time they divide." Marcus opened his mouth and then closed it. Priya almost smiled. "That is what we do here. We program cells the way you used to program computers."

Marcus would spend the next six months asking Priya to explain that again from first principles, in progressively more detail, until he could hold the whole picture in his head. This chapter is the first explanation. It does not assume a biology degree. It assumes you are a careful thinker who has just picked up a glowing petri dish for the first time and wants to know, precisely, what you are holding.

Why It Matters

Synthetic biology matters at every level you care to examine. At the company level, it opens product categories that did not exist five years ago: medicines designed for your genome, materials grown without fossil fuels, food produced without slaughter, sensors that detect disease before symptoms appear. At the industry level, it is reorganizing the competitive map of pharmaceuticals, agriculture, materials science, and energy simultaneously.

At the civilization level, it gives humanity a design interface to the biological world that no previous generation has possessed.

If you are an engineer, the relevance is structural: your field has extended into a new substrate. The design patterns you already know, feedback loops, modularity, abstraction layers, and iterative testing all apply. If you are an entrepreneur or investor, the relevance is strategic: this is a horizontal enabling technology that shifts competitive dynamics across every vertical it touches. If you are a policy professional or regulator, the relevance is governance. Every decision about what synthetic biology is permitted to do depends on understanding what it actually is at the engineering level.

Before we get to CRISPR, genetic circuits, engineered medicines, or bioremediation, this chapter answers three questions cleanly. What actually changed, and when? What is synthetic biology, precisely? And why is this the moment when it all became practical?

Diagram 1.1 - The Biology-Technology Convergence Timeline

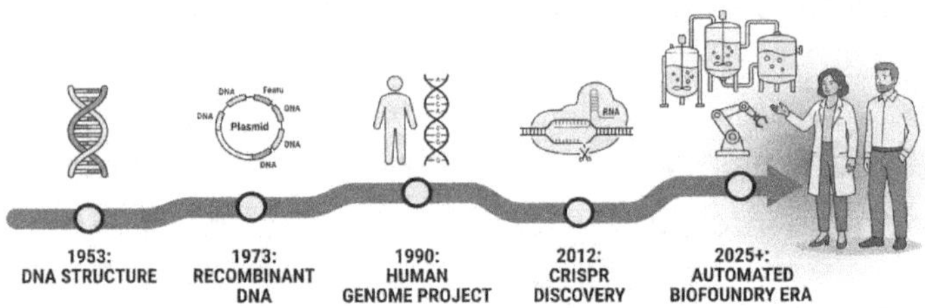

A visual journey tracing the accelerating impact of biological insights and technological capabilities, converging to enable complex engineering of life.

The timeline above compresses seventy years into a single image because the compression is instructive. Each node represents not just a discovery but a new capability: a door that opened and did not close again. The pace is also increasing. The time in calendar years between the Human Genome Project and the automated biofoundry is shorter than the time between the discovery of DNA structure and the first recombinant DNA experiments.

For the reader who thinks in terms of platform shifts, the pattern is familiar. Personal computers did not become commercially significant the moment the transistor was invented. The gap between foundational discovery and widespread application is often measured in decades. In biology, that gap has been shortening with each cycle. The question is not whether synthetic biology will matter. It is already mattering. The question is whether you will be fluent in its language when the decisions that affect you require that fluency.

From Observing Life to Designing It

For most of the history of science, biology was a discipline of observation. You studied organisms, cataloged their anatomy and behaviors, mapped their chemical reactions, and built accurate models of the machinery that evolution had been refining for 3.8 billion years. That work was profound. But something fundamental changed in the last thirty years, and the change can be described precisely. Biology became designable.

The best analogy is the shift from astronomy to aerospace. Astronomy is the science of observing the sky: cataloging stars, tracing orbits, and measuring the composition of distant atmospheres. It is a discipline of exquisite precision. Aerospace is something categorically different. It uses knowledge of the sky, gravity, and fluid dynamics not to observe but to navigate. The astronomer describes what is there. The aerospace engineer specifies what will happen, and then makes it happen.

Classical biology was astronomy. Synthetic biology is aerospace. Classical biology describes the living world with increasing precision. The synthetic biologist uses that description as a parts catalog and a set of operating rules, then builds systems the living world would never have built on its own. The shift is not a criticism of classical biology. It is recognition that a sufficient understanding of how living systems work eventually becomes sufficient to re-engineer them, and we have crossed that threshold in several domains simultaneously.

Diagram 1.2 - Astronomy to Aerospace: Observing vs. Designing Life

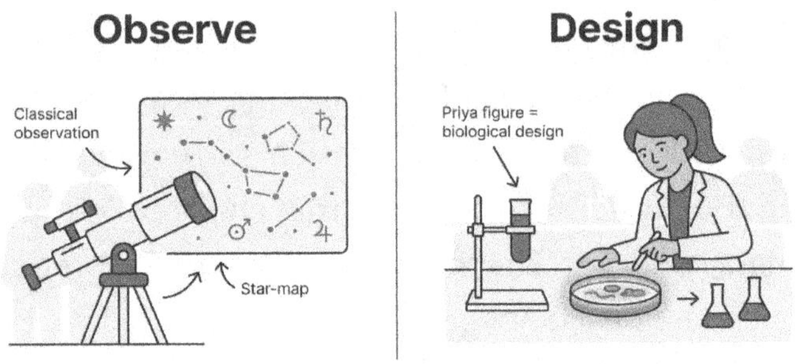

Mattnm caption comparisortes with board of an executive technical tone

When biology was observational, the bottleneck was knowledge. When it becomes designable, the bottleneck moves: the limiting factor becomes the ability to specify, build, and test biological systems quickly enough to learn from each iteration. That shift explains the emergence of the biofoundry, the automated design-build-test cycle, and the standardized parts registry. These are the institutional infrastructure of an engineering discipline that did not exist a generation ago.

Marcus, hearing this for the first time, leaned forward. "So the first generation of genetic engineers were more like astronomers than aerospace engineers. They could move a gene. They could not design a system." Priya nodded. "Exactly. A gene moved from one organism to another does one thing. A genetic circuit designed to sense a signal, process it, and produce a calibrated response does something qualitatively different. That is the gap between genetic engineering and synthetic biology, and it is not a small gap."

What Synthetic Biology Actually Is

The term synthetic biology is used loosely in the popular press. Some articles use it to mean CRISPR. Others use it to mean lab-grown meat. Others use it to mean any use of engineered organisms. None of those usages is precise enough to be useful. Here is a definition: Synthetic biology is the engineering of biological parts, devices, and systems that do not exist in nature, or the redesign of existing natural biological systems for new purposes, using the tools and workflows of an engineering discipline.

Every word carries weight. "Engineering" means there is a design phase, a build phase, a test phase, and an iteration cycle. The designer specifies what she wants the system to do before building it. She uses standardized components whose behavior is characterized. She measures actual output against intended output and uses the gap to improve the design. This workflow, familiar to anyone who has shipped software or designed a circuit board, is the organizing logic of synthetic biology.

"Parts, devices, and systems" is a three-level hierarchy borrowed directly from electrical engineering. A part is a basic functional unit: a DNA sequence that acts as a promoter (a power switch controlling whether a gene is read), or a ribosome binding site (a sequence controlling how efficiently a gene's instructions become protein). A device is a combination of parts that performs a specific function: a genetic toggle switch flipped between ON and OFF by a chemical signal. A system is a collection of devices that together produce complex behavior, sensing an input, processing it through defined logic, and generating a calibrated output.

Diagram 1.3 - Parts, Devices, Systems: The Three-Level Hierarchy

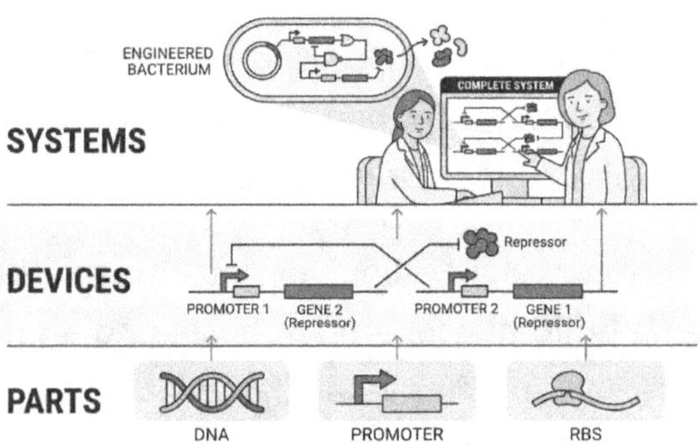

BUILDING BIOLOGICAL COMPLEXITY THROUGH HIERARCHICAL DESIGN.

The hierarchy matters because it enables the management of complexity. You design a genetic system by composing characterized parts into devices with known behavior, then composing those devices into systems. Each level of abstraction hides the complexity below, exactly as in software engineering: the developer writing a web application does not think about transistor states, and the synthetic biologist designing an engineered organism does not think about every base pair.

Synthetic biology is not a synonym for genetic engineering or for CRISPR. It is not simply using organisms to make products: that practice predates written history. Synthetic biology is the disciplined, engineering-style design of biological systems, and the word "engineering" is doing real work in that definition. The field exists because the tools for designing, building, and testing biological systems became precise and affordable enough to support a genuine engineering workflow.

Genetic Engineering vs. Synthetic Biology

The distinction between genetic engineering and synthetic biology trips up many smart readers. The confusion is understandable: both involve modifying DNA, both use molecular biology tools, and the boundary is not always sharp in practice. But the conceptual distinction is clean enough to state precisely, and it matters for everything that follows.

Genetic engineering, in its original and still most common usage, means transferring a gene or genes from one organism to another, or modifying a specific gene in place. Insulin-producing bacteria, the first major commercial product of genetic engineering, were created by inserting the human insulin gene into E. coli. The bacterium now carried a gene it did not have before and expressed it to produce insulin. This was a profound accomplishment given the limited systems logic: one gene was moved, one protein was produced, and one function was added.

Synthetic biology starts from a different premise. The question is not which gene to move but what system to design. The analogy Yuki uses is the difference between copying a paragraph from one document to another versus writing software from a standard library. Genetic engineering copies the paragraph. Synthetic biology specifies the architecture, selects parts from a characterized library, assembles them into functional modules, and tests system behavior against a design specification.

Diagram 1.4 - Genetic Engineering vs. Synthetic Biology: Copy vs. Design

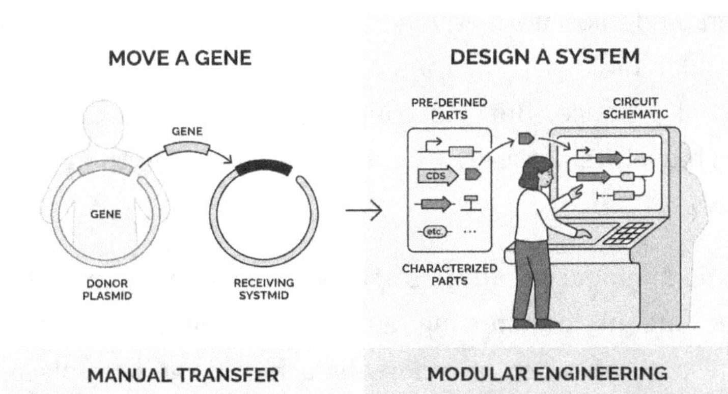

In practice, the distinction shows up in tools and intent. A genetic engineer works with a small number of well-characterized components and makes targeted changes to an existing organism. A synthetic biologist works with a library of standardized parts, designs multi-component systems with defined input-output behavior, and builds the genetic circuit from scratch using DNA synthesis. The key question shifts from 'does the transferred gene express correctly?' to 'does the designed system produce the specified behavior across all operating conditions I care about?'

Marcus recognized the systems challenge immediately. "It is like writing a plugin for an operating system you did not design and cannot fully inspect." Priya agreed, with a qualification. "Worse, actually, because the operating system is also evolving in response to your plugin. Cells are under selection pressure, and a genetic circuit that imposes a metabolic cost will be outcompeted over time by cells that find ways to silence it." That single insight, the biological substrate has its own agenda, explains a large fraction of the field's current research agenda.

Key Players: Real Companies in an Engineering Field

Synthetic biology has reached the stage where its most important applications are not hypothetical. Four companies illustrate the range of what the field is already doing at commercial scale. They will reappear throughout this book with full technical treatment; here, they serve as orientation points.

Ginkgo Bioworks, headquartered in Boston, has built an automated biofoundry modeled explicitly on semiconductor fabrication. A semiconductor fab takes a chip design and produces thousands of identical chips per run. Ginkgo takes a biological design, synthesizes the relevant DNA sequences, inserts them into host cells, and tests thousands of genetic variants per run. Automation is the business model: high-throughput testing makes the design-build-test cycle fast enough to be commercially viable.

Moderna's COVID-19 mRNA vaccine was designed in 48 hours after the viral genome was published in January 2020. That figure is not hyperbole. Once the SARS-CoV-2 genome was known, identifying the spike protein sequence and designing an mRNA to instruct human cells to produce it took less than two days. The remaining months before emergency authorization were spent on manufacturing scale-up, safety testing, and clinical trials rather than on design. The design was done in 48 hours. That is the power of treating biology as a programming language.

Diagram 1.5 - Four Pillars of Synthetic Biology Applications

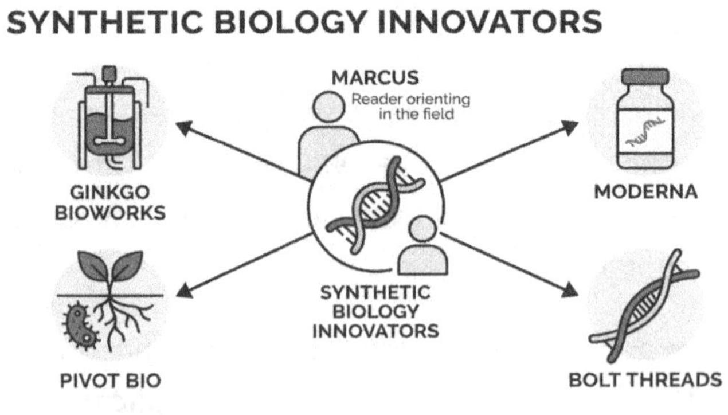

Bolt Threads produces Microsilk, a fiber made by engineered yeast carrying the spider silk gene. Spider silk is

stronger than steel by weight and tougher than Kevlar, but you cannot farm spiders: they are territorial and cannibalistic. Bolt Threads solved the problem by copying the spider silk gene into yeast, an organism that is easy to grow at a fermentation scale. The yeast executes a genetic program and produces a protein that can be spun into fiber with the mechanical properties of the original.

Pivot Bio has engineered soil microbes that fix atmospheric nitrogen for crops, reducing the need for synthetic fertilizer. The Haber-Bosch process, which makes synthetic nitrogen fertilizer, accounts for roughly one to two percent of global energy consumption. Pivot Bio redesigned the regulatory network that controls nitrogen fixation in soil microbes, upregulating the relevant genes. The result is a microbial product that replaces a portion of synthetic fertilizer without changing farming practices.

Why Now: The Cost Collapse That Made It All Possible

The question of why synthetic biology is happening now has a precise and satisfying answer. Two cost curves collapsed simultaneously, thereby changing the economics of working with biological information from prohibitive to accessible.

The first cost curve is DNA sequencing. Reading a human genome costs approximately $3 billion, as the Human Genome Project completed its first draft in 2003. By 2015, sequencing a human genome cost roughly $1,000. By 2025, several companies will offer it for under $200. The rate of cost decline in DNA sequencing has exceeded Moore's Law by a significant margin. Moore's Law roughly describes a 50 percent cost reduction every eighteen months for computing. DNA sequencing costs fell roughly tenfold faster than that for most of the 2000s and 2010s.

Diagram 1.6 - The Cost Collapse: Sequencing and Synthesis Cost Curves 2000 to 2025

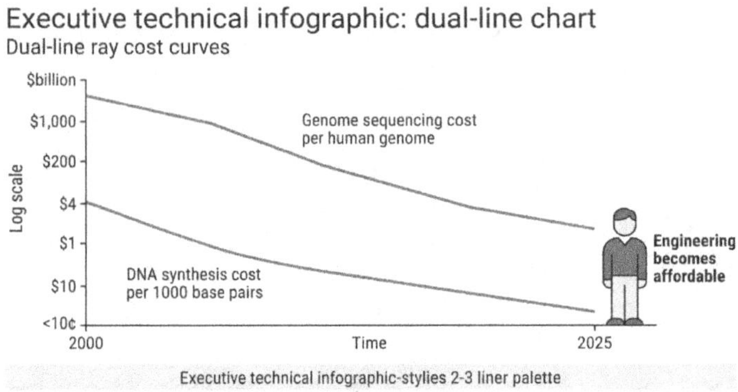

The second cost curve is DNA synthesis. Writing a custom DNA sequence cost roughly four dollars per thousand base pairs in the early 2000s. By 2025, synthesis costs had fallen to under ten cents per thousand base pairs, a reduction of approximately 97 percent. Today, a synthetic biologist can order a custom DNA sequence the way a programmer orders an API call: specify what you want, pay a few dollars, and receive the physical DNA in a few days.

The analogy to computing's cost collapse is instructive. In 1965, a transistor cost roughly one dollar. By 2020, a transistor cost about 0.000001 dollars, a reduction of eight orders of magnitude. That collapse made personal computers possible, then the internet, then smartphones, then machine learning at scale. None of those applications existed when transistors cost a dollar each. They became possible when computing was cheap enough that the bottleneck shifted from hardware to creativity. The same dynamic is now underway in biology.

When costs were high, biological research was limited to well-funded laboratories with patient timelines. As costs have fallen, the bottleneck has shifted: you can now test thousands of genetic variants in the time it previously took to test ten. You can sequence your engineered organism at the end of every experiment to confirm exactly what happened at the genetic level. Accelerated rates of learning in an engineering discipline produce compound improvements in capability, and the rate of learning in synthetic biology has been accelerating for over a decade.

Diagram 1.7 - The Three Enablers: Cost, Automation, and Data

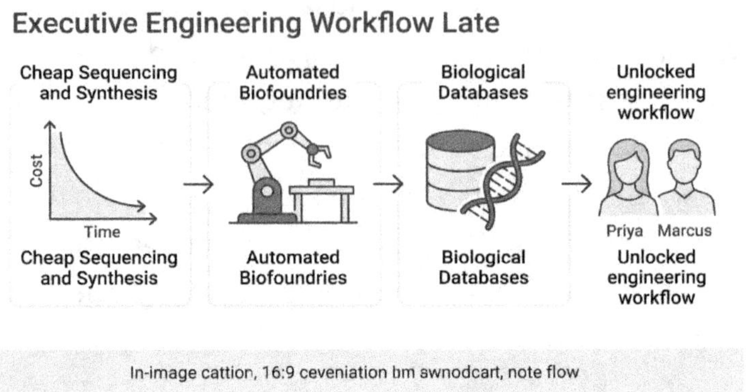

A third enabling factor is the rise of biological databases. The cost collapse of sequencing has produced enormous amounts of sequence data deposited into publicly accessible repositories. Every sequenced organism, every characterized gene, and every mapped protein structure are resources any synthetic biologist can query. The parts catalog grows every time a sequencer runs anywhere in the world. What the combination of cheap sequencing, cheap synthesis, and rich databases produces is a genuine engineering environment: specify a design, build it, measure performance against specification, and iterate quickly enough to make progress.

The Cell as a Programmable Machine

Priya's sentence to Marcus, "we program cells the way you used to program computers," is not a casual metaphor. It is a structural claim about how cells work, and it is worth unpacking carefully because it is the foundation on which everything else in this book rests.

A cell is, among other things, an information-processing system. Its genome is a sequence of instructions written in a four-letter chemical alphabet: adenine, thymine, guanine, and cytosine (A, T, G, C). Those instructions are read by molecular machinery, processed, and translated into proteins. Proteins are the functional outputs: they catalyze chemical reactions, transmit signals, build structures, and regulate which parts of the genome are active at any given moment. From an information-science perspective, this looks like running a program: reading instructions from a stored sequence, processing them through molecular machines, and producing functional outputs.

The analogy has real limits. A computer program runs on a substrate designed to run it. The instruction set is fixed, the memory architecture is known, and execution is deterministic. A cell runs its genetic program on a substrate shaped by evolution, subject to thermal noise, molecular crowding, and stochastic fluctuations in the concentration of every molecule involved. Treating it as a simple computer leads to real engineering mistakes. Priya insists on this. The cell is a noisy, complex, adaptive system that uses genetic information as one among many inputs.

Diagram 1.8 - DNA as Code: From Sequence to Protein Output

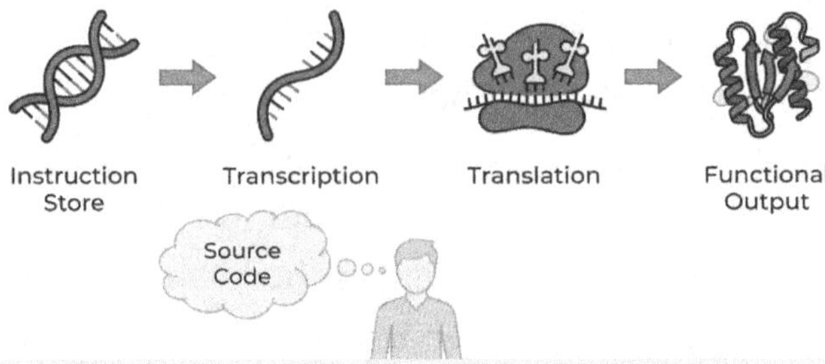

Marcus mind the ternraral istop flow an a engineering pipeline

With that caveat in place, the programming analogy does real explanatory work. The genome is structured into segments that map onto functional units: genes, which encode specific proteins; promoters, which are sequences upstream of genes that act like power switches controlling gene activity; operators and enhancers, which modulate gene activity in response to signals. The cell's molecular machinery reads these control sequences and uses them to decide which genes to express in response to the current environment and internal state.

At its most basic level, synthetic biology writes new sequences into this control architecture. A synthetic promoter can be designed to respond to a signal that the natural cell would not respond to. A synthetic genetic circuit creates a regulatory loop that senses an input, processes it through defined logic, and produces a calibrated output. The biological machinery executing these instructions is the cell's own. The instructions themselves are new. That is the operating definition of programming a cell.

The Scale of What Is Already Happening

It is easy to discuss synthetic biology in a way that makes it sound primarily like a research discipline, with commercial applications somewhere on the horizon. That framing is wrong. Synthetic biology has moved from research to revenue, and the scale of existing commercial deployment is large enough to deserve its own section.

In medicine, more than half of all approved insulin used globally today is produced by engineered bacteria or yeast. mRNA vaccines, of which Moderna and Pfizer-BioNTech delivered hundreds of millions of doses from 2021 onward, are synthetic biology products: the sequences were designed rather than copied from a natural source. CAR-T cell therapies, in which a patient's immune cells are genetically reprogrammed to recognize and attack the patient's specific tumor, have achieved remission rates in blood cancers that no previous therapy has approached. These are approved medical products in current use.

In materials, microorganisms engineered to produce the building blocks of plastics without petroleum as a feedstock are operating at an industrial scale. Industrial enzymes engineered for detergents and food processing, produced by engineered microorganisms, have largely replaced the harsh chemical processes they were designed to substitute. The biobased economy is already worth hundreds of billions of dollars globally each year.

Diagram 1.9 - Synthetic Biology at Commercial Scale: Four Sectors

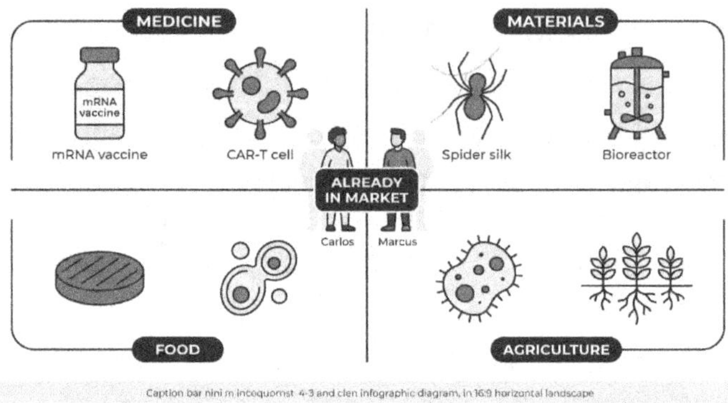

In food, precision fermentation, using engineered microorganisms to produce specific food proteins, is producing dairy proteins and animal fats without involving cows or chickens. Perfect Day produces whey protein identical to cow's milk protein using engineered yeast: the same protein, produced from the same genetic sequence, running in a different organism. UPSIDE Foods produces cultivated chicken, real animal muscle tissue grown from cells in a bioreactor, and received regulatory approval for commercial sale in 2023.

Yuki put it plainly during one of the team's early conversations. "The reason people consistently underestimate how much is already happening is that most of it is invisible. The insulin in a diabetic patient's pump does not announce that engineered bacteria made it. The detergent enzyme that dissolves protein stains at cold temperatures does not carry a label saying a synthetic biologist designed it. The products are there. The field has not yet become as visible as its output."

A Roadmap of the Twelve Chapters

This book is structured as an engineering curriculum: a sequence designed to produce understanding, not a textbook with complete coverage. The sequence matters, and making it explicit gives the reader a map for the journey ahead.

The first block, Chapters 1 through 5, covers foundations. Chapter 1 provides orientation. Chapter 2 gives the historical arc from the discovery of DNA's structure through the development of the tools that made synthetic biology possible. Chapter 3 introduces the genetic toolkit: the specific molecular components synthetic biologists use as the working parts of their designs. Chapter 4 is a deep treatment of CRISPR, what it actually is, how it works, and where it fits in the broader toolkit. Chapter 5 covers genetic circuits, the design patterns that allow synthetic biologists to build systems with logic-gate behavior, such as AND gates, toggle switches, and oscillators.

Diagram 1.10 - The Book as Engineering Curriculum: Three Blocks

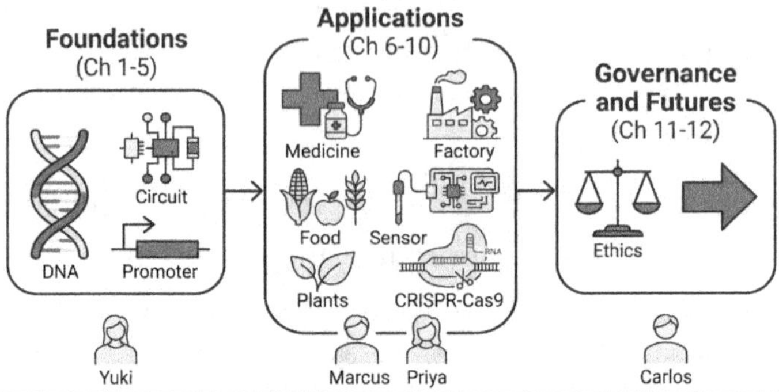

A concluing contiderac [illegible]ncluation is basict on synthetic biology journey

The second block, Chapters 6 through 10, covers applications. Chapter 6 covers medicine: mRNA vaccines, CAR-T therapies, and therapeutic organisms. Chapter 7 covers biomanufacturing: engineered microbes replacing petrochemical processes to produce materials, chemicals, and fuels. Chapter 8 examines engineered food: precision fermentation, cultivated meat, and nitrogen-fixing microbes. Chapter 9 covers biosensors, biological systems that sense and report on their chemical environment, with applications in diagnostics and point-of-care medicine. Chapter 10 covers biology as a planetary engineering tool: bioremediation, carbon capture by engineered organisms, and biological systems operating at the ecosystem scale.

The third block, Chapters 11 and 12, covers governance and futures. Chapter 11 examines the ethical landscape: the dual-use problem, germline editing and its implications, the environmental release question, and the regulatory structures governing the field. Carlos anchors this chapter with his FDA experience. Chapter 12 looks forward to the convergence of synthetic biology and artificial intelligence, the emergence of wholly designed organisms, and what a career in the field looks like today and beyond.

Every chapter opens with a Helix Forge scene and closes with a practical 'What This Means For You' section. The scenes are not decoration. They are the engineering context in which every concept in this book is actually used: a team of four people, each with a different perspective, building a company at the frontier of a fast-moving field. Their questions are your questions. This book is designed to give you their growing competence.

What This Means For You

You have now completed the orientation that every subsequent chapter of this book assumes. Before going further, it is worth translating what you have read into concrete capabilities.

If you are an engineer or technologist, you should now recognize that synthetic biology is not a separate discipline requiring you to start over. It is engineering thinking applied to a new substrate. The design patterns, abstraction hierarchies, and iterative test-and-learn cycle all transfer. What you are learning here is the vocabulary of the substrate: what the parts are, how they interact, and what the execution environment guarantees. By the end of Chapter 5, you will be able to describe a genetic circuit design and identify its failure modes. By the end of Chapter 10, you will be able to evaluate a startup's technical claims in any major application sector.

If you are an entrepreneur or investor, you should now understand why synthetic biology is a horizontal enabling technology rather than a vertical niche. The companies that win will not necessarily have the most impressive biology. They will identify the right application, build the right platform, and execute the design-build-test cycle faster than competitors. The structural advantage of a biofoundry model is operational: more experimental cycles per unit of time and cost means faster learning, and faster learning in a design discipline compounds into competitive advantage.

Diagram 1.11 - The Helix Forge Team as Reader Personas

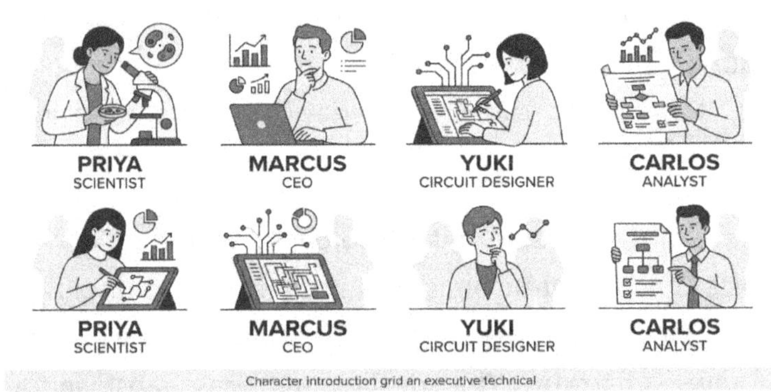

If you are a policy professional, regulator, or science communicator, you should now understand enough about the field's structure to know which questions matter. The most consequential regulatory questions in synthetic biology are not whether the science is real. It is. The questions are: where should the design-build-test cycle be allowed to operate, at what scale, with what oversight, and under what conditions should engineered organisms be permitted to leave controlled environments? Those questions require a technical understanding to be answered well.

For all readers, the most important shift this chapter asks you to make is conceptual: from thinking about biology as something that happens to living organisms to thinking about it as something that can be deliberately designed. That shift is not a philosophical claim about the nature of life. It is a description of what a generation of engineers has already done and continues to do in laboratories, biofoundries, and startups around the world. Accepting that description, even before you fully understand the mechanism, is the prerequisite for everything that follows in this book.

Takeaway

Biology has crossed a threshold. The scientific tradition of observing and characterizing living systems has been joined by an engineering tradition of designing and building them. Synthetic biology sits at the center of that second tradition: it applies the tools of engineering, standardized parts, quantitative design, iterative testing, and modular system architecture to the construction of biological systems that perform specified functions. This is not a prediction. It is a description of what is already happening in labs, biofoundries, and commercial facilities on every continent.

The field exists at this moment because two enabling cost curves collapsed. DNA sequencing fell from $3 billion per genome to under $200 per genome. DNA synthesis fell from four dollars per thousand base pairs to under ten cents. The result is an engineering environment where the design-build-test cycle is fast enough and cheap enough to support genuine iteration. The companies and research groups that have built infrastructure around this cycle are already producing commercial products at scale: medicines, materials, food ingredients, and agricultural inputs.

The structural metaphors that will guide the rest of this book are all grounded in real engineering practice. Cells are information-processing systems. DNA is code. Proteins are functional outputs. Genetic circuits are logic systems. The design-build-test-learn loop is the field's organizing workflow. These are not loose analogies. They are precise descriptions of how synthetic biologists actually work, and understanding them is the prerequisite for understanding everything the subsequent chapters cover.

Diagram 1.12 - Your Journey Through the Primer: From Orientation to Fluency

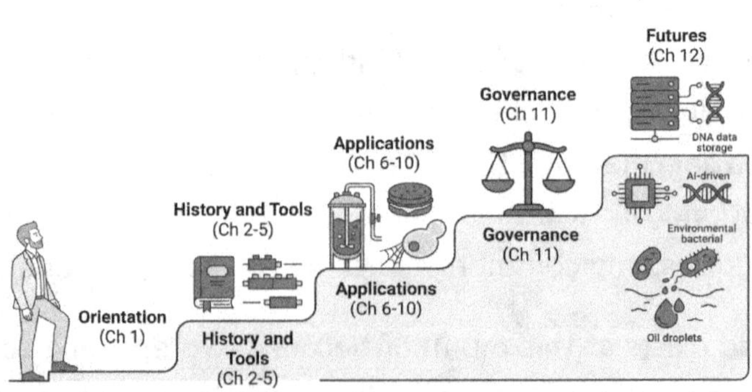

Your Journey Through the Primer: From Orientation to Fluency.

By the time you finish this book, you will have the technical fluency to evaluate synthetic biology from the inside: its claims, its investments, its regulatory debates, and its research directions. That fluency begins here, in a Boston lab, with a petri dish held up to the light. Marcus could not yet describe what he was looking at on his first morning at Helix Forge. Twelve chapters from now, you will be able to describe it precisely. The subject of everything that follows is the answer to the question Priya left hanging: what happens when you can program the living world?

2 A Brief, Wild History of Programming Life

Opening Scenario

The whiteboard in the Helix Forge conference room is not technically a whiteboard. It is a full wall of glass covered in so many layers of marker ink that Priya once joked it qualified as a geological formation. On a Tuesday morning in late October, Yuki Tanaka has taped a long roll of paper across the glass and is drawing a horizontal timeline in blue marker. The left edge reads 1953. The right edge reads today. She marks the decades, labels a handful of key moments, and steps back.

Marcus Webb leans in the doorway with his coffee and reads left to right. His eye catches the right-hand portion of the line, where the labels crowd together, and the pace of events visibly accelerates. At the far end, Yuki has pinned a printout: a student team from Thailand, which presented last week at the iGEM competition, had engineered a bacterial biosensor for detecting plastic pollution in water. Undergraduates. From a country with no legacy synthetic biology department. Building with standardized parts from a shared global registry.

Yuki caps her marker and turns. "Every company in this space is built on decisions made at three or four key moments in its history. If you do not know the history, you do not understand the field. And you definitely do not understand the risks." Marcus looks at the crowded right-hand edge of the timeline. "Walk me through it from the beginning," he says. "First principles."

Why It Matters

History, in science, is not decoration. It is a map of the assumptions your field is running on. When you understand where synthetic biology came from, you stop seeing it as a collection of disconnected technologies and start seeing it as a single, coherent engineering project that has been building momentum for 70 years. The tools changed. The organisms changed. The scale changed. But the underlying question has been the same since 1953: if genetic information is chemical, and chemistry follows rules, can we learn to write as well as read? The answer is yes. The path to that answer ran through a voluntary research moratorium, a regulatory framework built under pressure, years of frustrating standardization work, and a global student competition nobody expected to become the field's main training ground.

For anyone evaluating where synthetic biology is going next, understanding that path is not optional. Every company, tool, and policy debate in the chapters ahead is built on decisions made at specific moments described in this one. This is the context that makes everything else make sense. And it is, genuinely, a wild story.

The Double Helix and the Programmability Insight

The story starts in Cambridge in the spring of 1953, where James Watson and Francis Crick published a short paper in Nature describing the structure of DNA. It was famously understated. The final paragraph noted, in one careful word, an "interesting" implication for how hereditary information might be copied. What the paper was actually announcing was something far more radical: a mechanism by which biological information is stored, replicated, and, in principle, read.

The double helix is two chains of nucleotides wound around each other. Each nucleotide carries one of four chemical bases: adenine, thymine, guanine, or cytosine. The bases on opposite strands are complementary, adenine always pairing with thymine, and guanine always pairing with cytosine. When the cell divides, and the helix unzips, each strand serves as a template for rebuilding the full structure. The storage medium replicates itself.

What matters most to the synthetic biology story is a simpler observation: the genetic information in DNA is linear and digital. It is written in a four-letter alphabet, read sequentially. That is a code. And a code can be read, copied, modified, and rewritten. You do not have to know every detail of the molecular mechanism to see the implication: if DNA is code, then life is programmable. And programmable systems are things engineers work with.

Diagram 2.1 - The Double Helix as a Four-Letter Code

The practical implication of that insight took two decades to arrive. In the intervening years, the genetic code was cracked, the mechanism of transcription from DNA to RNA was worked out, and the ribosome's role in translating RNA into protein was described. Each discovery filled in more of the molecular mechanism and built the conceptual scaffolding for what came next. By the early 1970s, enough was understood that a new kind of experiment became thinkable: not just reading the genome, but writing it.

The Recombinant DNA Revolution

Herbert Boyer at UCSF was studying restriction enzymes, proteins that bacteria produce naturally to defend against viral DNA by cutting it at specific, predictable sequences. Boyer noticed that certain restriction enzymes left single-stranded overhangs at the cut site, short unpaired tails that were chemically "sticky." Two pieces of DNA cut with the same enzyme would have complementary sticky ends that could join together. Stanley Cohen at Stanford was working on plasmids, small circular DNA loops found in bacteria that replicate independently and can carry genes between cells. When Boyer and Cohen compared notes, the experiment nearly designed itself.

In 1973, they cut a plasmid with a restriction enzyme, inserted a fragment of frog DNA using matching sticky ends, resealed the circle, and introduced the recombinant plasmid into E. coli. The bacterium expressed the frog gene. This demonstrated something fundamental: genetic information is universal. The cell's protein-building machinery does not check the origin of a gene before reading it. A gene is a gene. If you can move it, you can move the function.

Diagram 2.2 - Recombinant DNA: Cut and Paste Across Species

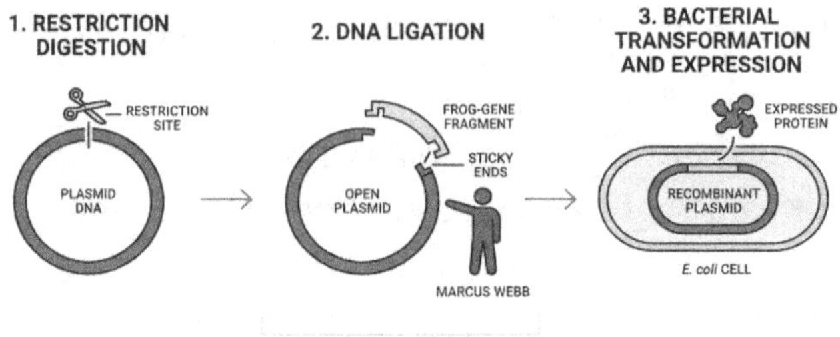

1973 Boyer and Cohen

Think of it through the software analogy this book uses deliberately. The Boyer-Cohen experiment was the discovery that files from one operating system could run on another, not similar files or compatible files, literally the same file, executed without modification. The ribosome reads the genetic code the same way in a frog and in a bacterium. The alphabet is the same. The grammar is the same.

The commercial implications were immediate. If any gene could be moved into bacteria, bacteria could produce any protein. Bacteria grow fast, reproduce exponentially, and scale in fermentation tanks. By 1982, Genentech had inserted the human insulin gene into E. coli and the FDA approved Humulin, the first recombinant DNA drug. Millions of people with diabetes have used it ever since. The technology did not require new industrial infrastructure. It required integrating a new biological component into the existing infrastructure. Living organisms are not just objects of study. They are manufacturing platforms.

Asilomar Pause: When Scientists Stopped Themselves

In February 1975, roughly 150 scientists gathered at a conference center in Asilomar, California, and did something almost without precedent in the history of research: they voluntarily agreed to pause their own most exciting work while they figured out whether it was safe.

The decision to call Asilomar began when Paul Berg at Stanford planned an experiment that troubled his peers. Berg intended to splice the genome of SV40, a tumor-causing virus, into E. coli, the most common bacterium in human guts. If the recombinant E. coli escaped and colonized human hosts, could it introduce tumor-causing material? Nobody knew. Berg had the skills and the permissions to run the experiment. He chose not to, and he and his colleagues sent a letter to scientific journals calling for a voluntary moratorium on the riskiest categories of recombinant DNA research until the risks could be assessed.

Diagram 2.3 - The Asilomar Conference: Voluntary Safety Governance in 1975

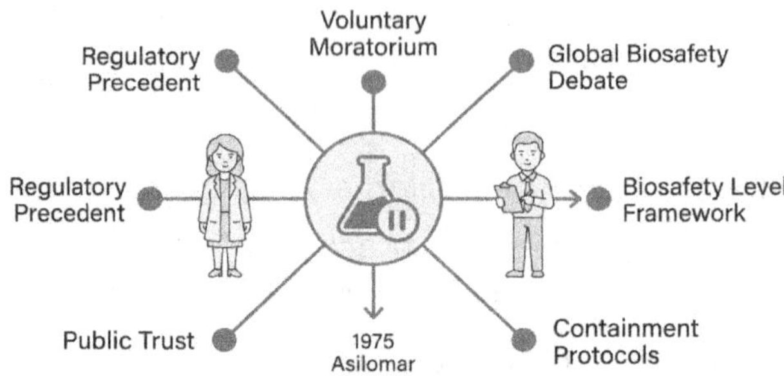

The conference that followed was chaotic, contentious, and extraordinary. Scientists argued about risk estimates for which no one had data to support, and about who had the right to make decisions affecting the public. Journalists and lawyers were present. The proceedings were broadcast. What emerged was a framework for biosafety that still governs recombinant DNA research today: biosafety levels that match containment requirements to estimated risk, physical containment standards, and a model for institutional biosafety committees to review research proposals before experiments begin. Research resumed, within those constraints, within months.

For the synthetic biology story, Asilomar matters in two ways. The first is practical: the biosafety infrastructure it created is the one every synthetic biology lab operates within today. The second is cultural. The scientists who had the most to gain from unrestricted research chose to restrict it, publicly, in dialogue with the public, because they believed that was the right thing to do. That precedent has been invoked in nearly every major biosafety debate since, including the CRISPR germline editing debates covered in full by Chapter 11.

The BioBrick Standard: A USB Port for Life

For roughly two decades after Asilomar, genetic engineering grew steadily but without a unifying engineering framework. Labs were inserting genes into organisms, producing proteins, and building new biological capabilities. But each lab reinvented the wheel. The same gene might be cloned and characterized dozens of times across different labs, using slightly different vectors and conditions. There was no shared vocabulary for what you had built, no registry to check whether someone had already experimented, no standard format for contributing your work to a common pool. Biology was being engineered, but not in the way engineering is.

Tom Knight noticed this. Knight was a computer scientist at MIT's AI Laboratory who had spent his career thinking about hardware abstraction layers. These interfaces let software run on hardware without needing to know the hardware's internals. In the late 1990s, he learned molecular biology from scratch and saw a field with extraordinary capabilities and almost no engineering infrastructure. No standard interfaces. No modular components. No shared parts library. In 2003, he proposed fixing this.

Diagram 2.4 - The BioBrick Standard: Interchangeable Biological Parts

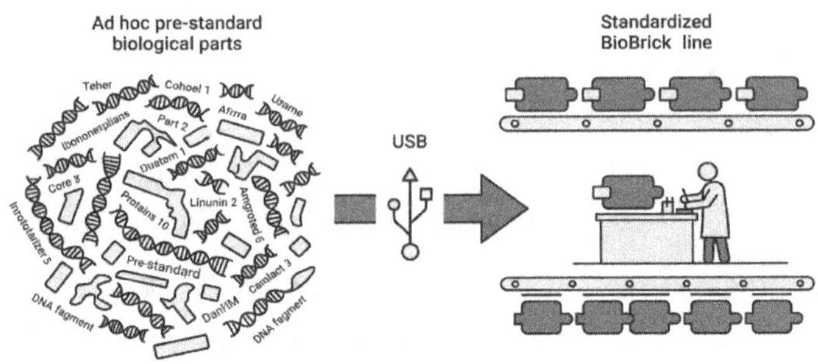

2003 MIT BioBrick Proposal

A BioBrick is a standardized DNA sequence encoding a biological function, flanked by specific restriction enzyme sites on both ends. Every BioBrick uses the same prefix on the left and the same suffix on the right, so any two BioBricks can be assembled using the same protocol. You do not redesign your cloning strategy for each new part. The interface is fixed. The parts are interchangeable.

The USB analogy is deliberate. USB was transformative not because serial data transfer was new but because every device, every port, used the same interface. BioBricks made the same bet for genetic parts. The Registry of Standard Biological Parts lets any lab deposit a characterized BioBrick and any lab in the world look it up, request a sample, and use it. The Registry grew slowly, then rapidly, as the iGEM competition adopted BioBricks and produced hundreds of new characterized parts each year. Today, the Registry holds thousands of parts from dozens of organisms. The field has since developed better assembly standards, but the BioBrick Registry established the principle that biological parts should be shared, documented, and reusable.

iGEM Movement: A Global Hackathon Grows a Field

The International Genetically Engineered Machine competition began at MIT in January 2003 as a month-long independent activities course. Five student teams. A handful of BioBrick parts. A simple challenge: build something biological and interesting. The first projects were modest: a bacterial oscillator that made cells blink rhythmically, a simple cell counter. The work was crude by later standards. But the format was right.

iGEM grew fast. By 2006, teams were competing from universities across the United States and Europe. By 2010, teams from Asia, South America, and Africa had joined. By the mid-2010s, iGEM drew over 300 teams from more than 50 countries, with a Jamboree in Boston every autumn that brought thousands of participants. The projects scaled too. Student teams have built bacterial biosensors that detect heavy metals in drinking water, yeast strains that produce antimalarial compounds, genetic circuit diagnostics, and, as Yuki's printout shows, a plastic pollution sensor from Thailand. Several iGEM projects have been published in peer-reviewed journals. A handful have been spun out as companies.

Diagram 2.5 - iGEM Growth: From Five Teams to a Global Movement

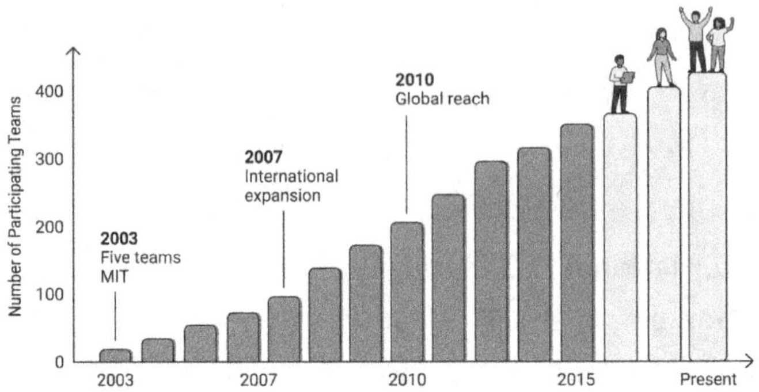

The deeper impact is not in any single project but in the alum network. The founders of Ginkgo Bioworks met while mentoring iGEM teams. Zymergen's founders have similar roots. Dozens of scientists and engineers now leading synthetic biology companies and regulatory agencies got their first hands-on experience through iGEM. The competition did for synthetic biology what the Homebrew Computer Club did for software: it created a culture of tinkering, sharing, and building that trained a generation of practitioners before the industry existed to train them.

The iGEM format also shaped field culture in ways that distinguish synthetic biology from older biotechnology. Every iGEM team is required to include a human practices component: a reflection on the social, ethical, and policy implications of their technology. This is not optional; it is judged. Carlos credits his own undergraduate iGEM mentorship with shaping how he thinks about science and policy needing to talk to each other. The requirement built that conversation into the curriculum before anyone had to mandate it.

Craig Venter and the Written Genome

In 2010, J. Craig Venter's team at the J. Craig Venter Institute announced the world's first synthetic cell. The headline was, as headlines about synthetic biology often are, simultaneously true and slightly misleading. What Venter's team had done: they synthesized, from scratch, the complete genome of a simple bacterium, Mycoplasma mycoides, 1.08 million base pairs of DNA written on a DNA synthesizer and assembled over several years into a single circular chromosome. They then inserted this human-written genome into an empty bacterial cell from which the original genome had been removed. The cell started running on the new genome. It reproduced. It passed the synthetic genome to its daughters.

This was not the creation of life from chemistry. The cellular machinery, the ribosomes, membranes, and metabolic enzymes, was borrowed from a living cell. Venter's team did not assemble a cell from scratch. What they did was write the instruction set from scratch and demonstrate that a living cell would execute it. The distinction matters because it tells you exactly what the achievement was and what it was not: a demonstration that the genome of a living organism can be written by humans, not just read, not just edited, but written from the first nucleotide to the last.

Diagram 2.6 - The Synthetic Cell: Writing a Genome from Scratch

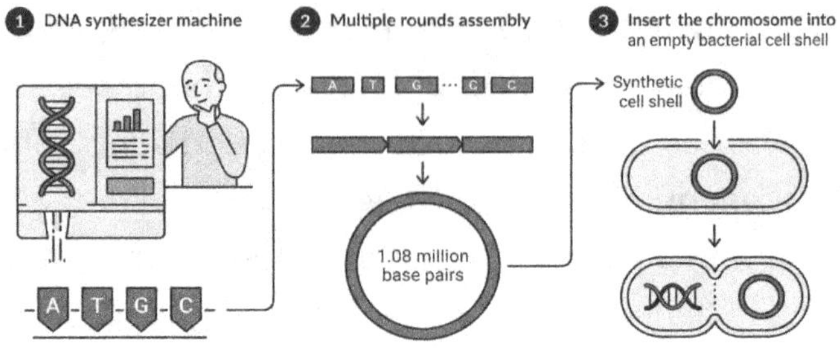

Venter Institute 2010

The ability to write a genome means that the information content of a living organism can be stored digitally, transmitted electronically, and reconstituted physically at any location with a DNA synthesizer. A genome is not a physical object that has to be transported in a sample tube. It is a file. You can email it. You can store it on a server. You can print it at any lab in the world with the right equipment. This has profound implications for vaccine production, the preservation of genetic diversity, and the distribution of biological manufacturing capabilities.

Venter's team also watermarked the synthetic genome with encoded messages and quotes from Feynman and Joyce, written as DNA sequences using a simple cipher. Not functional genes, just proof of authorship. The bacterium reproduced and passed the Feynman quote to its daughters. Life executing literature. It is a small detail, but it captures something true about what writing a genome means: you can put anything in there.

CRISPR Arrives and Changes the Pace of Everything

In 2012, a paper published in Science by Jennifer Doudna and Emmanuelle Charpentier described a molecular mechanism bacteria use to defend against viruses: a system called CRISPR-Cas9. CRISPR, an acronym for Clustered Regularly Interspaced Short Palindromic Repeats, refers to a pattern of repeated sequences in bacterial genomes that functions as a molecular immune memory. When a bacterium survives a viral attack, it stores a short fragment of the virus's DNA in its CRISPR locus. If the same virus attacks again, the bacterium uses that stored fragment to produce a guide RNA that directs a protein called Cas9 to the matching viral sequence. Cas9 cuts it. The virus is disabled.

What Doudna and Charpentier's paper demonstrated was that this system could be reprogrammed. The guide RNA is just an RNA sequence. Synthesize a guide RNA matching a sequence in any genome, and Cas9 will find and cut that sequence. The molecular scalpel is fully programmable. You change the target by changing the guide RNA, a routine task any graduate student can accomplish in a few days.

Diagram 2.7 - CRISPR-Cas9: A Programmable Molecular Scalpel

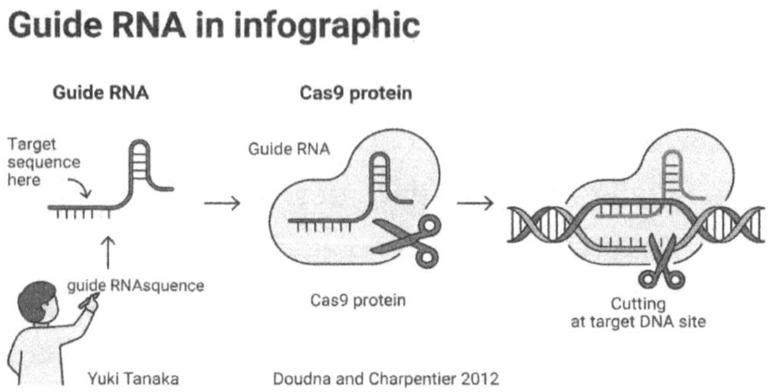

The practical effect was immediate. Before CRISPR, precise gene editing required specialized tools that took months to design per target site and cost tens of thousands of dollars per edit. With CRISPR, cost dropped by orders of magnitude, time dropped from months to days, and experiments that had been the province of large, well-funded groups became accessible to small labs, startups, and teaching laboratories.

CRISPR also made DIY biology real. The complexity of older editing tools had kept serious genetic engineering inside professional settings. CRISPR, with its simple, programmable guide RNA and off-the-shelf Cas9, was accessible enough that a motivated amateur with a basic bench could attempt simple editing experiments. This democratization is one of the most consequential things CRISPR has done for the field, not because amateur editing is currently producing scientific breakthroughs, but because it expanded the community of people who, at a hands-on level, understand what this technology can do.

Foundry-Scale Engineering: When Biology Started Running Like a Fab

By the mid-2010s, two things were true at once. The tools for designing and editing biological systems have never been more accessible. And the complexity of systems that commercial synthetic biology requires has never been higher. Engineering a microorganism to produce a target molecule at commercial yields meant making dozens, sometimes hundreds, of genetic modifications, each affecting the cell's metabolic balance in ways that were difficult to predict. The design-build-test cycle needed to run at an industrial scale, and that required infrastructure that no standard academic lab could provide.

The response was the biological foundry: a facility designed to run the design-build-test-learn cycle at high throughput, with automation, standardization, and computational integration. The founding vision is borrowed explicitly from semiconductor manufacturing. A semiconductor fab takes a chip design and executes fabrication with extreme precision, thousands of chips per run, every chip identical, every step logged. A biological foundry does the same for organisms: takes a genetic design, builds it in cells, tests its performance, feeds the results back into the design, all at a speed and scale a conventional lab cannot match.

Diagram 2.8 - The Biological Foundry: The Design-Build-Test-Learn Cycle at Scale

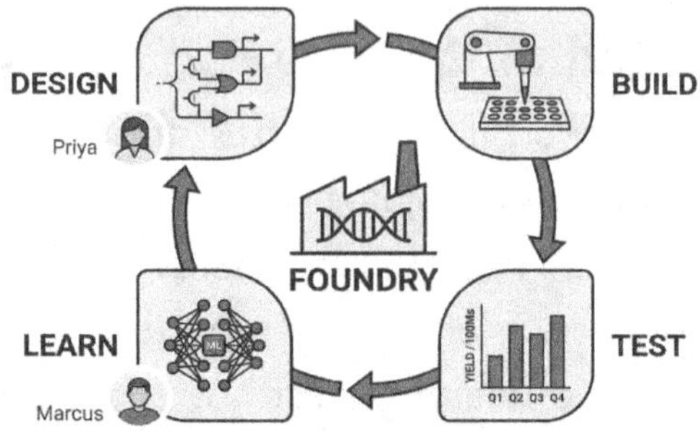

Executive technical op card-iv flow diagram

Ginkgo Bioworks, founded in 2009 by MIT graduates in biological engineering, built the first commercial biological foundry at scale. The Ginkgo Boston Foundry integrates automated liquid handling, high-throughput DNA synthesis, next-generation sequencing, and analytical tools into a software-driven workflow. Genetic designs are generated computationally, assembled by robots, tested in automated assays, and iterated, compressing what would take months in a conventional lab into weeks.

The foundry model separated design from execution. A customer contributes design intent and performance specifications; the foundry runs the engineering cycles. This is the biological equivalent of the fabless semiconductor model: design the chip, send it to a fab; design the organism, send it to a foundry. A foundry running thousands of experiments per year also generates the dataset that machine learning models use to predict genetic design behavior before anything is built, connecting directly to the AI convergence this book returns to in Chapter 12.

The DIY Biology Movement: Biology's Homebrew Computer Club

In 2008, a group of molecular biologists, artists, hackers, and curious professionals founded Genspace in Brooklyn, New York, a community biology laboratory with basic molecular biology equipment available to anyone through membership, outside university or corporate settings. The founding idea was explicit: biology should be accessible to people without an institutional lab. In the same way, the Homebrew Computer Club in the 1970s gave personal computer enthusiasts access to hardware that had been the exclusive province of large companies; Genspace gave biology enthusiasts access to tools previously locked inside professional labs.

BioCurious opened in Silicon Valley in 2010 with the same model. Other community labs followed: La Paillasse in Paris, Open Cell in London, and counterparts on every continent, growing into a global network. The tools available are basic compared to a university research facility. Still, they are real: PCR machines, gel electrophoresis equipment, microscopes, small fermenters, and, increasingly, CRISPR kits designed for community-lab contexts. The gap between community lab and university lab capability is much smaller than it was a decade ago and narrows each year as tools become cheaper and more automated.

Diagram 2.9 - The Global Community Biology Lab Network

An infographic style map is a central metaphor of a global network

The community biology movement means different things to different observers. For the innovation optimist, it is the leading edge of a democratization that could unleash the kind of creative tinkering that produced the personal computer and the early open-source software ecosystem. Carlos holds both views simultaneously, and he assesses that the culture of responsible practice that Genspace and BioCurious deliberately cultivate is a meaningful safeguard, and that real biosecurity risks come from well-resourced professional actors, not from community labs. The full discussion belongs in Chapter 11. The point here is simpler: the existence of community biology labs is itself a historical milestone. A field born in elite university laboratories is now, to some extent, accessible to anyone with curiosity and a membership fee.

Today's Pace: 70 Years of Acceleration, Compressed

Yuki finishes drawing the timeline. Marcus sets down his coffee. He points at the blank space after last week's iGEM result. "What goes here?" he asks. Yuki smiles. "That is what we are building."

The pace at which synthetic biology has moved in the last decade has no precedent in the field's history. The cost of DNA synthesis has fallen faster than Moore's Law: a base pair that cost one dollar in 2000 costs a fraction of a cent today. Whole-genome sequencing, which cost roughly 100 million dollars in 2001, now costs less than a thousand dollars and continues to fall. CRISPR compressed gene editing from months to days. Automated foundries compressed the engineering cycle for compressed organisms from years to weeks. Artificial intelligence is now beginning to compress the design phase, the most time-consuming part of the cycle, in ways that are only becoming clear.

Diagram 2.10 - The Falling Cost of DNA Synthesis and Sequencing Over Time

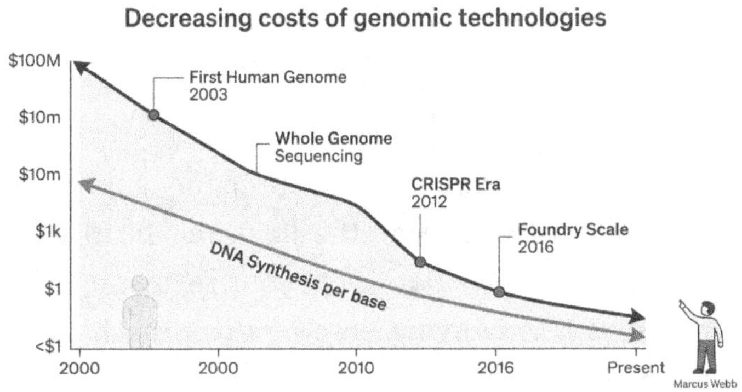

The combination of cheap sequencing, cheap synthesis, powerful editing tools, automated foundries, and AI-assisted design is producing something the field has been working toward since the discovery of the double helix: a genuine engineering discipline for living systems. Not a collection of tricks, but a complete stack: read the genome, design the modification, build it, test it, learn from the result, iterate. The same loop software engineers run when they ship a feature. The same loop semiconductor engineers run when they tape out a chip. But running inside living cells, with biological complexity layered on top.

For Marcus, the timeline has a specific shape: exponential. Quiet early decades, then recombinant DNA in the 1970s, BioBricks and iGEM in 2003, CRISPR in 2012, and now cheap synthesis, automation, and machine learning compounding in ways that make the 2010s look slow. He has seen this curve before, in software and semiconductors. He knows what the right side of an exponential cost curve looks like. He knows why Yuki wanted to draw the whole thing on the wall.

What This Means For You

If you are an engineer or entrepreneur approaching synthetic biology from outside the field, this history gives you the framework to evaluate what you are hearing. When a company says it is working on a new approach to DNA synthesis, you now know why that matters. When an article refers to the BioBrick Registry or the iGEM competition, you know what those are and why they were built. When someone invokes the Asilomar precedent in a debate about a new technology, you know what happened there, what was decided, and why the precedent carries the weight it does.

Diagram 2.11 - The Synthetic Biology Timeline: Key Milestones from 1953 to Today

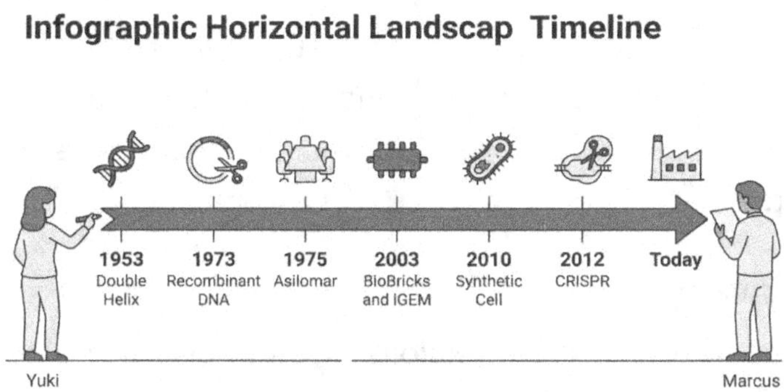

For the engineer, this is a history of infrastructure development. Each era gave the field a new layer: the double helix, the fundamental insight; recombinant DNA, the first practical tool; Asilomar, the governance culture; BioBricks component standardization; iGEM, the training pipeline; the synthetic cell, proof that writing was possible; CRISPR, a general-purpose editing tool; foundries, manufacturing scale. The layer now being built is intelligent automation. None of those AI design tools would exist without every layer beneath them. Each one depends on the one below it.

For the policy professional, this history shows that synthetic biology has a culture of self-governance that predates most of the regulatory frameworks governing it, as seen in Asilomar in 1975. The iGEM human practices requirement has been in place since the competition's earliest years. The biosafety protocols were developed by community labs operating without formal mandates. These are not the actions of a field that ignores risk. Effective regulation of synthetic biology will work with that culture rather than against it, and regulators who understand the history will be far more effective partners for the field than those who do not.

Takeaway

The history of synthetic biology is the story of a single radical idea working its way from insight to infrastructure over seventy years. The idea, first visible in the 1953 double helix, is that genetic information is a code and codes can be written. Everything that followed, recombinant DNA, restriction enzymes, plasmids, Asilomar, BioBricks, iGEM, the synthetic cell, CRISPR, biological foundries, is that idea acquiring tools, infrastructure, practitioners, and the industrial capacity to deliver on what it promised.

What makes this history unusual among technological revolutions is that it did not ignore its own risks. At two critical moments, the scientists leading the field built governance practices into its culture before being required to. Those decisions shaped everything that came after. The regulatory frameworks governing synthetic biology today have their roots at Asilomar. The culture of responsible innovation that characterizes the best companies and research groups in the field has its roots in the early iGEM community's insistence that building with biology carries responsibilities beyond the laboratory.

Diagram 2.12 - Seventy Years of Building: From Watson and Crick to the Helix Forge Team

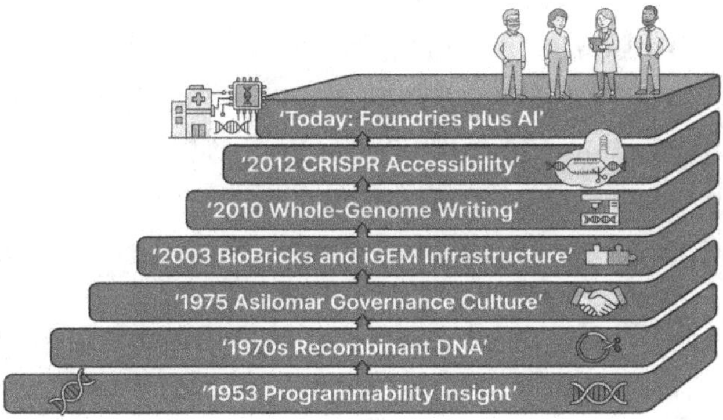

The pace today is faster than at any point in the field's history. Yuki's timeline will need more space on the right-hand side before long. Marcus is right that he has seen this curve before. And Yuki is right that understanding the history is not optional for anyone who wants to work in this field, invest in it, regulate it, or understand what is happening. Every company, every tool, and every argument in the chapters that follow is built on the decisions described in this one.

3 The Genetic Toolkit

Opening Scenario

The conference room at Helix Forge smells faintly of cold brew and dry-erase marker. It is a Tuesday morning in late October, and Yuki Tanaka has the main screen loaded with the iGEM Registry of Standard Biological Parts. This publicly accessible database, at first glance, looks like a very earnest GitHub repository for living systems. Thousands of entries, each with a name, a sequence, a functional description, a compatibility flag, and, if whoever submitted it was thorough, a set of characterization curves. Yuki navigates to a specific promoter entry and turns to face Marcus Webb.

"Think of this," she says, gesturing at the screen, "as npm for biology." Marcus leans forward. "You don't write every function from scratch. You pull packages other people have already built and tested." Yuki nods. "Exactly. Except when the documentation is wrong." She pauses just long enough. "Which is also like npm."

Priya Anand, seated across the table with a stack of printed sequences beside her coffee cup, smiles at this. Carlos Rivera opens his laptop and starts a new notes document. He has learned that when Yuki and Marcus start riffing on analogies, the next hour usually produces something worth writing down.

Why It Matters

Synthetic biology is an engineering discipline. That sentence sounds obvious until you try to practice it, because the engineering vocabulary of synthetic biology, the vocabulary of parts and components, and standardized interfaces, took decades to develop. In the early years of recombinant DNA technology, every laboratory had its own cloning strategies and its own conventions for naming and documenting genetic constructs. A promoter characterized in one lab was not easily transferred to another because the two groups were using incompatible molecular architectures. Progress was slow partly for a reason anyone who has worked in software before the era of package managers will recognize: the absence of a standard interface.

What changed was the deliberate application of engineering principles to biological construction. Synthetic biologists began asking questions that electronics engineers had answered decades earlier: What are the smallest functional units of a biological system? Can those units be characterized in a way that predicts their behavior? Can they be standardized to be interchangeable across designs? Can they be cataloged so that engineers who need a specific function do not have to build it from scratch? The answers produced the genetic toolkit, and the toolkit is what makes synthetic biology feel less like artisanal craft and more like design from a parts library.

Diagram 3.1 - The Genetic Parts Family Tree

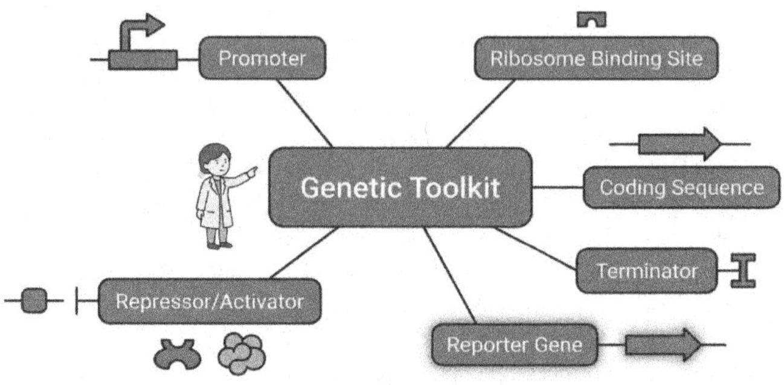

Parts as Components: The Language of Biological Building Blocks

Every engineered biological system is built from a small set of functional units called genetic parts: defined DNA sequences that each perform a specific, reproducible function in a living cell. The most important part in any genetic circuit is the promoter. A promoter is a short DNA sequence that sits directly upstream of a gene and serves as the landing platform for RNA polymerase, the cellular machinery that reads and copies that gene. When RNA polymerase encounters a promoter sequence, it binds and begins moving along the DNA strand, producing a single-stranded copy of the gene called messenger RNA. Ribosomes then translate that messenger RNA into a protein. The promoter is the switch that determines whether a gene is being actively transcribed or remains silent. Strong promoters drive high levels of gene expression. Weak promoters drive low levels.

Promoters come in two fundamental flavors. Constitutive promoters are always on: they drive gene expression continuously, regardless of what signals are present inside or outside the cell. Inducible promoters are off by default and are switched on by a specific chemical or physical signal. The canonical example in the toolkit is the lac promoter, borrowed from E. coli, which is normally repressed but switched on in the presence of a synthetic analog called IPTG. Inducible promoters are the programmable inputs of genetic circuits: they let you trigger gene expression on demand, from outside the cell, by adding the right molecule to the growth medium. This is the feature that makes biological systems responsive and eventually programmable.

Diagram 3.2 - Constitutive vs. Inducible Promoters

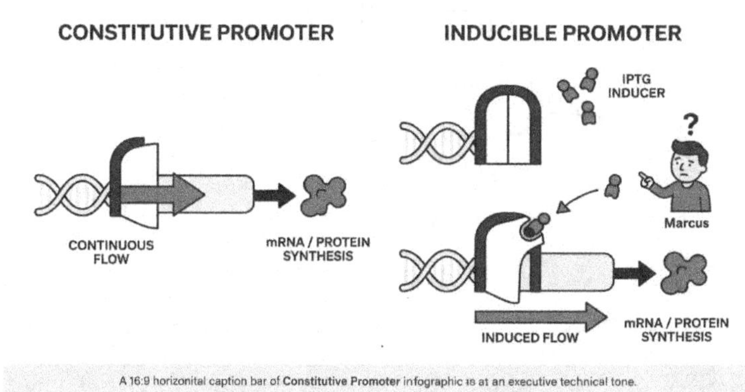

Downstream of the promoter, the ribosome binding site (RBS), a short sequence on the messenger RNA, is recognized by ribosomes and bound before translation into protein. RBS strength is one of the primary volume knobs available to a synthetic biologist: if a promoter controls whether a gene is on or off, the RBS controls how loudly the gene is expressed when it is on. Every gene expression event must also end, and the genetic element responsible is the terminator, a DNA sequence that causes RNA polymerase to terminate transcription. Without a well-placed terminator, transcription continues past the intended gene boundary. A circuit without clean terminators leaks signal in ways that are difficult to diagnose.

Diagram 3.3 - A Complete Genetic Part on a DNA Strand

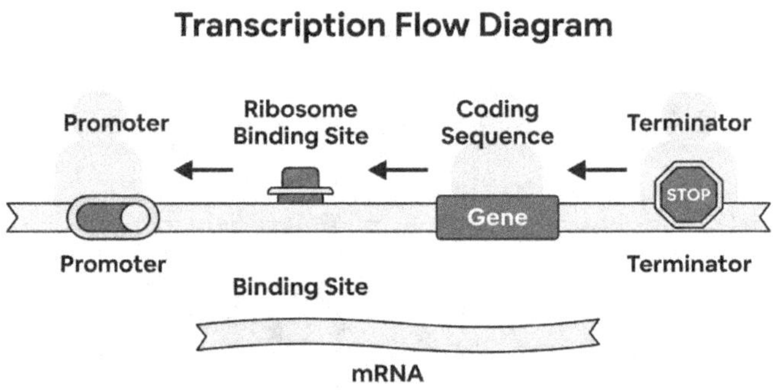

Repressors & Activators: Circuit Breakers & Amplifiers

Repressors are proteins that bind to a specific short DNA sequence called an operator, located near or within a promoter. When a repressor protein binds to its operator, it physically blocks RNA polymerase from accessing the promoter, preventing transcription from starting. The gene downstream goes silent. The repressor has flipped a switch off, not by altering the DNA sequence but by physically occupying the landing site that the transcription machinery needs. The lac repressor in E. coli works exactly this way, binding to the lac operator and blocking transcription until lactose arrives and changes the repressor's shape, releasing the operator and allowing transcription to proceed.

Activators work in the opposite direction. An activator protein binds near a promoter and enhances RNA polymerase binding, increasing the rate of transcription. Where a repressor is a circuit breaker, an activator is an amplifier. In many natural and synthetic genetic networks, repressors and activators work in combination: one gene's product activates a second gene, whose product represses a third, whose repression releases a fourth. This cascading architecture is how cells implement complex regulatory programs from simple molecular parts, and it is how digital logic circuits implement complex Boolean operations from simple transistors. The parallel is not accidental. A repressor gene construct is a biological NOT gate: when the repressor protein is present, the target gene is off; when the repressor is absent, the target gene is on. AND gates, OR gates, toggle switches, and oscillators can all be built from combinations of repressors and activators. Chapter 5 walks through how those constructions work in detail.

Diagram 3.4 - Repressor and Activator Action at a Promoter

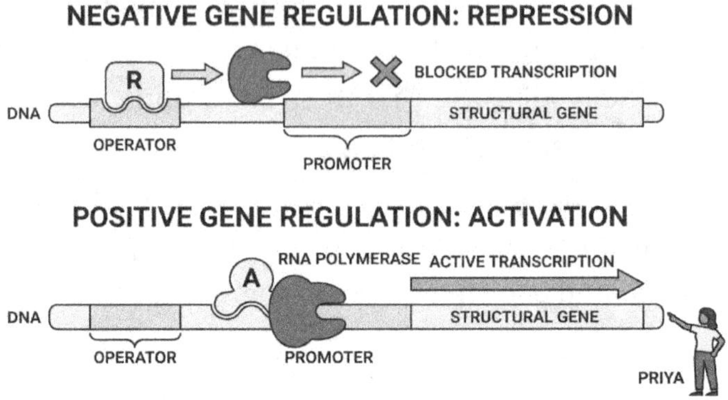

Reporter Genes: The Console.log of Synthetic Biology

You cannot debug a system you cannot observe. In software, you instrument your code with logging statements. In biology, the equivalent question is: how do you see whether a genetic circuit is actually running? The cell is opaque. Proteins are invisible. Transcription and translation are molecular-scale events happening inside a structure you cannot observe directly without specialized equipment. The genetic toolkit's answer is the reporter gene, a coding sequence whose protein product produces a detectable signal.

The most famous reporter gene in synthetic biology is GFP, which stands for green fluorescent protein, originally isolated from the jellyfish Aequorea victoria. The protein folds into a barrel structure that, when exposed to blue or ultraviolet light, re-emits it as green fluorescence. When you insert a GFP coding sequence downstream of a promoter in your genetic circuit, the cell that expresses GFP glows green under a fluorescence microscope. You can directly see whether your promoter is active, measure its intensity to estimate expression levels, and watch gene expression turn on in response to an inducer or off in response to a repressor. GFP is precisely the console.log of synthetic biology: a visibility tool that makes the invisible machinery of gene expression readable. The development of GFP as a tool was recognized with the 2008 Nobel Prize in Chemistry, awarded to Osamu Shimomura, Martin Chalfie, and Roger Tsien. Since then, a full palette of fluorescent protein variants has emerged, fluorescing in yellow, cyan, red, and near-infrared, allowing experimenters to label multiple different proteins in the same cell simultaneously.

Diagram 3.5 - GFP Reporter Gene in Action

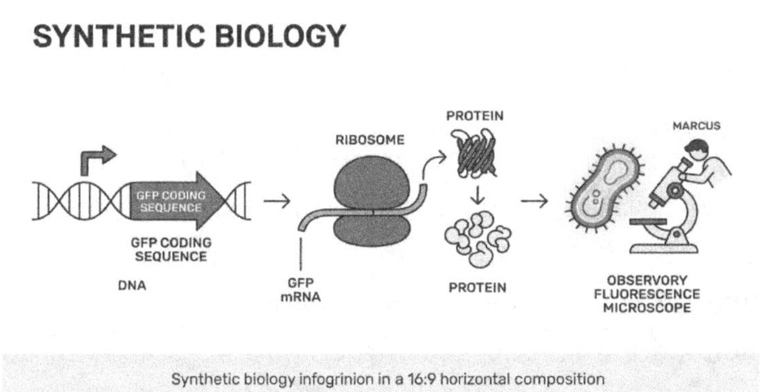

Luciferase, borrowed from fireflies, catalyzes a chemical reaction that produces light spontaneously as long as its substrate luciferin is available. Unlike GFP, which requires an excitation light source, luciferase produces light on its own, making it useful for measuring very low expression levels where cellular autofluorescence would obscure a faint GFP signal. The availability of reliable reporter genes is architecturally necessary, not merely convenient. The design-build-test-learn cycle that governs synthetic biology practice depends entirely on the ability to measure what a circuit is doing. A circuit you cannot measure is a circuit you cannot improve. Reporter genes are the measurement layer that enables iterative engineering.

The Standardized Registry: BioBricks and the iGEM Parts Registry

Parts are only useful at scale if they can be shared, and sharing requires standardization. The BioBrick standard was developed in the early 2000s, primarily through work at MIT, as a direct attempt to solve the interface problem that plagued early recombinant DNA research. A BioBrick is a genetic part that has been flanked by a specific set of restriction enzyme sites in a standardized configuration. The key property of the BioBrick configuration is that when two BioBricks are assembled, the resulting sequence is itself a valid BioBrick. BioBrick assembly is composable: you can join two parts, then join the result with a third, building up a multi-part genetic construct from standardized components using a repeatable, predictable protocol.

The iGEM Registry of Standard Biological Parts is the public repository built around the BioBrick standard and its successors. iGEM stands for the International Genetically Engineered Machine Foundation, originally a competition for undergraduate teams to design and build biological systems from standard parts. The Registry grew from the parts library that teams deposited after each year's competition into a community-maintained database of characterized genetic parts covering promoters, RBS sequences, coding sequences, terminators, reporter genes, plasmid backbones, and entire genetic circuits. The Registry contains well over twenty thousand entries, each including the part's DNA sequence, a functional description, characterization data where available, and notes on the cellular contexts in which the part has been tested.

Diagram 3.6 - BioBrick Assembly: Composing Parts Like Software Modules

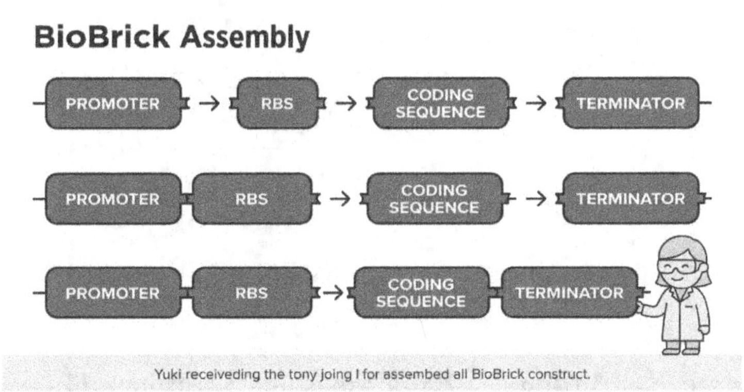

The npm analogy is worth pushing further. npm changed the pace of JavaScript development by giving every developer access to a shared library of pre-built, pre-tested code modules, dropping the cognitive overhead of building and allowing teams to compose more complex systems from reliable parts. The iGEM Registry represents the same logic applied to genetic parts: promoters, RBS sequences, and terminators that every project needs do not have to be characterized from scratch. There are important differences, however. npm packages, once tested, are deterministic: the same code in the same runtime produces the same output every time. Biological parts carry no such guarantee, and the reasons why are the subject of this chapter's final technical section.

Diagram 3.7 - The iGEM Registry as a Biological Parts Shelf

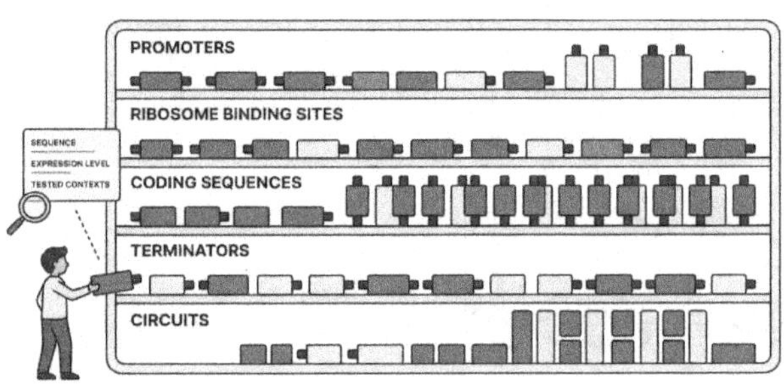

Plasmids as Chassis: Delivering Parts into Cells

A genetic part sitting in a database is like a software library in a repository: it only becomes useful when it is running in the right environment. For genetic parts, the primary delivery vehicle into a living cell is the plasmid. A plasmid is a small, circular molecule of double-stranded DNA that replicates independently of the cell's main chromosome. Plasmids occur naturally in bacteria and have been central to molecular biology since 1973, when Stanley Cohen and Herbert Boyer demonstrated that you could cut a gene from one organism, insert it into a plasmid, and have that plasmid replicate inside a bacterial cell. That experiment is one of the founding events of recombinant DNA technology.

In synthetic biology, a plasmid serves as the chassis that holds your assembled genetic circuit. You design the circuit, physically assemble the DNA sequence by combining your parts, insert the assembled sequence into a plasmid vector, and introduce that plasmid into your host organism. The plasmid carries its sequence into the cell, and because plasmids replicate autonomously, every daughter cell inherits a copy of the plasmid and therefore a copy of your circuit. For many applications, running the circuit from a plasmid is sufficient, with the significant advantage that you can remove the circuit from the organism simply by eliminating the plasmid.

A plasmid vector used in synthetic biology typically contains several functional elements beyond the circuit you are inserting. There is an origin of replication that tells the cell's DNA-copying machinery how many copies to maintain. High-copy-number plasmids replicate to hundreds of copies per cell, driving very high levels of expression. Low-copy-number plasmids maintain only a few copies, giving more moderate, stable expression. There is also a selectable marker, most commonly an antibiotic resistance gene, that allows researchers to select for cells that successfully took up the plasmid: cells that lack the plasmid die in media containing the antibiotic, and cells that carry it survive and proliferate.

Diagram 3.8 - Anatomy of a Plasmid Vector

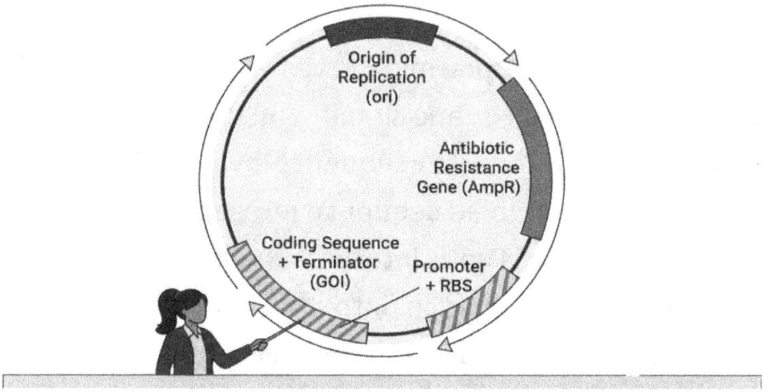

Beyond standard plasmids, synthetic biologists have developed a vocabulary of vector types optimized for different applications. Integrating vectors insert themselves into the host organism's chromosome at a specific location, which is useful when stability is more important than removability. Viral vectors, particularly those based on adeno-associated virus (AAV), are used to deliver genetic circuits into mammalian cells. These vectors borrow the natural ability of viruses to enter cells and deliver genetic material, but have been engineered to remove the genes responsible for viral replication and pathogenicity. Several approved gene therapies on the market today use AAV-based vectors to deliver corrective genes to patients with inherited genetic diseases.

Transformation: Getting Parts into Cells

Designing a plasmid carrying your assembled circuit is the design phase. Getting that plasmid into living cells is the build phase, and introducing foreign DNA into a cell is called transformation. The ability of cells to internalize and express foreign DNA is the physical mechanism that makes all of synthetic biology possible. Without transformation, there would be no way to test a design in a living system, and without testing, there would be no engineering cycle.

For bacterial cells, particularly E. coli, transformation is a routine laboratory procedure. Chemical transformation uses calcium chloride and heat shock to temporarily make the cell membrane permeable, allowing plasmid DNA to enter. The procedure is fast, cheap, and reliable. Electroporation, which uses a brief pulse of electrical current to create temporary pores in the cell membrane, achieves higher transformation efficiency when the DNA construct is large. Transforming mammalian cells is more technically demanding. Lipofection uses lipid nanoparticles to encapsulate DNA and fuse with the cell membrane. Viral transduction using engineered viral vectors is the most efficient delivery method for many cell types and the standard approach for clinical-grade gene therapy.

Diagram 3.9 - Transformation: Delivering a Plasmid into a Bacterial Cell

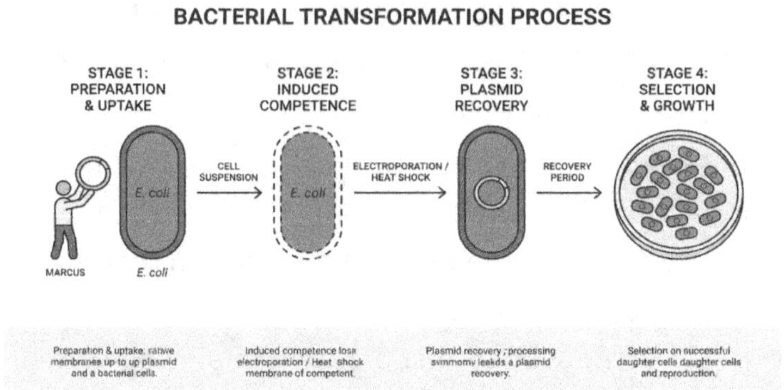

Vector Design: Engineering the Delivery System

The design of the vector that carries a genetic circuit is tightly coupled to the design of the circuit itself. The vector's properties, copy number, selectable markers, and integration behavior directly influence the circuit it carries. An experienced synthetic biologist like Priya Anand does not think about the circuit design and then separately choose a vector as if selecting a shipping box. She thinks about them together as a system, because the vector's contributions to the cell's overall genetic load, to the expression levels of the circuit's parts, and to the long-term stability of the construct are all design variables that shape the final behavior of the engineered organism.

One of the most consequential vector design decisions is copy number. High-copy-number plasmids can replicate to hundreds of copies per cell, dramatically amplifying expression levels. But this also creates a metabolic burden problem. Every copy of the plasmid is being replicated and maintained by the cell's molecular machinery, consuming transcription and translation resources. Under sufficient metabolic burden, cells slow their growth and eventually evolve mutations that delete or silence the very genes you were trying to express. High-copy-number expression is a short-term strategy, not a long-term one, and the difference between a research prototype and a manufacturable product often comes down to solving the metabolic burden problem. Another critical decision is the choice of a selectable marker. Antibiotic resistance markers work reliably, but in food and therapeutic contexts, they raise biosafety and regulatory concerns, and regulatory agencies have increasingly pushed for antibiotic-free selection systems based on auxotrophic markers that make the cell dependent on a nutrient it can produce only while maintaining the plasmid.

Diagram 3.10 - Vector Copy Number and Its Effects on Expression

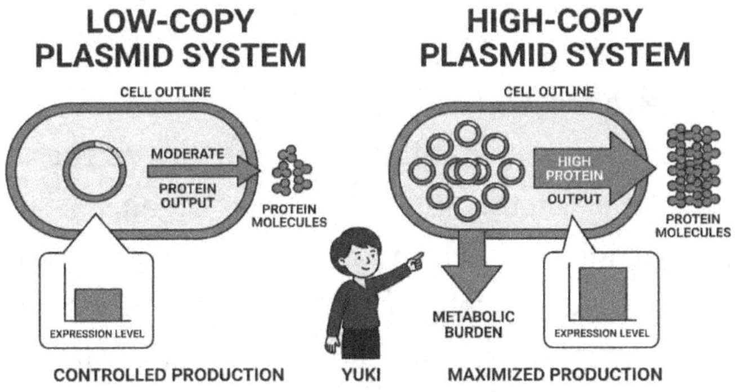

The Design-Build-Test-Learn Cycle: A Preview

The parts are the vocabulary. The vector is the delivery mechanism. The organism is the execution environment. But none of these elements guarantees that a genetic circuit will behave as designed. Biology is not deterministic in the way that software is deterministic, and the gap between what a circuit is designed to do and what it actually does when placed inside a living cell is the central practical problem of synthetic biology. The field's response is the design-build-test-learn cycle, and understanding it at a conceptual level is essential to making sense of how synthetic biology projects progress from idea to a working prototype.

In the design phase, a team like Helix Forge specifies the parts they intend to use, their arrangement on a vector, the expected expression levels based on characterized part data, and the predicted behavior of the assembled circuit. In the build phase, the team physically assembles the designed construct, synthesizes DNA sequences, performs restriction enzyme digestions and ligations to join parts, inserts the assembled sequence into a vector, and transforms the vector into the host organism. Gene synthesis technology, which allows any specified DNA sequence to be chemically synthesized from scratch, has dramatically accelerated this phase. Companies like Twist Bioscience and Integrated DNA Technologies can produce synthesized DNA of thousands of base pairs in a matter of days, at costs that have fallen by more than a thousandfold since 2000.

In the test phase, the team measures the behavior of the constructed circuit using reporter genes and other quantitative readouts. They compare measured behavior to predicted behavior. Almost always, there is a gap, and the task of the test phase is to understand why: which assumption in the design model was wrong, and which part behaved differently than its datasheet predicted. The learning phase translates test results into updated knowledge that feeds back into the next design iteration, and the cycle starts again. At Ginkgo Bioworks, the entire cycle is automated: robotic platforms cycle through thousands of design variants in the time it would take a traditional lab to cycle through a dozen. The scale of iteration is one of the primary advantages of synthetic biology foundry platforms, and Chapter 7 examines how that scale advantage translates into commercial value.

Diagram 3.11 - The Design-Build-Test-Learn Cycle

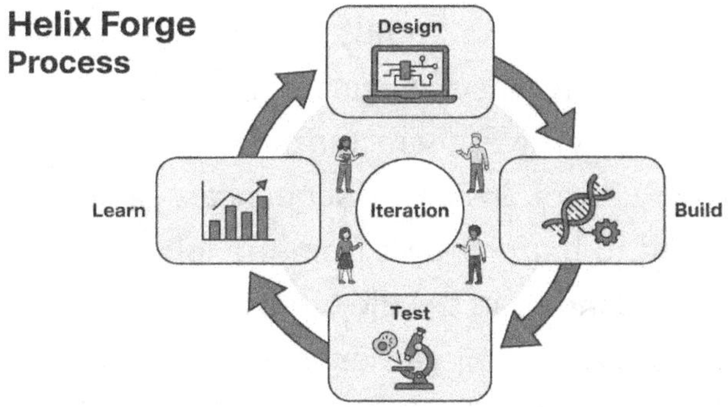

Caption: The Helix Forge, full Helix Forge team or cycle is ucique in an executive technical tone

Context-Dependence: When Parts Don't Behave as Expected

Marcus Webb, who came to synthetic biology from a career building distributed software systems, has a specific phrase he uses when a genetic circuit behaves unexpectedly: "the documentation was wrong." He is being only half-facetious. Biological parts are less predictable than electronic components. A promoter that drives high expression in E. coli may drive low expression in yeast, and moderate expression in a mammalian cell line. An RBS sequence that produces a specific protein output level in one genetic context may produce a very different output level when its surrounding sequence is changed. This property is called context-dependence, and it is the central reliability challenge of the genetic toolkit.

Context-dependence arises from several distinct sources. The first is sequence context: the DNA and RNA sequences immediately surrounding a part influence its behavior in ways that are difficult to predict from the part's behavior in isolation. Changes in the secondary structure of the mRNA upstream or downstream of an RBS can dramatically alter ribosome-binding efficiency. Engineering around these effects requires extensive characterization in each new context or the use of insulator sequences, short DNA spacers designed to buffer a part from the influence of its neighbors. The second source is the cellular environment: a part characterized in E. coli carries characterization data specific to E. coli's transcription and translation machinery, and many of those parameters differ significantly across yeast, mammalian cells, or other production hosts. A repressor protein characterized in bacteria may fold incorrectly in a mammalian cell, degrade rapidly, or encounter competing interactions with endogenous proteins that alter its behavior.

The third source of context-dependence is metabolic state. Cells under different growth conditions, at different stages of their cell cycle, or under different nutritional constraints are not equivalent execution environments. A circuit that behaves stably in a well-fed, exponentially growing E. coli culture may behave very differently when the culture enters the stationary phase. The synthetic biology community has made genuine progress through improved characterization practices, computational tools that model sequence-context effects on RBS strength, and insulator design. But the problem remains unsolved. Biology is not a predictable compiler. The cell is not a deterministic processor. This fundamental tension, between the engineering aspiration of composable, predictable parts and the biological reality of context-dependent behavior, is what motivates the design-build-test-learn cycle as an operational necessity: when you cannot fully predict, you must iterate.

Diagram 3.12 - Context-Dependence: One Part, Different Outcomes

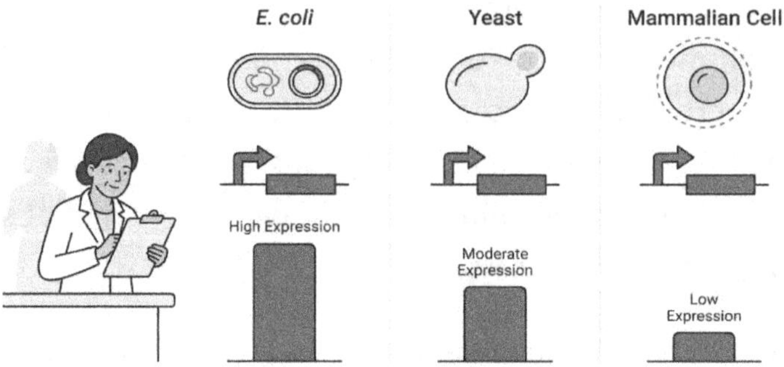

Priya Anand (44 years old, etd). one genetic part produces different outcomes across different organisms.

What This Means For You

If you are an engineer evaluating a synthetic biology platform, the parts vocabulary you have acquired in this chapter is exactly what you need to ask the right technical questions. When a company claims a novel promoter system or a proprietary RBS library, you now know what those claims mean and what to ask: How was it characterized? In what cell type? Across what range of conditions? What is the expression level relative to standard reference parts? How stable is expression over extended culture? These are not difficult questions for a competent technical team to answer, and a team that cannot answer them clearly has immature characterization practices. Characterization rigor is one of the clearest signals of engineering sophistication in this field.

If you are an entrepreneur considering a business model in synthetic biology, the parts and standards layer is one of the most promising areas to compete in. The history of every engineering discipline shows that companies controlling standardized parts infrastructure can extract disproportionate value from the ecosystem that builds on top of them. In semiconductors, TSMC manufactures the chips designed by the ecosystem. In cloud computing, AWS provides the infrastructure on which applications run. In synthetic biology, the equivalent infrastructure layer, the high-quality characterized parts libraries, the assembly standards, the design tools, and the organism engineering foundries are still being built and contested. Companies like Ginkgo Bioworks, Twist Bioscience, and Benchling are competing to own different layers of this infrastructure stack, and understanding what each layer does is the prerequisite for understanding why that competition matters.

Takeaway

The genetic toolkit is a set of functional DNA parts, promoters, ribosome binding sites, coding sequences, terminators, repressors, activators, and reporter genes, each with a defined molecular function and a standardized interface. Assembled on a plasmid vector and introduced into a host organism through transformation, these parts form the building blocks of every synthetic biological system in existence, from the simplest reporter construct to the most complex therapeutic cell circuit. The BioBrick standard and the iGEM Parts Registry gave the field a shared vocabulary and shared infrastructure, accelerating the pace of biological engineering in a way that is genuinely analogous to the acceleration that package managers brought to software development.

The design-build-test-learn cycle is the operational backbone of synthetic biology practice. It exists because prediction is imperfect: the gap between a designed circuit and a working circuit must be closed by measurement and iteration. Reporter genes like GFP and luciferase are the measurement layer that enables iteration. Without observable outputs, you cannot close the feedback loop, and without closing the feedback loop, you cannot improve. The combination of characterized parts, standardized vectors, and iterative testing allows a team like Helix Forge to move from a biological design specification to a validated prototype with engineering discipline rather than relying on pure trial and error.

The most important thing to carry forward from this chapter is the honest assessment of the toolkit's limits. Biological parts are not electronic components. Context-dependence means that a part characterized in one organism or one sequence context will not necessarily perform identically in another. The field is making genuine progress through improved characterization, computational modeling, and insulator design, but the problem remains unsolved. The predictability gap between a genetic circuit and an electronic circuit is real and consequential. It is the primary reason that Chapter 5 on genetic circuits must devote as much time to engineering challenges as to engineering achievements. Knowing the toolkit is the beginning. Knowing its limits is what makes you useful.

Chapter 9, on biology that listens, will show what happens when the design-build-test-learn cycle is applied not just to production systems but to sensing systems, where the genetic toolkit's parts are assembled to detect specific molecular signals and produce a measurable response. The promoter's sensitivity to specific transcription factors, the repressor's ability to translate a molecular input into a gene expression output, and the reporter gene's ability to make that output visible: all of those properties become the functional elements of biosensor design. The toolkit does not change. What changes is the intent and the problems you choose to solve with it. That is the enduring lesson of synthetic biology's history, and it is the theme that runs through every remaining chapter of this book.

4 CRISPR and the Precision Revolution

Opening Scenario

The conference room at Helix Forge had two cell images on the main monitor. On the left, red blood cells from a patient with sickle cell disease: crescent-shaped, rigid, prone to jamming in the small vessels that feed organs and joints. On the right, cells from the same patient line after a CRISPR editing session: round, pliable, and indistinguishable from healthy donor cells. A single point mutation, one letter in three billion, had been corrected. Priya had done it herself, twice, in the same week.

One of the investors leaned forward. "So that's it," he said. "CRISPR solves everything." Priya set down her pointer. "CRISPR is a chapter," she said. "Synthetic biology is the whole book. Today I want to make sure you understand the difference." Marcus, watching from the back of the room, typed a note to himself: find-and-replace versus designing the document. The rest of the afternoon would prove both halves of that sentence.

Why It Matters

CRISPR is the most widely recognized tool in modern biology. In roughly a decade, it moved from a curiosity in bacterial immunology to a Nobel Prize-winning platform that enabled the first FDA-approved gene-editing medicine. No other biotechnology tool has traveled that far that fast. If you work anywhere near life sciences, biotech investment, pharmaceutical development, or health policy, you have almost certainly encountered the word. What is less common is a clear mechanistic understanding of what CRISPR actually does, what it cannot do, and how it fits into the broader engineering toolkit.

That gap has practical consequences. Engineers and entrepreneurs who understand CRISPR only at the headline level tend to make the same mistake: they treat it as a general-purpose solution for any problem involving genetics. It is not. CRISPR is a precision editor. It can find a specific location in a genome and change what is there. It cannot design a genetic circuit, engineer a metabolic pathway, or create a new biological function from parts.

Chapter 4, therefore, does two jobs: giving you a complete understanding of CRISPR and its successors, and drawing the boundary line that makes the rest of this book legible.

Diagram 4.1 - CRISPR in the Synthetic Biology Toolkit

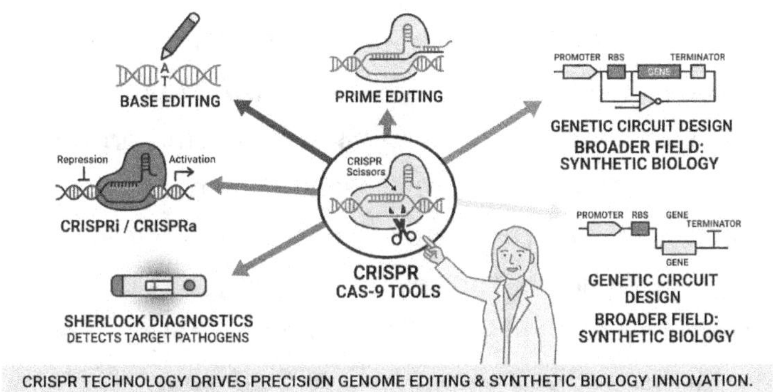

Bacterial Immune System: Where CRISPR Came From

To understand why CRISPR works the way it does, you need to understand why bacteria evolved it. Bacteria have been locked in an arms race with bacteriophages, the viruses that infect them, for billions of years, and CRISPR is one of their most sophisticated defensive adaptations: an adaptive immune system that learns from past infections. CRISPR stands for Clustered Regularly Interspaced Short Palindromic Repeats, a description of the pattern of repeated and unique sequences in the bacterial chromosome where viral memories are stored.

When a bacteriophage injects its DNA into a bacterial cell, specialized proteins capture a short snippet of the viral DNA, typically 20 nucleotides long, and insert it into the CRISPR array as a spacer, a molecular memory of the infection. When the same virus attacks again, the cell transcribes the CRISPR array into guide RNAs that carry those 20-letter addresses. Each guide RNA travels with a protein called Cas9, short for CRISPR-associated protein 9. When the guide RNA finds a matching sequence in the viral DNA, Cas9 docks and cuts both strands, destroying the virus before it can replicate. The key insight: targeting is entirely determined by the guide RNA sequence. Change the 20-letter address, and you change where Cas9 goes.

Jennifer Doudna at UC Berkeley and Emmanuelle Charpentier, then at the Helmholtz Center for Infection Research, with contributions from Feng Zhang at the Broad Institute, showed in 2012 and 2013 that programmable recognition could be redirected to target any DNA sequence in any organism. Their work launched one of the fastest technological transitions in the history of molecular biology and earned Doudna and Charpentier the 2020 Nobel Prize in Chemistry. The bacterial origin explains the architecture of the tool: CRISPR's precision is not the product of human engineering cleverness but of billions of years of evolutionary pressure that selected for a recognition system accurate enough to distinguish viral sequences from the cell's own DNA.

Diagram 4.2 - The Natural CRISPR Immune System in Bacteria

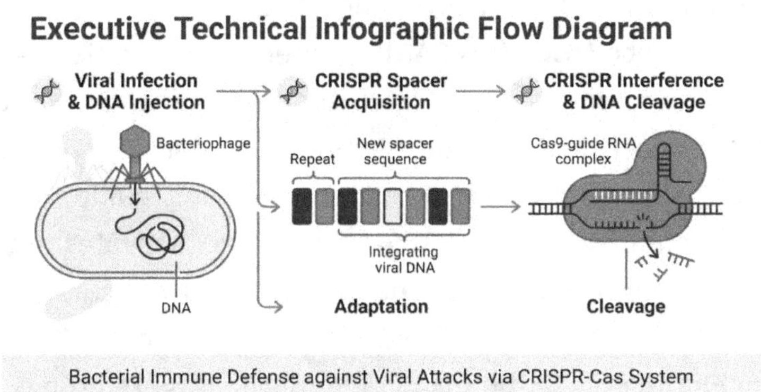

The Mechanism of Cas9: How the GPS Find-and-Replace Works

The CRISPR-Cas9 editing system in laboratory form has two components: the guide RNA, which provides the address, and the Cas9 protein, which performs the cut. The guide RNA is a single molecule roughly 100 nucleotides long. The first 20 nucleotides are the targeting sequence, designed to be complementary to the DNA target via Watson-Crick base-pairing that holds the double helix together. When the guide RNA finds a complementary sequence in the genome, it binds to one strand and alters the shape of Cas9, thereby activating its cutting machinery.

Cas9 does not cut at any target where its guide RNA lands. There is a second requirement: the target sequence must be immediately flanked by a short sequence called a PAM (protospacer adjacent motif). For the most widely used Cas9, from Streptococcus pyogenes, the PAM is the three-letter sequence NGG. This PAM requirement is a molecular confirmation code, a safety latch that evolved to prevent Cas9 from accidentally cutting the bacterial cell's own CRISPR array. When both conditions are met, guide RNA complementarity and PAM recognition, Cas9 activates two cutting domains: RuvC cuts one strand, and HNH cuts the other. The result is a double-strand break, a complete cut through both rails of the DNA ladder at the targeted rung.

A double-strand break triggers one of two cellular repair pathways. Non-homologous end joining, or NHEJ, rejoins the broken ends quickly but imprecisely, often introducing small insertions or deletions called indels at the cut site. If the cut falls within a protein-coding gene, indels typically disrupt the gene's function, effectively knocking it out. Homology-directed repair (HDR) uses a provided DNA template to precisely repair a break, allowing the researcher to correct a mutation or insert a new sequence. HDR is more precise but requires cells to be actively dividing, which limits its use in non-dividing tissues like neurons and heart muscle. The delivery question is equally consequential: getting Cas9 and its guide RNA into the right cells in the right tissue, using adeno-associated viruses, lipid nanoparticles, or electroporation, is often the rate-limiting engineering challenge in any clinical program.

Diagram 4.3 - Cas9 Cutting at the PAM Site

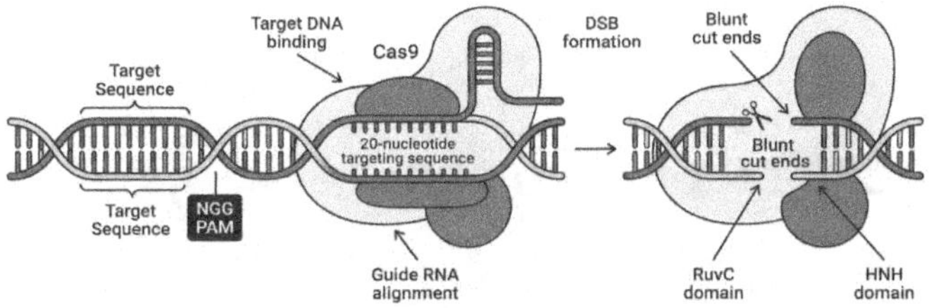

Diagram 4.4 - NHEJ vs. Homology-Directed Repair After a Double-Strand Break

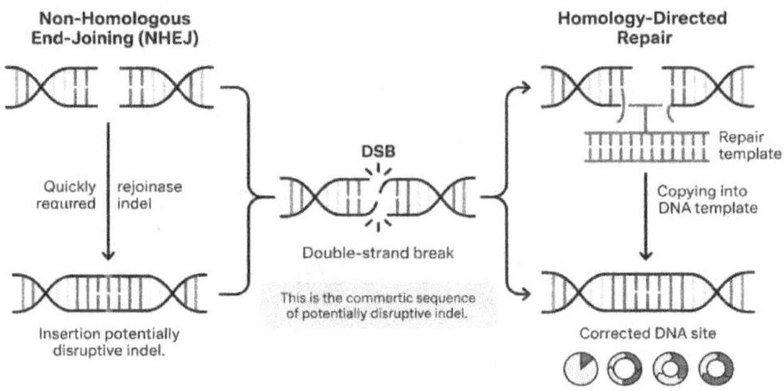

What CRISPR Can Do: Clinical Examples and the Sickle Cell Breakthrough

In December 2023, the FDA approved Casgevy, developed by Vertex Pharmaceuticals and CRISPR Therapeutics, for the treatment of sickle cell disease and transfusion-dependent beta-thalassemia. It was the first CRISPR-based medicine approved anywhere in the world, and it arrived as both a clinical milestone and a proof of concept that the precision gene-editing era in medicine had formally begun.

Sickle cell disease is caused by a single point mutation in the HBB gene, which encodes the beta-globin subunit of hemoglobin. The mutation replaces glutamic acid with valine at one position in the protein chain, causing hemoglobin molecules to polymerize under low-oxygen conditions, forming rigid fibers that distort red blood cells into a crescent or sickle shape. Sickle cells are fragile; they are rapidly cleared from circulation, causing anemia, and they clog small blood vessels, causing pain crises, organ damage, stroke, and shortened life expectancy. Roughly 100,000 people in the United States and over 25 million worldwide live with the disease.

Casgevy takes a biologically elegant detour rather than directly correcting the HBB mutation. During fetal development, the body uses a different gene, HBB-gamma, to produce fetal hemoglobin, or HbF, which does not polymerize the way sickle hemoglobin does. Shortly after birth, a protein called BCL11A shuts fetal hemoglobin production off and activates adult hemoglobin. People with natural variants that partially disable BCL11A continue making HbF into adulthood and, critically, do not develop severe sickle cell disease even carrying the HBB mutation. Casgevy uses CRISPR to disrupt a BCL11A enhancer in the patient's own hematopoietic stem cells, the bone marrow cells that produce all blood cells, editing them ex vivo before reinfusing them. The result is sustained high levels of fetal hemoglobin production. In clinical trials, the vast majority of treated patients became free of severe pain crises, many achieving hemoglobin levels in the normal range for the first time in their lives.

Diagram 4.5 - Sickle Cell Red Blood Cell Before and After CRISPR Editing

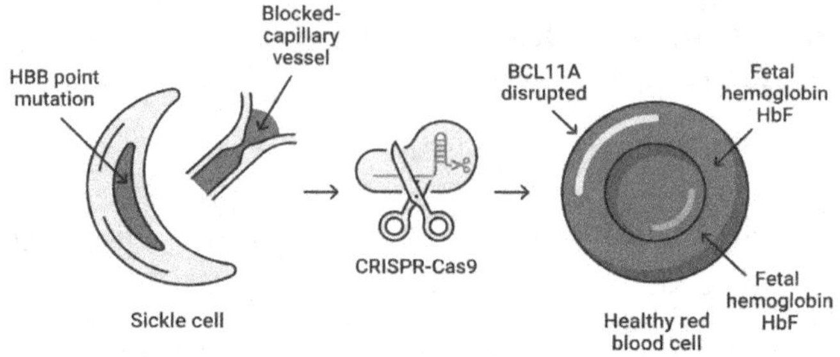

Conminiolist metaphist of the therapeutic gene editing process jnt palettis

Beyond sickle cell disease, the clinical CRISPR pipeline spans several disease areas. Intellia Therapeutics demonstrated in clinical trials that in vivo CRISPR editing, delivering Cas9 mRNA and a guide RNA via lipid nanoparticles directly into the bloodstream, substantially reduces levels of the misfolded TTR protein responsible for transthyretin amyloidosis, a progressive disease damaging the heart and nervous system. This was the first demonstration of clinically meaningful in vivo CRISPR editing in humans, which matters enormously because it extends the technology beyond settings requiring the complex ex vivo stem cell infrastructure of Casgevy. In oncology, CRISPR is being used to engineer allogeneic CAR-T cells from donor material by editing out genes that would otherwise cause rejection or graft-versus-host effects, enabling off-the-shelf T-cell therapies at a commercial scale. Several such programs are in early clinical trials with promising preliminary data.

Off-Target Effects and the Limits of CRISPR Editing

No tool this powerful operates without a failure mode, and CRISPR's primary failure mode is the off-target edit: a cut at a genomic location other than the intended target. Off-target edits occur because guide RNA binding does not require perfect complementarity. The human genome is three billion base pairs long, and most 20-nucleotide sequences occur, with one or two mismatches, at a handful of other locations. When Cas9 cuts one of these near-miss sites, it results in an unintended change. Depending on where it falls, the consequences range from inconsequential to potentially serious, including disruption of a tumor suppressor gene or activation of an oncogene.

The field has responded with several strategies that substantially reduce off-target risk. High-fidelity Cas9 variants, engineered through directed evolution and rational protein design, with names such as eSpCas9 and HiFi Cas9, exhibit orders-of-magnitude lower off-target activity than wild-type Cas9. Paired Cas9 nickase strategies use two modified Cas9 molecules that each cut only one strand, requiring both to bind to nearby sites for a double-strand break to occur, thereby multiplying the precision requirement. Delivery as mRNA or as pre-assembled ribonucleoprotein complexes limits the window of Cas9 activity to hours rather than days, reducing the number of opportunities for off-target engagement. Clinical-grade CRISPR programs now routinely use whole-genome sequencing of edited cell populations to verify off-target profiles before proceeding to human use.

Diagram 4.6 - Off-Target Editing Risk and Mitigation Strategies

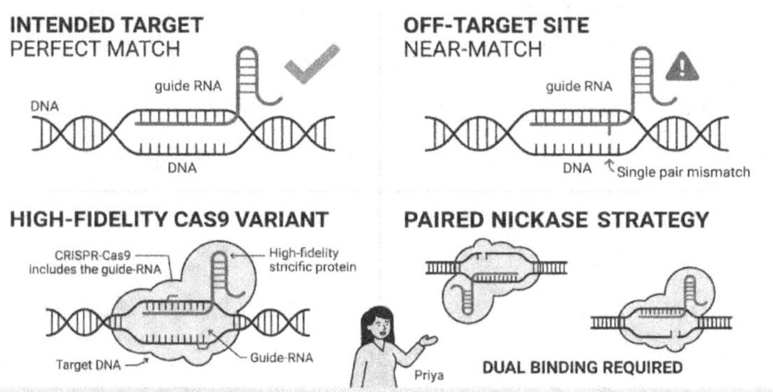

CRISPR-Cas9 variants also paired nickase strategies, our strand at indereemhance arn executive technical.

Beyond off-target editing, the limits of CRISPR as a class of tools deserve direct statement, because they define what the rest of this book is about. CRISPR edits what is already present in a genome. It disrupts genes, corrects point mutations, inserts short sequences, and deletes segments. What it does not do is design a new biological function. It cannot construct a genetic circuit that responds to a stimulus and produces a programmed output. It cannot engineer a metabolic pathway that builds a new compound. It cannot create a regulatory logic layer that coordinates gene expression across multiple signals. Those functions require the design toolkit introduced in Chapter 5. CRISPR gets you to the page where the edit needs to happen. Synthetic biology gives you the grammar, the architecture, and the story itself.

Base Editing: Changing a Letter Without Breaking the Spine

By 2016, the CRISPR field had acknowledged a problem. The double-strand break Cas9 produces is powerful but imprecise: the cell's choice of repair pathway is not fully controllable, NHEJ-induced indels are random in size and position, and HDR rates are low in non-dividing cells. For diseases caused by point mutations, where a single DNA letter is wrong, the ideal edit would be more like correcting a typo than cutting out a sentence and pasting a new one. David Liu's laboratory at the Broad Institute developed exactly that capability, calling it base editing.

Base editors combine a catalytically impaired Cas9, one that binds its target through guide RNA guidance but cannot cut both strands of the DNA, with a chemical enzyme that directly converts one DNA base into another. The first class, cytosine base editors (CBEs), carries a cytosine deaminase that converts cytosine (C) to uracil (U), which the cell then reads as thymine (T), producing a C-to-T edit without any double-strand break. The second class, adenine base editors (ABEs), convert adenine (A) to inosine (I), which the cell reads as guanine (G), producing an A-to-G edit. Together, CBEs and ABEs cover all four transition mutations, the most common class of disease-causing point mutations, addressing roughly 30,000 known pathogenic variants in the human genome. Because no double-strand break is created, the primary source of unintended indels is eliminated. Because no repair template is required, base editing works efficiently in non-dividing cells where HDR is impractical. Early clinical programs using base editors are now in Phase 1 and Phase 2 trials for elevated LDL cholesterol, sickle cell disease, and certain leukemias.

Diagram 4.7 - Base Editor Pencil Tip Mechanism

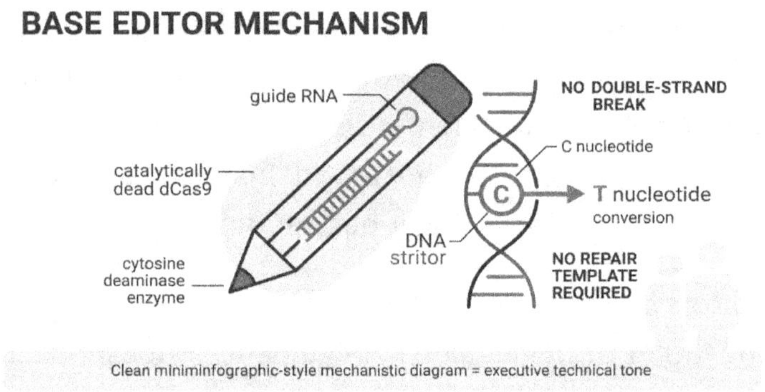

Prime Editing: The Search-and-Replace Function

David Liu's laboratory did not stop at base editing. In 2019, they published prime editing, which they explicitly described as a genome-wide search-and-replace operation. The description is precise: prime editing can install any small insertion, deletion, or any of the twelve types of point mutation at a target site, without a double-strand break and without a separate donor DNA template. This combination covers the vast majority of known Mendelian disease-causing mutations.

A prime editor consists of a Cas9 nickase, which cuts only one strand of DNA rather than both, fused to a reverse transcriptase, which reads an RNA molecule and synthesizes a complementary DNA strand. The system is guided by a pegRNA, short for prime editing guide RNA, which has the standard 20-nucleotide targeting sequence plus an extension at its end that encodes the desired edit as an RNA template. When the prime editor nicks one strand of DNA at the target site, the pegRNA extension hybridizes to the nicked strand, and the reverse transcriptase reads the template, synthesizing a new DNA segment containing the desired edit. Cellular processing then integrates this new segment into the chromosome. Because only a single-strand nick is involved, the cell does not trigger the crisis-mode repair responses associated with double-strand breaks, and the profile of unintended edits is correspondingly cleaner. Prime Medicine was founded specifically to commercialize this platform, and early preclinical data across multiple disease models are encouraging.

Diagram 4.8 - Prime Editor with Template Tail Architecture

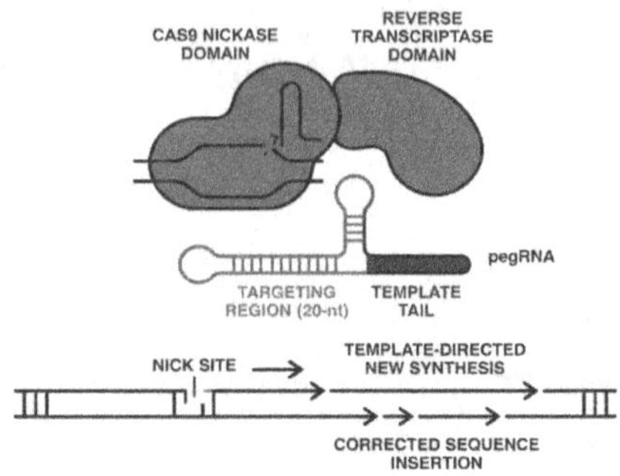

Mechanistic metaphor per central specific synthesiis per image (optional)

CRISPRi and CRISPRa: Dimmer Switches for Gene Expression

Not every application requires a permanent change to DNA. Sometimes the goal is to turn a gene up or down without altering its sequence. CRISPRi and CRISPRa address this need by building on a version of Cas9 with its cutting activity disabled: catalytically dead Cas9, or dCas9. This modified protein retains its guide RNA-directed binding but cannot cut the DNA it lands on. CRISPRi, or CRISPR interference, directs dCas9 to a gene's promoter, the DNA region where the transcription machinery binds to begin RNA production. A dCas9 protein parked at the promoter physically blocks the machinery, reducing gene expression without deleting or mutating the gene. CRISPRa, or CRISPR activation, fuses transcriptional activator domains to dCas9, so that when it binds near a gene's promoter, it recruits the transcription machinery rather than blocking it, increasing expression of any gene the guide RNA addresses. Both tools work in non-dividing cells, and multiple guide RNAs can operate simultaneously in the same cell, allowing several genes to be modulated at once.

The significance of CRISPRi and CRISPRa for genetic circuit design is direct and practical. When Yuki's team at Helix Forge designs a circuit that needs to switch a gene on or off in response to a cellular signal, CRISPRi and CRISPRa are among the most versatile components available. Because the only thing that determines which gene is affected is the guide RNA sequence, these tools can be incorporated into multi-input regulatory logic: a gene can be held silent by CRISPRi until a specific signal degrades the interfering complex, or switched on by CRISPRa in response to a detected metabolite. This programmability is what makes them not just silencing and activation tools but genuine circuit components, and their role in genetic circuit design will be explored in detail in Chapter 5. At a large scale, CRISPRi screens in which thousands of guide RNAs simultaneously silence different genes across a cell population have been used to identify which genes confer drug resistance or sensitivity, generating maps of gene function with a comprehensiveness that earlier methods could not match.

Diagram 4.9 - CRISPRi and CRISPRa as Gene Expression Dimmer Switches

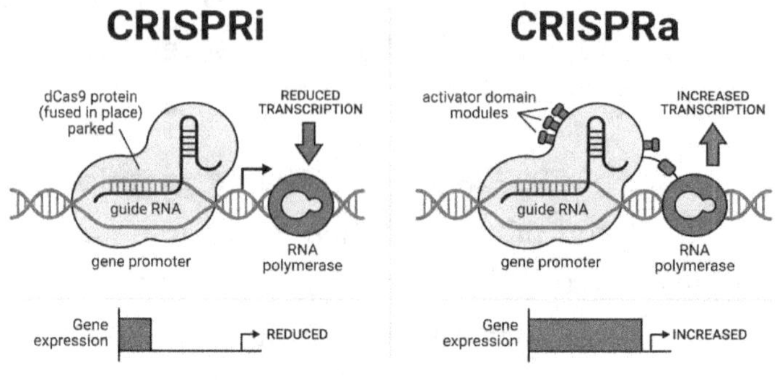

CRISPRi infographic diagnationmath geneoris dCase9 in place on parked dr elect inihitiation in gene transcription

CRISPR Diagnostics: SHERLOCK, DETECTR, and the Pandemic Proof of Concept

The molecular recognition machinery at the core of CRISPR, the ability of a guide RNA to find a specific nucleic acid sequence with high specificity, can be repurposed for a completely different job: detecting whether a sequence is present in a sample at all. This is the basis of CRISPR diagnostics, and during the COVID-19 pandemic, two platforms, SHERLOCK and DETECTR, demonstrated that the approach could deliver laboratory-quality sensitivity in a format readable on a paper strip outside a laboratory setting.

SHERLOCK stands for Specific High-sensitivity Enzymatic Reporter UnLOCKing. Developed in Feng Zhang's laboratory at the Broad Institute, it uses a CRISPR protein called Cas13, which targets RNA rather than DNA. Cas13 has collateral cleavage activity: when its guide RNA directs it to the target

RNA, the protein becomes activated and begins cleaving nearby RNA molecules indiscriminately. In the SHERLOCK system, short reporter molecules carry a fluorescent dye on one end and a quenching molecule on the other. When Cas13 is activated by target RNA, it cleaves the reporter, separating the dye from the quencher and generating a detectable signal. DETECTR, which stands for DNA Endonuclease Targeted CRISPR Trans Reporter, was developed in Jennifer Doudna's laboratory and uses Cas12a, which targets DNA and, upon target recognition, activates collateral cleavage of single-stranded DNA reporters. Both platforms can detect their targets at attomolar concentrations, finding a single target molecule among ten billion irrelevant molecules, with a sensitivity comparable to PCR.

Diagram 4.10 - CRISPR Diagnostic Chip Using SHERLOCK

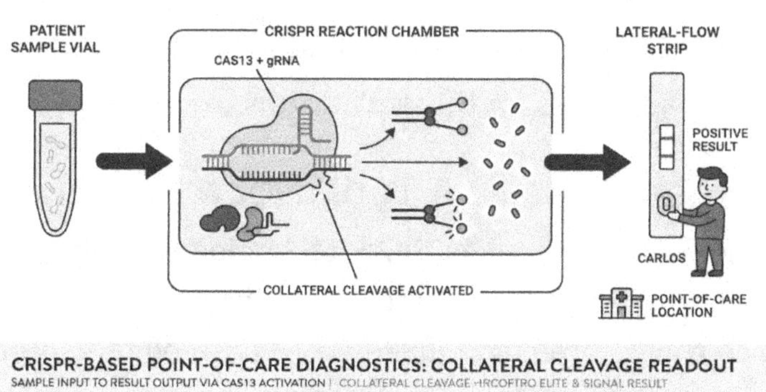

During the COVID-19 pandemic, both platforms were validated against SARS-CoV-2 RNA in clinical samples, delivering sensitivity and specificity competitive with PCR-based tests and producing results in under an hour without laboratory equipment. PCR-based diagnostics require thermal cyclers, trained personnel, and controlled environments. They are excellent tools, but they are laboratory tools. CRISPR-based diagnostics, because their readout can be configured as a visible line on a lateral flow strip, can in principle be manufactured and deployed at the cost and scale of home pregnancy tests, reaching health clinics in low-resource settings where laboratory infrastructure is unavailable. Beyond infectious disease, guide RNAs can be designed to detect cancer-associated mutations in cell-free DNA from blood samples, antibiotic resistance mutations in bacterial pathogens, or somatic mutations in tumor biopsies, extending the diagnostic reach of CRISPR's molecular recognition specificity across a broad range of clinical applications. Mammoth Biosciences, co-founded by Doudna, and Sherlock Biosciences, co-founded by Zhang, are the primary commercial vehicles pursuing regulatory approvals for these platforms.

CRISPR in Context: A Tool, Not a Platform

With the full landscape of CRISPR technologies in view, the most important conceptual move this chapter can make is to place them correctly. CRISPR-Cas9, base editors, prime editors, CRISPRi, CRISPRa, and CRISPR diagnostics are all expressions of a single insight: that a guide RNA's programmable sequence recognition can be harnessed for a wide range of molecular operations. They represent the precision editing layer of the synthetic biology toolkit. When you need to change a specific sequence, silence or activate a specific gene, or detect a specific sequence, this family of tools gives you unprecedented molecular control. The reason they are so powerful is the same reason a well-designed text editor is powerful: precise operations at a known address, with reliable results.

But synthetic biology is not primarily an editing field. It is a design field. The question that drives the discipline is not how to change a specific sequence but how to construct a biological system that does something new. Constructing a genetic toggle switch requires designing promoters, ribosome binding sites, and feedback loops. Engineering a metabolic pathway requires selecting enzyme-encoding genes, tuning their expression, and iterating against a production target. Constructing a biosensor requires designing a biological information processing system. None of the CRISPR tools in this chapter can do that work on their own. CRISPR gets you to the page where the edit belongs. Synthetic biology is the pen, the grammar, and the story itself.

Diagram 4.11 - Editing vs. Design: CRISPR and Synthetic Biology as Distinct Layers

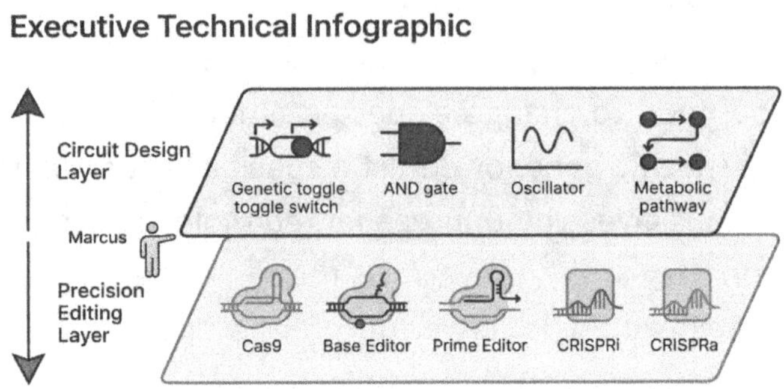

This distinction has direct consequences for how to evaluate companies and research programs. A company with CRISPR editing capabilities has a powerful molecular tool, but that tool alone does not constitute a designed biological system. A company that can design genetic circuits, assemble biological parts into functional systems, and iterate those systems through a disciplined engineering cycle has something qualitatively different: a platform. This is the distinction Priya was drawing for the advisors in the conference room. The most sophisticated applications combine both layers: a CAR-T cell that has been CRISPR-edited to remove immune checkpoint genes and simultaneously engineered to express a synthetic receptor with a genetic circuit controlling the timing and magnitude of its response is not just a CRISPR product. It is a designed biological system in which CRISPR editing played a necessary role. Understanding both layers is what makes it possible to reason about the field with genuine clarity.

What This Means For You

For engineers and product developers, this chapter provides a comprehensive mechanistic picture of the tools that will define precision medicine and biotechnology over the next decade. You can evaluate a CRISPR-based clinical program and ask the right questions: What is the guide RNA targeting, and what is the off-target evidence? Is the therapy editing ex vivo cells or delivering editors in vivo, and what does that imply for delivery risk and manufacturing complexity? Is the editing mechanism standard Cas9, a base editor, or a prime editor, and how does that choice affect the risk of unintended genomic changes? These questions distinguish informed technical evaluation from reading press releases.

For the entrepreneur, the clinical examples here, Casgevy's approval for sickle cell disease, Intellia's in vivo transthyretin results, and the first base-editing clinical programs, reveal a pattern worth recognizing. Each success came from identifying a specific disease, gene, editing operation, delivery route, and patient population. The specificity is the business model. Generic CRISPR capability is not a competitive moat. Specific validated programs with delivery solutions for specific tissues are the moat, and the companies that understand this distinction most clearly are consistently the ones making clinical progress.

For the policy professional, the editing-versus-design distinction is arguably the most important conceptual tool in the synthetic biology regulatory toolkit. Regulatory frameworks for CRISPR-based therapies currently treat these interventions as gene therapies, a well-established category with clear FDA oversight pathways for somatic cell editing. But as CRISPR is combined with genetic circuit design into more complex engineered biological systems, particularly in applications involving germline editing or environmental release, the regulatory frameworks will need to evolve to address the designed system as a whole, not just the individual editing operations within it. Understanding where today's regulations were written and where the technology is heading is a prerequisite for doing that work well.

Takeaway

CRISPR-Cas9 is one of the most consequential molecular tools in the history of biology. A bacterial immune system, evolved over billions of years to recognize and destroy viral invaders, was decoded, simplified, and redirected by a group of researchers whose insights were as much about engineering elegance as about molecular biology. The guide RNA's programmable address, Cas9's precise cutting, the PAM sequence confirmation, and the cell's own repair machinery working together produce a system capable of targeted changes to the genome of any living organism. The 2023 approval of Casgevy for sickle cell disease placed a capstone on the first decade of clinical CRISPR work. It opened a second decade in which base editing, prime editing, and in vivo delivery will define what is possible.

But this chapter has also drawn a boundary, and that boundary is as important as the capability itself. CRISPR edits what is already there. Synthetic biology designs what does not yet exist. The guide RNA can direct Cas9 to any address in any genome, and the system's variants can change individual letters, silence genes, amplify expression, or detect sequences in a sample. None of these operations, however precise, constitutes designing a new biological function. The genetic circuits, metabolic pathways, and programmed cellular behaviors that make synthetic biology a genuine engineering discipline require a design toolkit that CRISPR alone does not provide. Understanding that distinction is the most important thing this chapter set out to accomplish, and it is the foundation on which the rest of this book rests.

CRISPRi and CRISPRa are the family members that most naturally bridge editing and design, because programmable gene regulation is a component around which genetic circuits can be built. CRISPR diagnostics extend the molecular recognition framework into real-world sensing and detection, demonstrating the field's characteristic pattern of taking a validated mechanism and engineering it toward every job it can do. The diversity of the CRISPR family tree is itself a lesson in synthetic biology's approach to tool development: discover a mechanism that evolution already optimized, characterize it completely, then redirect it toward every problem its architecture can address.

Diagram 4.12 - The CRISPR Family Tree: From Bacterial Immunity to Clinical Tools

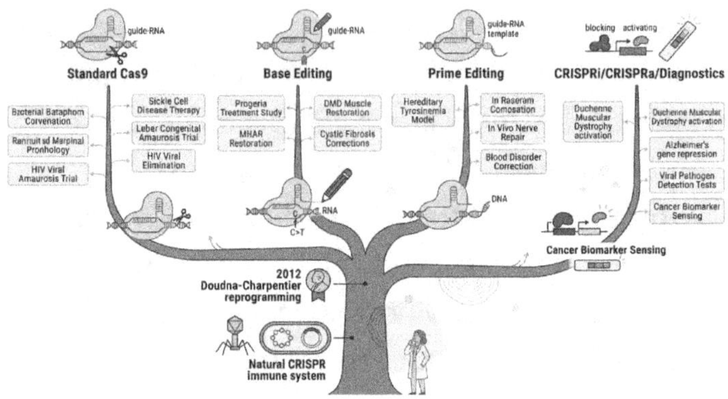

Chapter 5 introduces the design layer that sits above the editing layer described here. Genetic circuits, the toggle switches, logic gates, and oscillators that allow biological systems to process information and respond in programmed ways, are the subject of the next chapter. Those tools will use what CRISPR provides, particularly CRISPRi and CRISPRa as circuit components, but will operate according to a different kind of engineering logic: not find-and-change, but design-and-build. Priya was right in the conference room. CRISPR is a chapter. Next comes the book's architecture.

5 Designing Genetic Circuits

Opening Scenario

The whiteboard in Helix Forge's design lab is a controlled mess. Yuki Tanaka stands with a blue marker uncapped, her back to the window that looks out over the Cambridge rooftops, drawing two rectangles connected by arrows that loop back on themselves. She labels one rectangle "Gene A" and the other "Gene B". An arrow runs from Gene A down to a flat-headed symbol at Gene B's promoter, the shorthand for repression in circuit diagrams: Gene A makes a protein that shuts Gene B off. Then she draws the opposite: an arrow from Gene B pointing back, with the same flat-headed symbol, to Gene A's promoter. Gene B encodes a protein that shuts off Gene A. Two genes, each silencing the other, locked in a molecular standoff.

Marcus Webb is leaning against the opposite wall with his arms crossed, reading the diagram the way a programmer reads an unfamiliar codebase, tracing the data flow. He follows the arrows. He traces the loop. He goes quiet for a moment, and then he says: "That's a flip-flop." Yuki sets the marker down. "Yes." Marcus straightens up. "A memory bit. You built a memory bit out of DNA." Yuki picks the marker back up. "Welcome to genetic circuit design," she says. "Now let me show you an oscillator." She uncaps a red marker for emphasis, then puts it back and reaches for blue instead. Oscillators do not provide negative information. They are, in their own way, one of the most beautiful things in engineering: a system that makes time out of nothing but molecular interactions.

The toggle switch and the oscillator that Yuki drew on that whiteboard were not invented at Helix Forge. They are canonical designs from the year 2000, the founding circuits of a field. But the fact that Yuki can draw them, that Marcus can recognize them, that a startup in Cambridge can pick them up and deploy them in a living cell as naturally as a software team picks up a design pattern from a textbook, is the thing this chapter is about. Genetic circuit design has a vocabulary, a set of proven patterns, a growing library of parts, and a rigorous engineering workflow. This chapter explains all of it.

Why It Matters

If you have been reading this book as a software engineer, a technologist, or an entrepreneur, you have probably been waiting for the chapter where biology stops feeling like chemistry and starts feeling like programming. This is that chapter. Genetic circuit design is a part of synthetic biology where the engineering analogy is not a simplification or a metaphor. It is a precise description of what is actually happening at the molecular level inside a living cell.

The stakes are real and growing. Every engineered organism that does something useful, whether it produces a medicine, detects a disease biomarker, cleans a contaminated waterway, or synthesizes a chemical feedstock, does those things because it contains a genetic circuit that processes signals from its environment and produces a programmed response. The toggle switch is the core of a synthetic gene drive. The logic gate is the heart of a cellular diagnostic. The oscillator is the clock signal of a biological timing device. Understanding genetic circuits is not background knowledge for synthetic biology applications; it is the foundation on which they are built.

For the software engineer reading this chapter, the mental model you are about to acquire is genuinely transferable. The design patterns you will learn here, feedback loops, bistable switches, oscillators, and Boolean logic, are the same patterns you already know from control theory, digital logic, and distributed systems. They run on a different substrate, and that substrate has properties with no analog in silicon. But the patterns themselves are real, and recognizing them in a research paper or a startup pitch deck is a practical skill with immediate commercial value.

For the entrepreneur or investor, this chapter serves as a toolkit for due diligence. A company whose genetic circuits are built on characterized parts assembled with a rigorous design-build-test-learn workflow is a different investment from one whose circuits are held together with a biological equivalent of duct tape. After this chapter, you will be able to tell the difference.

What a Genetic Circuit Actually Is

A genetic circuit is a network of regulatory interactions between genetic parts that takes one or more molecular inputs and produces one or more molecular outputs according to a designed logical relationship. That definition is precise, and it is worth unpacking word by word, because each piece of it does real work.

Start with "regulatory interactions between genetic parts." The parts are the components from Chapter 3: promoters, ribosome-binding sites, coding sequences, and terminators. The regulatory interactions are the molecular conversations between these parts: a protein produced by one gene binding to the promoter of another gene and either activating or repressing its transcription. A transcription factor, which is a protein that controls whether a gene is read by binding to specific DNA sequences near the gene's start point, is the fundamental connector in any genetic circuit. When a transcription factor is a repressor, it silences its target. When it is an activator, it turns its target on. These two operations, repression and activation, are the fundamental Boolean operations of biological logic.

Now the inputs. A molecular input to a genetic circuit can be a small molecule that binds to a transcription factor and alters its shape, thereby changing whether it can bind DNA. It can be a light signal absorbed by a photosensitive protein that then changes its DNA-binding activity. It can be a change in temperature, a specific quorum-sensing molecule produced by a bacterial colony, or the concentration of a particular metabolite in the cell. The circuit senses these inputs through its regulatory proteins, and the inputs determine the circuit's behavior.

The outputs are equally varied: proteins that catalyze a reaction, proteins that produce a visible signal such as a fluorescent reporter, proteins that alter the cell's metabolism, or regulatory RNAs that feed back into the circuit's own operation. A sigma factor, which is a protein subunit that helps RNA polymerase recognize a specific promoter sequence, can serve as a circuit output in one layer and a regulatory input in the next. The layering of inputs and outputs, circuits controlling circuits, is how complexity is built.

Diagram 5.1 - Anatomy of a Genetic Circuit

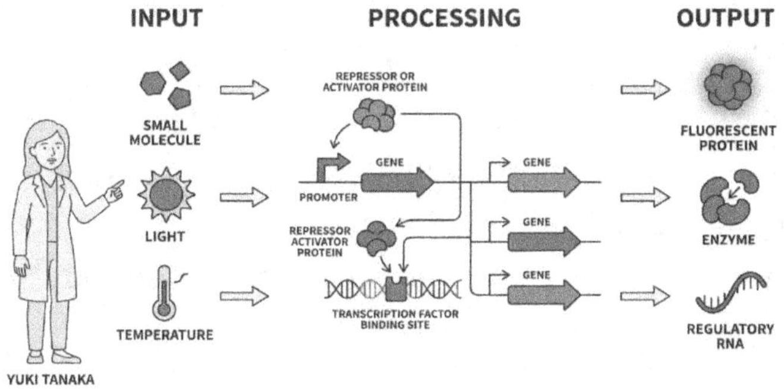

The electronic circuit analogy is precise rather than loose. In an electronic circuit, a voltage signal passes through transistors that amplify, invert, or combine it, and the result drives a load: a motor, a speaker, or another circuit. In a genetic circuit, a molecular concentration signal passes through transcription factors that activate, repress, or combine it. The result drives an output: an enzyme, a fluorescent protein, or another layer of regulation. The wires are for molecular diffusion. The transistors are transcription factors. The power supply is the cell's own metabolism, which provides the energy and raw materials to transcribe and translate every gene in the circuit. The substrate is alive, which means it grows, divides, mutates, and dies. But the information-processing architecture is the same.

The field that studies and designs these circuits was deliberately named after electronics. Synthetic biology's founders were electrical engineers and physicists who had moved into biology and who recognized not just a metaphor but a genuine structural analogy between molecular regulatory networks and electronic circuits. The vocabulary they adopted, logic gates, toggle switches, oscillators, and amplifiers, was not borrowed for marketing purposes. It was borrowed because the underlying mathematics is the same: Boolean algebra for logic gates, ordinary differential equations for dynamic behavior, and control theory for feedback loops.

A ribosome binding site, a short RNA sequence that controls how efficiently a ribosome attaches to messenger RNA and begins translating it into protein, functions in a genetic circuit the way a resistor functions in an electronic circuit: it sets the gain of the signal. A stronger ribosome binding site produces more protein from a given message, amplifying the signal. A weaker one attenuates it. A terminator is a DNA sequence that signals RNA polymerase to stop transcription and release the RNA, determining where one gene's signal ends and the next begins, analogous to the boundary between logic stages in a circuit. Characterization, the process of precisely measuring a biological part's behavior across a range of conditions, is analogous to measuring a resistor's tolerance or a transistor's gain curve. You cannot design a reliable circuit without characterized parts, and the synthetic biology field has invested enormous effort in building libraries of parts whose behavior has been rigorously measured to be trusted in designs.

Diagram 5.2 - Transcription Factor as Molecular Transistor

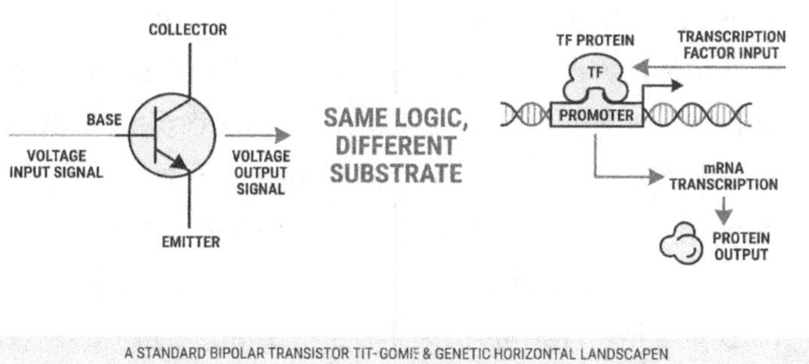

The Toggle Switch: Biology's First Memory Bit

The year 2000 was when synthetic biology announced itself to the world, and it did so in a single issue of Nature, with two papers published back-to-back. One of them, by James Collins and Timothy Gardner at Boston University, described a genetic toggle switch. The other, by Michael

Elowitz and Stanislas Leibler at Princeton, described a repressilator. Together, these two circuits established that genetic circuit design was a real engineering discipline, that real digital and dynamic behaviors could be programmed into living cells using only DNA and protein, and that the engineering of biological systems had graduated from wishful analogy to demonstrated fact.

The toggle switch is elegant in its simplicity. Take two genes, call them Gene 1 and Gene 2. Gene 1 produces a repressor protein, Repressor 1, that binds to the promoter region of Gene 2 and silences it. Gene 2 produces a repressor protein, Repressor 2, that binds to the promoter region of Gene 1 and silences it. Each gene is suppressing the other. The question is: which one wins? The answer depends on the initial conditions. If at startup the cell contains more Repressor 1 than Repressor 2, Gene 1 will dominate: it will suppress Gene 2, which means less Repressor 2 is produced, which means Gene 1's promoter is more active, which means even more Repressor 1 is produced. The system runs away from any intermediate state and snaps to one of two stable configurations. In one configuration, Gene 1 is fully on, and Gene 2 is fully off. In the other case, Gene 2 is fully on, and Gene 1 is fully off.

This is bistability, a system with exactly two stable states and an unstable middle ground. In electronics, this is precisely the behavior of a flip-flop circuit, the basic one-bit memory element that underlies every register, every cache, and every RAM cell in every computer ever built. Marcus's recognition on the whiteboard was technically correct: a genetic toggle switch is a one-bit memory element implemented in DNA and protein. The cell remembers which state it was kicked into, and it stays there even after the kicking signal is removed.

The "kicking signal" is how you switch the toggle. Collins and Gardner designed their switch so that two different small molecules, one for each gene, could temporarily override the repressor's binding. Adding the first chemical derepresses Gene 2, which floods the cell with Repressor 2, which shuts off Gene 1, allowing Gene 2 to maintain its dominance even after the chemical is washed away. The system has flipped. Add the second chemical, and it flips back. This is the operational principle of a bistable switch in biological systems: a transient perturbation is sufficient to permanently change the state, and the system stores that state in its own molecular dynamics without any external memory element.

The applications of bistability go beyond the theoretical. Living cells that need to make irreversible fate decisions, a stem cell committing to a particular lineage, a bacterium deciding to enter dormancy, a virus deciding to integrate or replicate, use toggle-switch logic implemented in their own natural regulatory networks. Collins and Gardner were not inventing a new biological concept. They were demonstrating that synthetic biologists could implement a known biological logic pattern from scratch, using designed parts, with predictable and tunable behavior. That demonstration, the proof that you could engineer a biological memory bit, was the founding moment of the field.

Diagram 5.3 - Genetic Toggle Switch and Electronic Flip-Flop

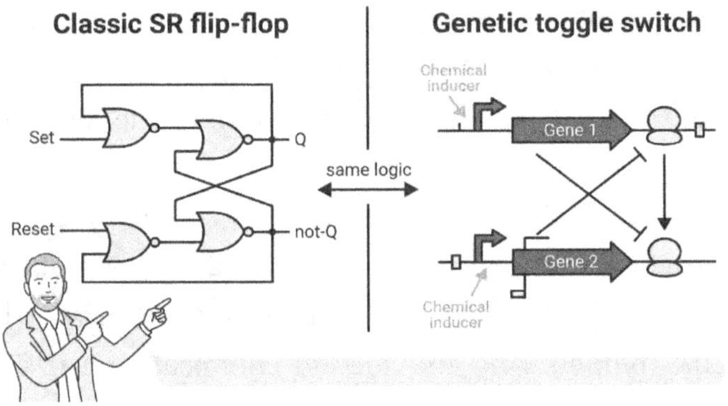

One aspect of the toggle switch that is easy to underestimate is the role of the parts' quantitative properties in its operation. The switch needs its repressors to be strong enough to maintain their dominant state in the presence of the noise of the molecular environment. It needs its promoters to be tuned so that one gene's repressor output is sufficient to overcome the other's promoter activity. Getting these quantitative relationships right requires not just the right parts but characterized parts, parts whose repressor binding strengths and transcription rates have been measured carefully enough to allow computational prediction of whether the switch will actually be bistable in the cell. The history of the field is littered with genetic circuits that looked bistable on paper but failed in the cell because a key part behaved differently than expected. Characterization is the unglamorous work that makes circuit design reliable.

Repressilator: Engineering an Oscillator from Scratch

The second paper in that landmark issue of Nature described a circuit with no natural analog: a self-sustaining biological oscillator built entirely from non-oscillating parts. Michael Elowitz and Stanislas Leibler called their circuit the repressilator. This name combines "repressilate" with "oscillator," and the circuit they described has become the most widely known designed oscillator in synthetic biology.

The repressilator uses three genes arranged in a ring. Gene A produces a repressor that silences Gene B. Gene B produces a repressor that silences Gene C. Gene C produces a repressor that silences Gene A. If you trace that loop, you will notice that it creates a cycle with an odd number of inversions: A represses B, B represses C, C represses A. An odd number of inversions in a feedback loop is the hallmark of an oscillator. In control theory, this is an unstable feedback configuration, and in a biological circuit, that instability manifests as a sustained oscillation rather than a fixed point.

The dynamics work as follows. Suppose Gene A is highly expressed at the start. The large amount of Repressor A silences Gene B, so Repressor B levels are low. With low Repressor B, Gene C is free to be expressed, producing large amounts of Repressor C, which then silences Gene A. With

Gene A silenced, Repressor A levels fall. With low Repressor A, Gene B is derepressed. Now Repressor B rises, silencing Gene C. With Gene C silenced, Repressor C falls. With low Repressor C, Gene A is derepressed again. The cycle repeats. The cell blinks rhythmically, expressing each gene in sequence, because the ring of repressors chases itself around the loop without ever catching up.

Elowitz and Leibler made the oscillation visible by attaching a green fluorescent protein reporter to one of the genes. Under a microscope, individual bacterial cells lit up with a gentle, periodic green fluorescence pulse, each pulse representing one cycle of the repressilator. The degradation rates of the repressor proteins and the transcription and translation rates of each gene set the oscillation period. Adjust those parameters to change the clock speed.

Diagram 5.4 - Repressilator Three-Gene Oscillator Loop

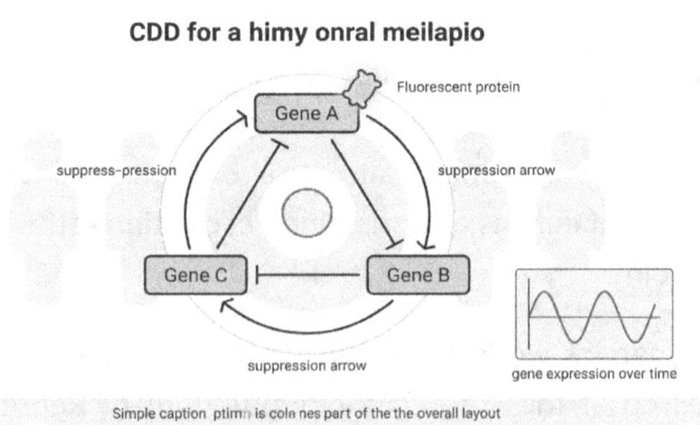

In electronic terms, the repressilator is a ring oscillator: an odd number of inverters connected in a loop, which is the simplest possible circuit that generates a clock signal from nothing but logic gates. The three-stage CMOS ring oscillator is a standard building block in digital design, generating a periodic signal at a frequency determined by the propagation delay of each inverter stage. Elowitz and Leibler's repressilator is its biological equivalent, with transcription and translation delay playing the role of gate propagation delay, and protein degradation setting the "reset" that allows the oscillation to continue rather than latching into a fixed state.

The repressilator was not just a proof of concept for oscillation. It was a demonstration that complex dynamic behavior, behavior that changes over time in a designed pattern rather than just settling into a stable state, could be engineered from scratch into living cells. This mattered because some of the most valuable biological behaviors are dynamic: the circadian clock that governs the daily rhythm of metabolism, the cell cycle that controls when a cell divides, and the oscillatory signaling that patterns embryonic tissue during development. None of these processes could ever be engineered without the ability to design oscillatory circuits. The repressilator proved that the ability existed.

It also revealed something important about the limits of the electronics analogy, a recurring theme in this chapter. The repressilator's actual behavior in cells was not a clean, perfectly regular sine wave. Different cells in the same culture oscillated at slightly different periods. Some cells fell out of phase with their neighbors. Occasionally, a cell's oscillator would stall or spontaneously shift phase. This irregularity was not a design flaw, exactly. It was a fundamental property of the biological substrate, a consequence of the small number of molecules involved and the intrinsic randomness of gene expression. Elowitz and Leibler observed it, measured it, and reported it honestly. Their circuit worked, and it was noisy. Both things were true. Understanding why both things could be true simultaneously is the key to understanding what makes genetic circuit engineering genuinely hard.

Diagram 5.5 - Repressilator Output: Designed Oscillation vs. Biological Noise

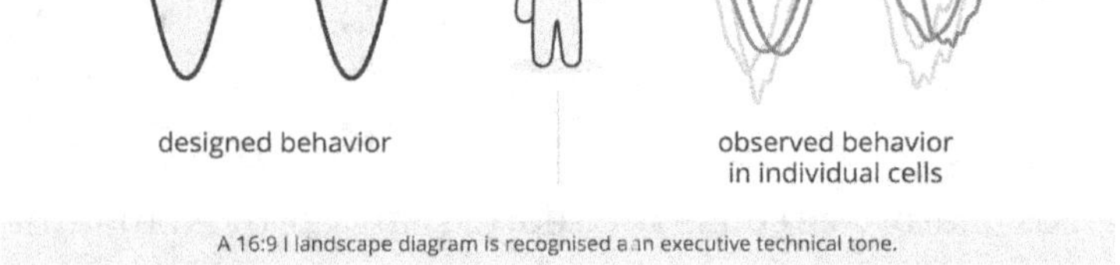

Boolean Logic in Living Cells: AND, OR, and NOT Gates

Boolean logic is the mathematics of true and false, one and zero, on and off. Every digital system in existence, from a pocket calculator to a supercomputer, is built from combinations of three primitive operations: AND, which outputs true only when all its inputs are true; OR, which outputs true when any of its inputs are true; and NOT, which inverts its input. These operations can be combined in any configuration to compute any logical function, and the physical devices that implement them, the logic gates, are the universal building blocks of digital computation.

Genetic logic gates implement the same Boolean operations using the same molecular machinery we have been discussing: transcription factors, promoters, and their regulatory interactions. A genetic NOT gate, the simplest case, is implemented by a repressor: when the input protein is present, the repressor binds the output gene's promoter and silences it. Input high, output low. Input low (repressor absent), output high. This is logical inversion, implemented by a single transcription factor binding a single promoter.

A genetic AND gate requires both input signals to be present before it produces an output. One way to implement this is with a two-input promoter that requires two activating transcription factors to bind simultaneously before RNA polymerase can initiate transcription. Both inputs must be present. Another implementation uses a cascade: the first input activates an intermediate gene, and the output gene requires both the intermediate protein and the second input to be expressed. The output gene is transcribed only when both conditions are satisfied simultaneously. Input A AND Input B equals output on.

A genetic OR gate activates its output when either input is present. This can be implemented by a promoter with two separate binding sites for two different activators: either activator alone is sufficient to recruit RNA polymerase and initiate transcription. Input A OR Input B equals output on. The AND gate and OR gate differ only in how their promoters are architecturally structured, because at the molecular level, "and" means "both binding sites must be occupied, while "or" means "either binding site is sufficient.

These are real, functional circuits that have been built, measured, and published. Genetic AND gates have been constructed in bacteria, yeast, and mammalian cells, and they behave in ways that closely match their Boolean logic specification. The outputs are not perfectly binary, because gene expression is continuous rather than truly digital, but the circuits exhibit threshold behavior: below a certain input concentration, the output is low; above the threshold, the output is high. The thresholds are tunable by selecting promoters and ribosome-binding sites with the right quantitative properties.

Diagram 5.6 - Genetic AND, OR, and NOT Gates

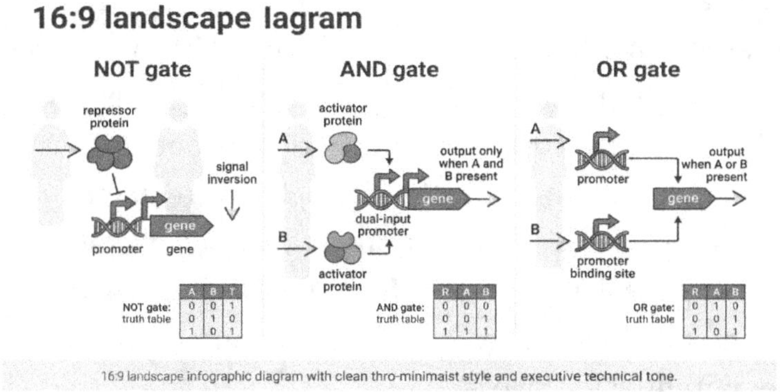

The applications of genetic logic gates are not merely theoretical. One of the most powerful uses of the AND gate in practice is in cellular diagnostics and therapeutics. Consider a cell therapy intended to kill cancer cells. A cancer cell is not absolutely distinct from a normal cell: it often overexpresses some proteins that normal cells also express at lower levels, and it may underexpress others. A single-input genetic circuit that activates a kill switch whenever it detects any amount of Protein X will produce false positives, activating in normal cells that happen to express moderate levels of Protein X. An AND gate that activates only when both Protein X AND Protein Y are above their thresholds is far more specific. Two simultaneous conditions must be met, and the probability that both are met in a normal cell is the product of two small probabilities, which is a very small number indeed.

This kind of two-input specificity has been implemented in engineered T cells designed to selectively target tumor cells based on a combination of surface markers. The genetic AND gate inside the T cell processes the two marker signals and activates the cell's therapeutic function only when both are present simultaneously. A three-input AND gate, which requires three simultaneous signals, would be even more specific, but at the cost of additional circuit complexity and the characterization work that complexity requires. The gate architecture is a direct translation from digital logic design, and the design trade-offs are the same: more inputs mean greater specificity but greater complexity and a higher potential for failure.

Genetic logic also enables more sophisticated computation. By wiring gates together in series, a genetic circuit can evaluate complex logical expressions: "activate the output if (A AND B) OR (C AND NOT D)." These multi-layer circuits are called cascades or layered circuits, and building them requires solving a problem that electronics engineers know well: fan-out. When one logic gate drives two downstream gates, the output signal must be strong enough to drive both. In a genetic circuit, this means that the transcription factor produced by the first gate must be present at a sufficiently high concentration to bind both downstream gate promoters simultaneously. Fan-out problems have led to many genetic circuit designs failing, and their resolution is a central engineering challenge in the field.

Diagram 5.7 - Layered Genetic Circuit for Tumor-Specific T Cell Activation

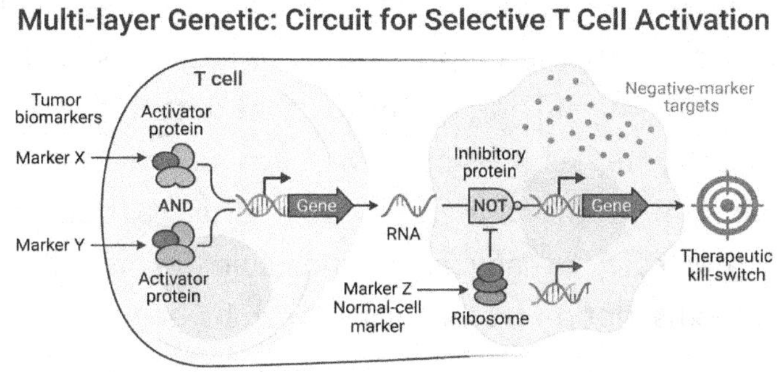

Multi-layer genetic circuit for selective T cell activation, or selective T cell activation

Sensor-Actuator Circuits: The Full Signal Chain

A logic gate is an abstract functional unit. A real genetic circuit for a real application is a complete signal chain: a sensor that detects the input signal, a processing layer that applies the logic, and an actuator that produces the physical output. Understanding how these three stages are implemented at the molecular level and how they are connected is what separates knowing the theory of genetic circuits from being able to read a circuit description and understand what it actually does.

The sensor stage is implemented by proteins that respond to specific molecular signals. A common architecture uses an allosteric transcription factor, a protein that can bind DNA but whose DNA-binding activity is conditional on its prior binding of a small-molecule ligand. In the absence of the ligand, the protein binds DNA tightly and represses downstream gene expression. When the ligand is present, it binds to a different part of the protein, changes its shape, and reduces its DNA-binding affinity. The gene is derepressed. The transcription factor has sensed the presence of the ligand and converted that detection into a change in gene expression. The ligand can be an environmental toxin, a metabolite, a drug, a quorum-sensing molecule, or any small molecule for which an allosteric transcription factor exists or can be engineered.

Light-responsive circuits use a different sensor architecture: photosensitive proteins that change their conformation upon absorbing specific wavelengths of light. These proteins can be engineered to interact with transcription factors, so that illuminating a cell with red light turns a gene on, and blue light turns it off, or vice versa. This optogenetic approach to sensing gives the circuit designer exquisite temporal and spatial control over the input signal: you can turn genes on in individual cells within a tissue with millisecond precision by shining a focused beam of light. For circuits designed to operate in tissues or on the skin, light sensing offers a non-invasive and highly controllable input interface that no chemical input can match.

The actuator stage translates the circuit's logical output into a physical action. The simplest actuator is a reporter gene: a gene encoding a fluorescent protein that glows when transcribed, making the circuit's output state directly visible. Reporters are used during the test phase of the design-build-test-learn cycle to verify that the circuit is behaving as designed, and the choice of reporter, green fluorescent protein for one output, red fluorescent protein for another, allows multiple outputs to be monitored simultaneously in the same cell.

In therapeutic circuits, the actuator produces a functional protein, such as an enzyme, cytokine, surface receptor, or toxin. In biosynthesis circuits, the actuator activates the metabolic genes required to produce a target compound. For diagnostic circuits, the actuator produces a detectable signal, a color change, a fluorescent pulse, or an electrochemical signal that the operator can read as a yes-or-no answer about the sample. In each case, the actuator's job is to convert the abstract logical output of the processing layer into a physical consequence in the world.

Diagram 5.8 - Sensor-Processing-Actuator Signal Chain

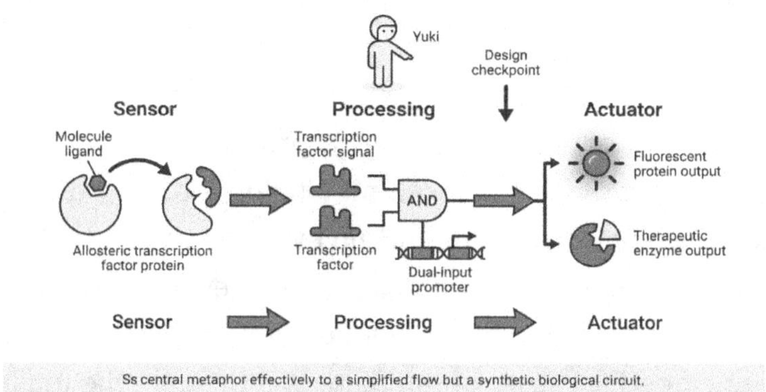

One of the most important design considerations in sensor-actuator circuits is what engineers call retroactivity. Retroactivity refers to the loading effect that occurs when a downstream component draws heavily on an upstream signal. In an electronic circuit, this is called loading:

connecting a low-impedance load to a high-impedance output degrades the output signal. In a genetic circuit, retroactivity occurs when a downstream transcription factor binds so much of its upstream activator that it depletes the activator's free concentration, changing the apparent signal level seen by other parts of the circuit that also depend on that activator. A circuit that works beautifully in isolation may behave differently when connected to an actuator that absorbs a large fraction of the intermediate signaling protein.

Managing retroactivity is one reason genetic circuit designers spend so much time on quantitative modeling before building anything. The circuit's behavior depends not just on the logic of its connections but on the concentrations of all its components, and those concentrations are influenced by everything in the cell, including other circuits, the cell's growth state, and the metabolic cost of producing all those proteins. A circuit that works in a rapidly dividing cell may fail in a slow-growing cell, because the dilution of protein by cell growth, which is a normal mechanism for reducing protein levels, works at a different rate. These context-dependent effects are the daily engineering reality of the field, and they are the main reason that building a genetic circuit is harder than drawing one on a whiteboard.

Computer-Aided Design: From Truth Table to DNA Sequence

In 1980, designing an integrated circuit required a team of engineers with specialized training, years of experience, and a carefully managed library of cell designs. By 1995, hardware description languages such as VHDL and Verilog allowed engineers to specify a circuit's behavior in software, simulate it, and then automatically synthesize the physical implementation using standardized cell libraries. This shift from manual design to automated synthesis compressed the design cycle, enabled far more complex circuits, and opened electronic design to a much broader pool of engineers. Synthetic biology is undergoing an analogous transition right now.

Benchling is a cloud-based platform for genetic design that functions as the synthetic biologist's IDE. In this integrated development environment, sequences are written, parts are retrieved from databases, plasmids are assembled, and experiments are designed and tracked. On Benchling, a circuit designer can retrieve characterized parts from integrated repositories, drag and drop them into a linear or circular construct, visualize the regulatory interactions, and export the design for synthesis. It is the CAD tool for genetic parts, and its adoption across the field, at both academic institutions and commercial companies, reflects the broader trend toward software-assisted biological design.

Cello is a more radical departure from manual design: it is a genetic circuit compiler. To use Cello, you do not start with a list of parts. You start with a truth table, a complete specification of the circuit's output for every possible input combination. You specify the input sensors available to the circuit (for example, which small molecules or light signals can be detected), the output actuators available (which reporter or functional genes are on the menu), and the library of characterized regulatory parts that the compiler can use. Cello then searches through the space of possible circuit designs and finds one that correctly implements your truth table using those parts, in the same organism you are targeting.

Christopher Voigt and colleagues at MIT developed the Cello compiler and first published it in 2016. It represented a genuine conceptual breakthrough: for the first time, it was possible to specify the desired behavior of a genetic circuit in abstract logical terms and have a software tool design the physical DNA sequence that implements that behavior. The analogy to hardware synthesis from VHDL is exact: in both cases, you describe what the circuit should do, not how it should do it, and the compiler figures out the how. Cello's circuit designs have been experimentally validated in bacteria, demonstrating that the compiled designs work in living cells rather than just in simulation.

The limitations of Cello are instructive. The compiler works well for circuits up to moderate complexity, roughly six to seven layers deep, within the constraints of a specific organism and a specific library of parts. Beyond that complexity, the number of possible circuit topologies explodes combinatorially, and the compiler's search space becomes intractable. The accuracy of the compiler's predictions also depends heavily on the quality of the characterization data for each library part. If a part's behavior model is inaccurate, the compiler may design a circuit that looks correct in simulation but fails in the cell. Garbage in, garbage out applies as much to genetic circuit compilers as to any other software tool.

More recent work has extended the CAD approach with machine learning. Rather than relying on hand-curated mathematical models of each part's behavior, machine learning models can be trained on large datasets of measured circuit behavior to predict how new circuit designs will perform. This closes a gap that has limited Cello and similar tools: the requirement for accurate mechanistic models of every part. A machine learning predictor can learn the effective behavior of parts from experimental data without requiring a complete mechanistic understanding of why they behave as they do. The same shift, from mechanistic models to learned statistical models, is playing out across engineering biology, and it is one of the most significant things happening in the field right now.

Diagram 5.9 - Genetic Circuit Compiler: Truth Table to DNA Sequence

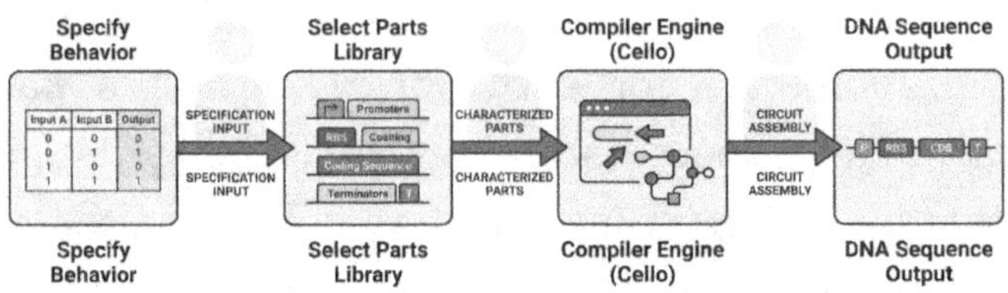

The Design-Build-Test-Learn Cycle

Every engineering discipline has its fundamental workflow, the iterative loop that converts intent into reality. In software development, it is the agile sprint: design a feature, implement it, test it, measure how users interact with it, and revise the design based on what you learned. In hardware design, it is the tape-out cycle: design the chip, fabricate it, test it, and iterate. In synthetic biology, it is the design-build-test-learn cycle, abbreviated DBTL, and it is the operational heartbeat of every synthetic biology company, foundry, and academic lab worldwide.

The Design phase begins before a single physical molecule is made. Working from a library of characterized parts and a set of computational tools, the designer models the circuit's intended behavior in silico, predicting the concentrations of key proteins as a function of input signals and estimating the circuit's steady-state and dynamic behavior. Modern design tools range from deterministic ordinary differential equation models, which predict the average behavior of the circuit across many cells, to stochastic simulations that model the behavior of individual molecules and capture the effects of biological noise. The designer selects parts from characterized libraries whose quantitative properties fit the circuit's needs, checking that the stoichiometry and kinetics are compatible. The design phase ends when the designer has a specific DNA sequence, a parts list, and a prediction of the circuit's behavior.

The Build phase converts the design into physical DNA. This begins with DNA synthesis: the circuit's sequence is ordered from a commercial synthesis provider, which will deliver a tube of synthetic DNA encoding the designed construct. Depending on the circuit's complexity, the build phase may also involve cloning, the process of inserting a synthesized fragment into a plasmid, a small circular DNA molecule that can replicate independently inside a host cell. The assembled construct is then transformed into the target organism, the process of introducing the plasmid into the cells, typically by briefly disrupting the cell membrane to allow DNA to enter. The cells that have successfully incorporated the plasmid are selected using antibiotic resistance genes designed into the construct for this purpose.

The Test phase measures what the circuit actually does in living cells. The primary tool is the reporter gene: a gene encoding a fluorescent protein or an enzyme whose activity produces a measurable signal, wired to the circuit's output. By measuring reporter output under different input conditions, the designer can directly observe the circuit's input-output behavior. For a logic gate, this means testing all input combinations and verifying that the output is high when it should be and low when it should be. Flow cytometry, which measures fluorescence in thousands of individual cells per second, is the workhorse measurement technology for this purpose: it produces not just an average output level but also a distribution of outputs across the cell population, revealing whether the circuit behaves consistently or exhibits high cell-to-cell variability.

DNA sequencing is performed at multiple points during the test phase to verify that the constructed sequence matches the designed sequence exactly. A single-base-pair mutation introduced during synthesis or cloning can change a promoter's strength, disrupt a ribosome-binding site, or introduce a premature stop codon that truncates a protein. The build phase is not error-free, and sequencing is the quality control step that catches these errors before they contaminate the experimental results. This is why the build and test phases are so tightly coupled in practice: you are simultaneously checking whether the construct was built correctly and whether the correct construct behaves as designed.

The Learn phase is where the design cycle closes the feedback loop. The measurements from the test phase are compared to the predictions from the design phase. Where predictions and measurements agree, the model is validated. Where they disagree, the model must be updated. The source of discrepancy might be a part whose behavior was miscalibrated in the library, a context-dependent effect that the model did not account for, or a biological interaction between the synthetic circuit and the cell's native regulatory network that was not included in the model. The Learn phase extracts the maximum information from the experimental results and incorporates it into an updated model that will be used for the next design iteration. The quality of the learning step determines how quickly the team converges on a working design.

Diagram 5.10 - The Design-Build-Test-Learn Cycle

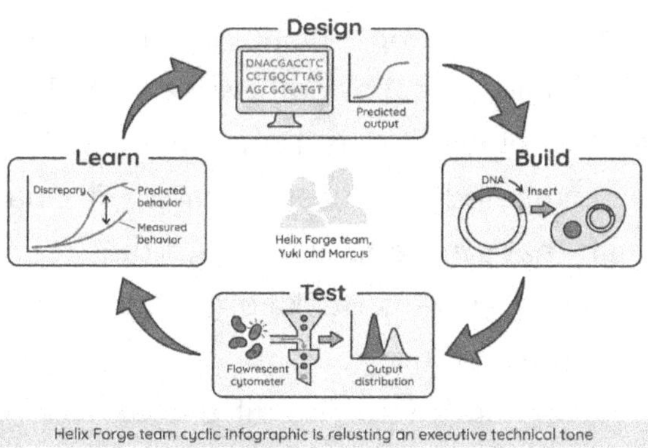

The speed of the DBTL cycle is the central competitive metric in synthetic biology, and this fact alone explains the rise of the biological foundry as an industry model. A lab performing DBTL iterations manually, with individual researchers handling every pipetting step, every transformation, every measurement, runs perhaps a few iterations per month. A biological foundry with automated liquid handling, robotic colony picking, high-throughput

DNA sequencing, and integrated data pipelines can run hundreds of DBTL iterations in parallel, reducing the time from design to measured result from months to days. Ginkgo Bioworks' foundry model in Boston is built on exactly this principle: the company's competitive advantage is not any particular circuit design, but the industrial-scale capability to run DBTL cycles faster than any individual lab can match. Speed of iteration, not initial cleverness of design, is the winning strategy in a complex biological design space.

The analogy to software development is not casual. The DBTL cycle is agile development for living systems. The Design phase is the sprint planning and architecture session. The Build phase is the coding sprint. The Test phase is the QA and CI pipeline. The Learn phase is the sprint retrospective combined with user research. The parallel is precise enough that synthetic biology startups founded by software engineers, such as Helix Forge, often adopt agile project management frameworks for their biological work almost without modification. The differences are real and matter, but the underlying discipline of iterative, data-driven improvement with rapid cycles remains the same.

Biological Noise and the Limits of Determinism

Here is the uncomfortable truth that Yuki will always tell Marcus when he gets too enthusiastic about the electronics analogy: biology is not silicon. An electronic logic gate is deterministic. Given the same input voltage, it produces the same output voltage every time, within tolerances so tight that, for practical purposes, the output is perfectly reproducible. A genetic logic gate is stochastic. Given the same average input concentration, it will produce a distribution of outputs across a population of cells, because the individual molecular events that constitute gene expression are fundamentally random.

Biological noise refers to the random variation in gene expression that arises from the probabilistic nature of molecular events. Gene transcription is not a continuous flow of RNA molecules; it is a series of discrete events, each triggered when an RNA polymerase molecule randomly collides with and successfully binds to a promoter. The number of transcription events per unit time follows a statistical distribution rather than a fixed rate. Translation of each mRNA molecule is similarly stochastic. Each ribosome binding event is a probabilistic collision, and the number of protein molecules produced from a single mRNA copy before it is degraded varies randomly from molecule to molecule.

The consequence is that even genetically identical cells in the same environment, with the same circuit and the same inputs, will express different levels of circuit proteins. In a population of bacteria all containing the same toggle switch, some cells may be in the high-Gene-1 state and others in the high-Gene-2 state, because small random fluctuations in protein levels during early growth pushed them to different stable configurations. In a population of cells all containing the same AND gate, some cells will produce sufficient amounts of both activators to cross the activation threshold, and others will not, purely by chance. This cell-to-cell variability is not a bug in a specific circuit design. It is a property of the biological substrate that cannot be eliminated, only managed.

Managing biological noise is one of the central engineering challenges in genetic circuit design, and the strategies for doing so are direct translations from noise management in analog electronic circuits. The first strategy is to increase the signal-to-noise ratio by increasing the signal. A circuit that uses strong promoters and strong ribosome binding sites to produce high concentrations of its key proteins is less sensitive to random fluctuations, because the noise, which has a roughly fixed absolute magnitude, becomes smaller relative to the signal. This is why synthetic biologists often prefer strong promoters in their circuits even when a weaker promoter would logically suffice: the stronger promoter provides a higher copy number of the key regulatory proteins, which reduces the relative contribution of random fluctuations.

The second strategy is to design circuits with built-in hysteresis, snap-through behavior that makes the circuit resistant to being nudged out of its current state by small fluctuations. The toggle switch is inherently hysteretic: once it has snapped to one stable state, it requires a large perturbation to flip to the other state, not just a small fluctuation. This hysteresis means that random noise fluctuations, which are small compared to the energy barrier between states, cannot cause the circuit to flip spontaneously. The circuit remembers its state robustly even in a noisy molecular environment.

The third strategy is negative feedback, which in a genetic circuit means designing a regulatory loop where the output protein represses its own expression. When protein levels get too high, the repression increases, pulling levels back down. When protein levels drop below a set point, repression decreases, and expression rises. This autoregulatory feedback stabilizes protein concentrations around a set point, smoothing out the random fluctuations that would otherwise cause levels to wander. Negative feedback is one of the most powerful tools in any engineer's repertoire, in electronics, in control systems, in economics, and in genetic circuit design, because it converts the noisy output of an open-loop system into the stable output of a closed-loop system.

Retroactivity, mentioned earlier in the context of sensor-actuator circuits, is also a noise management issue. When a downstream circuit draws heavily on an upstream signaling molecule, it creates fluctuations in the upstream molecule's concentration that propagate back through the circuit as noise. Insulating genetic circuit modules from one another, so that downstream loading does not affect upstream signal levels, is an active area of research and a practical consideration in every circuit design. Just as electronic circuit boards use buffer amplifiers to isolate signal sources from downstream loads, synthetic biologists are developing genetic insulator parts, characterized by regulatory elements that prevent downstream circuits from loading the upstream signal.

Diagram 5.11 - Noise Management Strategies in Genetic Circuits

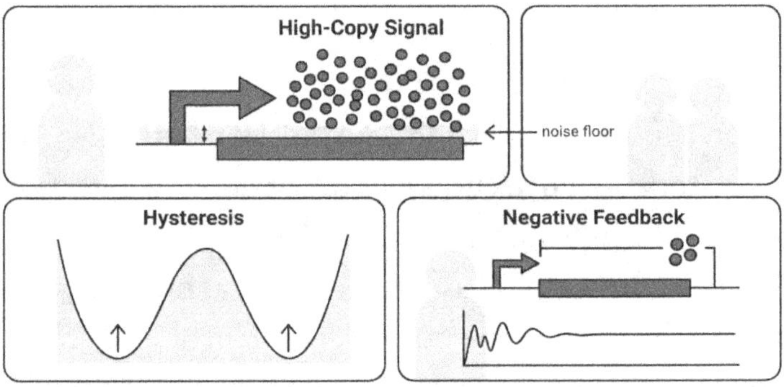

Random variation is small in an executive technical tone

Where the Electronics Analogy Breaks Down

Yuki has a rule at Helix Forge. You are allowed to use the electronics analogy to explain a circuit to Marcus. You are not allowed to use it to predict how a circuit will behave in a cell without running the numbers first. The analogy earns its keep as a conceptual map. It fails as a quantitative model. Understanding why it fails is as important as understanding why it works, because it determines how much confidence you can place in a circuit design before you build it.

The first fundamental difference is that electronic components are manufactured to a tolerance. A resistor labeled 10 kilohms will have a resistance between 9.9 and 10.1 kilohms, or between 9 and 11 kilohms depending on its grade, but it will not have a resistance of 5 or 50 kilohms. Genetic parts do not come with tolerances stamped on them. The same promoter sequence, when transformed into ten different bacterial strains or expressed from ten different plasmid constructs, will produce ten somewhat different transcription rates because the chromosomal context around the insertion site, local DNA structure, nearby transcription from other genes, and dozens of other factors affect its behavior. The sequence is identical; the behavior is variable. This is the context-dependence problem, and it is the reason why a circuit that works in one strain may fail in another, even if both strains are nominally the same species.

The second difference is that biological circuits operate within a living cell that has its own regulatory networks, metabolism, and evolutionary agenda. An electronic circuit sits on a passive substrate. A genetic circuit competes with thousands of other genes for the cell's transcription and translation machinery. When a synthetic circuit is highly expressed, it creates a metabolic burden on the cell by consuming ribosomes, RNA polymerase, and raw metabolites. The cell responds to this burden by reducing its growth rate, which in turn changes protein dilution rates and, ultimately, protein concentrations in ways not predicted by the designer's model. In extreme cases, cells under heavy synthetic circuit burden evolve mutations that reduce the circuit's expression, providing a selective advantage for cells that partially break the circuit. Evolution is always in the room when you are engineering biology.

The third difference is that electronic circuits operate on a timescale set by the speed of electrons in conductors, which is essentially instantaneous from a human perspective. Genetic circuits operate on the timescale of gene expression: the time required to transcribe a gene into mRNA, translate that mRNA into protein, and allow enough protein to accumulate to cross a functional threshold. This timescale is minutes to hours, not nanoseconds. The consequence is that a genetic circuit's transient behavior, how it responds to a change in input, is slow and involves significant overshoot and ringing before settling to its new steady state, in ways that are difficult to predict without detailed kinetic models. For applications that require fast responses, the slow dynamics of gene expression impose a fundamental speed limit that no amount of design cleverness can circumvent.

The fourth difference is modularity, or rather, the limited modularity of genetic parts. In electronics, the transistor is a universal building block: you can wire transistors together in any combination, and the behavior of the composite circuit is predictable from the behavior of the individual transistors, because transistors are designed to be modular. Genetic parts interact with the cell's molecular environment in ways that electronic components do not. A transcription factor in a genetic circuit is not just a regulator of its designed target gene: it may also bind, at low affinity, to hundreds of other sites in the genome, producing off-target effects. Two circuits placed in the same cell may interact through shared resources, competing for the same pool of transcription factors or ribosomes. The assumption of modularity, which is foundational to electronic circuit design, must be earned in genetic circuit design through careful characterization and experimental validation.

None of these differences makes genetic circuit design impossible. They make it harder, slower, and less predictable than electronic circuit design, and they are the reason that the design-build-test-learn cycle requires so many iterations before a circuit works reliably. The field is aware of all of these problems. It is actively working on solutions: insulator sequences to reduce context dependence, orthogonal transcription systems that do not compete with the cell's native machinery, cell-free expression systems that remove the evolutionary pressure, and machine learning models that capture context dependence empirically rather than trying to model it mechanistically. Progress on each of these fronts is accelerating. But the honest engineering reality, the one that Yuki enforces at Helix Forge and that every serious synthetic biologist acknowledges, is that building a genetic circuit is not like writing code, and expecting it to work on the first build is not a plan. It is a hope.

Diagram 5.12 - Electronics Analogy: Where It Works and Where It Breaks Down

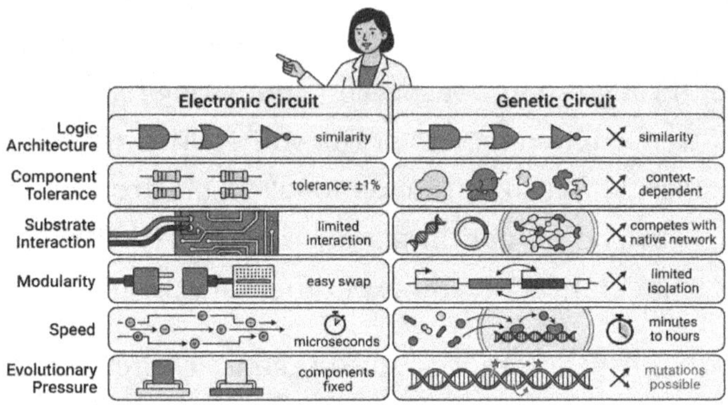

What This Means For You

If you are a software engineer reading this chapter, the single most valuable thing you have just acquired is not a list of biological facts. It is a working mental model that lets you read a genetic circuit description and understand it in structural terms. When a research paper describes a two-input AND gate that activates a therapeutic output only in the presence of two specific cancer biomarkers, you now know what that means at the molecular level: two activating transcription factors, a dual-input promoter, and a threshold behavior that requires both inputs above a set concentration simultaneously. You can evaluate the design on its merits, ask meaningful questions about characterization, and assess whether the noise management strategy is robust enough for the application. That is a genuine, non-trivial analytical capability, and it is the foundation for evaluating every synthetic biology application described in the chapters that follow.

If you are an entrepreneur or investor, the DBTL cycle framework gives you a concrete way to assess the maturity of a synthetic biology company's technology. A company that is on its second or third DBTL iteration for a core circuit is in a very different position from one that is on its fifteenth, with a validated computational model and a library of characterized parts that make each subsequent iteration faster and more predictable. The number of DBTL iterations completed is a more honest indicator of technical progress than any description of the circuit's intended behavior, because it tells you how well the team's model matches reality. Ask about iteration speed, characterization depth, and model accuracy. The answers will tell you more about technical risk than the circuit topology will.

For policy professionals and ethicists, the circuit design framework matters because it changes the nature of what it means to engineer a living organism. A genetic circuit is not a random perturbation of a cell's biology: it is a designed information-processing system with specified inputs, specified logic, and specified outputs. The fact that circuits can be designed, characterized, and validated in controlled ways means that their behavior is, in principle, predictable and auditable. It also means that circuits can fail, behave unexpectedly in new environments, or interact with the cell's native networks in unintended ways. The regulatory frameworks that govern engineered organisms need to account for both the predictability that circuit design provides and the residual uncertainty that biological noise and context-dependence introduce. This is not a reason for alarm; it is a reason for technically informed regulation.

For every reader in every category: the honest caveat in this chapter, that biology is not silicon, that genetic circuits are noisier, slower, and more context-dependent than electronic circuits, is not a counsel of despair. It is a description of the engineering frontier. The toggle switch worked in 2000. The repressilator worked in 2000. Genetic AND-gates are used today in clinical cell therapy applications. The DBTL cycle works. The CAD tools are getting better. The characterization libraries are growing. The machine learning models are improving the predictive accuracy of designs. The honest difficulty of genetic circuit engineering is not a ceiling: it is a research program, and it is one of the most active and rapidly improving areas in all of engineering.

Takeaway

Genetic circuits are real information-processing systems running in living cells. The toggle switch is a biological memory bit, a one-bit flip-flop implemented from DNA and protein that stores a state without any external memory element. The repressilator is a biological clock, a self-sustaining oscillator built from three mutual repressors that drives periodic gene expression in cells that have no native oscillator. AND, OR, and NOT gates in genetic circuits implement Boolean logic using the same mathematical principles as their electronic counterparts, with transcription factors as transistors, promoters as logic stages, and molecular concentrations as signal levels. These are not metaphors. They are functional descriptions of characterized systems that have been built, measured, and validated in living cells.

The design-build-test-learn cycle is synthetic biology's engineering workflow, its answer to the question of how you systematically converge on a working design in a domain where the parts are noisy, and the substrate is alive. Design means modeling in silico and selecting characterized parts. Building means assembling DNA and introducing it to cells. Test means measuring circuit output with reporter genes and flow cytometry. Learning means comparing measurements to predictions and updating the model. The speed of this cycle is the central competitive metric of the field, which is why biological foundries that can automate and parallelize DBTL iterations are reshaping the industry's economics.

Biological noise is real and manageable. The stochastic nature of gene expression means that genetic circuits produce output distributions rather than deterministic values, that cell-to-cell variability is unavoidable, and that context dependence can make the same parts behave differently across genetic or cellular environments. The engineering response to noise, stronger signals, hysteretic design, negative feedback, circuit insulation, is the same toolkit that analog engineers have used for decades, applied to a new substrate. The electronics analogy is precise and powerful as a structural map. It fails as a quantitative prediction tool unless you do the characterization work and run the numbers.

Marcus's recognition on the whiteboard, "that's a memory bit," was correct in the deepest engineering sense. Biology has been running logic gates, toggle switches, and oscillators for billions of years: they are the molecular mechanisms of cellular decision-making, circadian rhythms, and developmental patterning. What synthetic biology has done is give engineers the ability to design, build, and test their own versions of those circuits, with parts they choose, logic they specify, and behavior they model and measure. The field is young, the tools are improving rapidly, and the circuits that Yuki draws on whiteboards today will be running in medicines, sensors, and living factories tomorrow. The engineering is real. The biology is alive. Both things are true at once, and that combination is exactly what makes this the most interesting engineering frontier of the century.

6 Medicine Reimagined

Opening Scenario

The conference room at Helix Forge is quiet except for the low hum of the ventilation system. Priya stands at the front of the room, a single slide projected behind her, which contains nothing but a timeline. On the left edge, the year

1990. On the right edge, January 13, 2020. Between them, a sequence of milestones rendered in small text: Katalin Karikó's first mRNA transfection experiments at the University of Pennsylvania; the discovery that chemically modified nucleosides could silence the immune alarm that unmodified mRNA triggered; the development of ionizable lipid nanoparticles that could carry a fragile mRNA molecule through the body without destroying it; and then, at the very end of the line, a single bold entry: Moderna's COVID-19 vaccine sequence finalized. Forty-eight hours after the viral genome was published.

A board member, seated near the back, leans forward. "Forty-eight hours," she says. It is not quite a question. Priya nods. "The speed was not luck," she says. "It was infrastructure. Every piece of the system, the delivery vehicle, the modified chemistry, the synthesis platform, had been built and tested over thirty years. When the genome was published, the only thing Moderna's team had to do was design a new sequence and load it into a platform that already worked. The vaccine was software. The cell was the computer. And the platform was already running." Marcus, sitting to Priya's left, opens his laptop and pulls up the design files for Helix Forge's own diagnostic circuit, the one that uses logic gates to detect two disease biomarkers simultaneously before triggering a response signal. He looks at the slide. He looks at his screen. He says, quietly, "We're building on the same principle." Priya looks at him. "Yes," she says. "We are."

This chapter is about what happens when engineering logic, the same logic that designs circuits and writes software, is applied to human medicine. Not as a metaphor. As the actual operational framework behind therapies that are, right now, curing cancers considered incurable, preventing pandemics in hours instead of years, and programming bacteria to act as living pharmacies inside the human body. The scale of what is becoming possible is genuinely difficult to absorb. This chapter is an attempt to absorb it carefully, without losing the engineering ground beneath it.

Why It Matters

For most of human history, medicine worked by subtraction. You identified a harmful agent, a bacterium, a virus, a malignant cell, and you found a way to remove or suppress it. Antibiotics kill bacteria. Chemotherapy killed fast-dividing cells, malignant and healthy alike. Surgery removed tumors. Even the best conventional treatments were often blunt instruments, powerful but imprecise, effective in aggregate but costly in collateral damage.

Synthetic biology changes the equation by introducing a new category of medical tool: programmable biological agents that do not merely suppress a disease but actively engage with it using the same molecular vocabulary the body already uses. An mRNA vaccine does not inject a weakened pathogen or a foreign chemical. It delivers a temporary instruction to the body's own cells, asking them to produce a specific protein that trains the immune system. A CAR-T cell, which is short for Chimeric Antigen

Receptor T cell, is not a drug in any conventional sense. It is a genetically reprogrammed immune cell, taken from the patient's own body, engineered to carry a synthetic receptor that recognizes cancer with precision, and returned to the patient as a living, self-replicating therapeutic agent. An engineered bacterium, administered to a patient with a metabolic disorder, is a genetic circuit running inside a living organism that senses the patient's internal chemistry and responds in real time.

For engineers and entrepreneurs, this matters for a specific reason. The transition from chemistry-based medicine to biology-based medicine is a platform transition. It follows the same structural logic as every previous platform transition in technology: a new abstraction layer appears, it enables a class of applications that was previously impossible, and the entire industry reorganizes around it. mRNA therapeutics are not new drugs. It is a new platform. Once the delivery infrastructure is in place, any new therapeutic is just a new sequence. CAR-T cell therapy is not a new surgical technique. It is a programmable cell manufacturing process, and the engineering challenges that remain, making it faster, cheaper, and more automated, are systems engineering problems as much as they are biology problems. Understanding this chapter means understanding the platform architecture of modern medicine. That architecture is being built right now.

For the curious professional who has read about CRISPR babies or cancer remissions in the news and wondered what is actually happening at the molecular level, this chapter provides the engineering explanation. Not the headline. The mechanism.

Diagram 6.1 - The Platform Architecture of Programmable Medicine

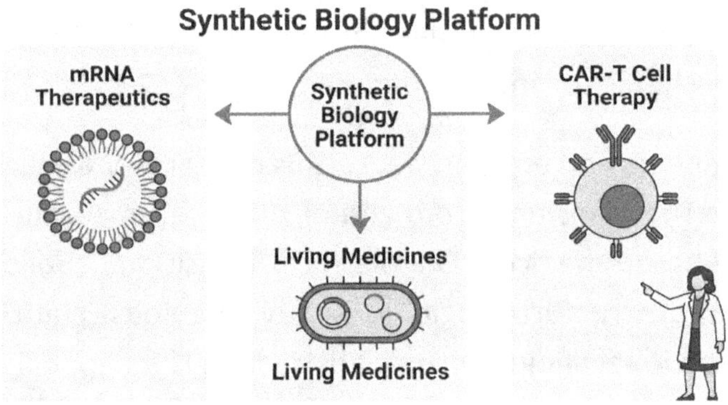

The three pillars of programmable medicine shown above, mRNA therapeutics, CAR-T cell therapy, and living medicines, each represent a different engineering approach to the same goal: giving the body precise, programmable instructions for fighting disease. Each will receive its own full treatment in the sections that follow.

The Instruction Manual Delivered to the Cell: mRNA Therapeutics

To understand mRNA therapeutics, you need to understand what mRNA is and what it does in a living cell. Start with the central dogma of molecular biology, one of the foundational operating principles of every cell in your body: DNA is transcribed into messenger RNA, and messenger

RNA is translated into protein. DNA is the master archive, stored safely in the cell's nucleus. mRNA is the working copy, a single-stranded molecule that carries the instructions from the archive to the ribosome, which is the cell's protein-building machinery. The ribosome reads the mRNA sequence and assembles a protein, one amino acid at a time, according to the instructions encoded in the sequence. When the ribosome is done, the mRNA is degraded, and the protein remains.

An mRNA vaccine or therapeutic works by delivering a synthetic mRNA molecule to the cell. The cell's ribosomes read that synthetic message, build the specified protein, and the immune system or metabolic machinery responds. For a vaccine, the specified protein is a viral antigen, such as the surface protein of a pathogen, such as the spike protein of SARS-CoV-2. The immune system recognizes the antigen as foreign, mounts a response, and stores the memory of that response. If the real pathogen appears later, the immune system already knows how to fight it. For a therapeutic application, the specified protein might be a missing enzyme, a cytokine regulator, or a cancer-fighting agent. The delivery mechanism is the same—only the sequence changes.

This sounds simple in principle. In practice, it took roughly thirty years to make it work. The core problem was the immune system. Unmodified mRNA, the kind that cells produce naturally, contains a molecular signature that the body's innate immune system recognizes as foreign and attacks. Injecting unmodified synthetic mRNA into a mammal triggered a ferocious inflammatory response that destroyed the mRNA before it could reach a ribosome. Every attempt at mRNA therapeutics in the 1990s and early 2000s ran directly into this wall.

The breakthrough came from Katalin Karikó and Drew Weissman at the University of Pennsylvania. Their key insight was that naturally occurring RNA in the body, particularly transfer RNA and ribosomal RNA, contains chemically modified forms of the standard nucleosides, the building blocks of RNA. These modifications, particularly the substitution of pseudouridine for uridine at specific positions, signal to the immune system that the RNA is not foreign. Karikó and Weissman showed in a landmark 2005 paper that incorporating pseudouridine into synthetic mRNA dramatically reduced the inflammatory response, allowing the mRNA to survive long enough to reach ribosomes and produce protein. This discovery, which eventually earned Karikó and Weissman the 2023 Nobel Prize in Physiology or Medicine, removed the primary roadblock to mRNA therapeutics.

Diagram 6.2 - Modified Nucleoside Chemistry: How mRNA Escapes the Immune Alarm

Unnodified mRNA vs. m pseudouridine : translation

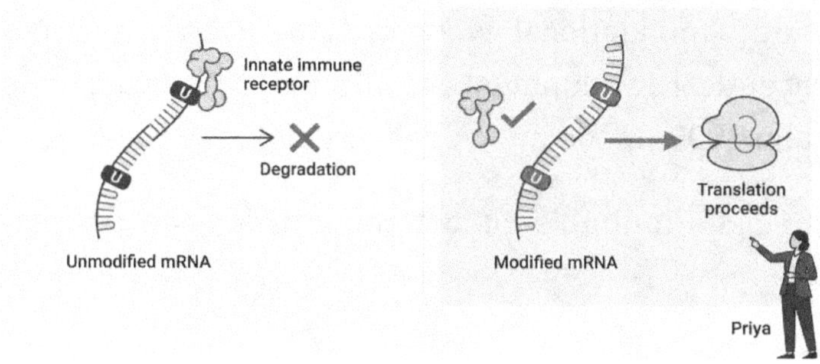

Solving the immune evasion problem was essential, but it left a second challenge: delivery. mRNA is a fragile molecule. It degrades rapidly in biological fluids, is too large to diffuse across cell membranes on its own, and is quickly destroyed by circulating enzymes. Getting a synthetic mRNA molecule from an injection site into the interior of a target cell, intact, required a delivery vehicle.

The solution was ionizable lipid nanoparticles, or LNPs. A lipid nanoparticle is a tiny sphere, roughly one hundred nanometers in diameter, made of lipid molecules that can spontaneously form a protective shell around an mRNA cargo. The "ionizable" part is the critical engineering innovation: at neutral pH, the lipid molecules carry no charge, so they do not trigger an inflammatory response in the bloodstream. But when the nanoparticle enters the acidic environment of a cell's endosome, which is the cellular compartment that the nanoparticle is taken up into, the lipids become positively charged, destabilize the endosomal membrane, and release the mRNA into the cytoplasm, where the ribosomes are. The nanoparticle is a

Trojan horse that is inert in transit and activates on arrival. Pieter Cullis at the University of British Columbia contributed foundational work on LNP design, and the pharmaceutical development of ionizable LNPs through the 1990s and 2000s made mRNA delivery clinically viable.

Diagram 6.3 - Ionizable Lipid Nanoparticle: The Delivery Vehicle

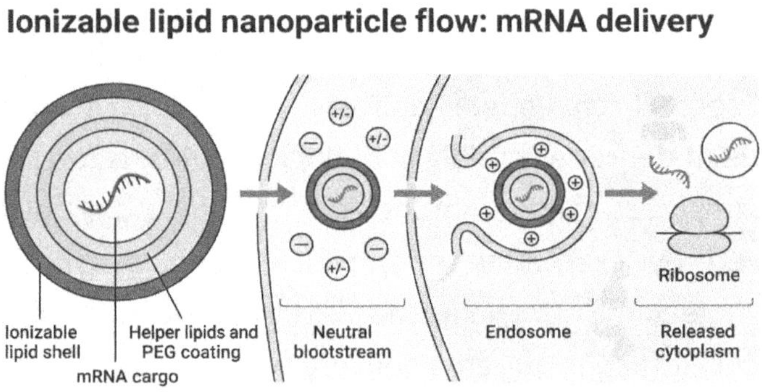

With modified nucleosides and LNPs in hand, the core mRNA platform was technically functional. What remained was to build the manufacturing and scale-up infrastructure and to demonstrate clinical efficacy. Moderna and BioNTech both built mRNA manufacturing platforms through the 2010s, optimizing synthesis, purification, and formulation. When the SARS-CoV-2 genome was published on January 10, 2020, both organizations had platforms ready to receive a sequence. Moderna's team, led by Barney Graham and Jason McLellan's structural work on the prefusion-stabilized spike protein and Moderna's own design team, finalized the vaccine sequence on January 13,

2020. The vaccine design was complete before the first confirmed case of COVID-19 in the United States.

The clinical trial results, announced in November 2020, reported efficacy rates above ninety percent for both mRNA vaccines. Mass deployment followed. The speed of the response was unprecedented in vaccine history, and it was made possible precisely by the platform architecture: the delivery system, the modified nucleoside chemistry, and the manufacturing process were already in place. Only the sequence was new, and the sequence was code.

One Platform, Endless Applications: From Pandemic Vaccines to Cancer Neoantigens

The most consequential feature of mRNA therapeutics is not what it did for COVID-19. It is what the COVID-19 experience revealed about the platform's broader potential. The infrastructure, the ionizable LNP delivery system, the modified nucleoside chemistry, and the mRNA synthesis and purification process remain constant across applications. Only the mRNA sequence changes, and mRNA sequences can be designed computationally. This means that for any disease where a protein can be identified as a useful therapeutic or immune target, an mRNA therapeutic is theoretically designable. The limiting factor shifts from chemistry to sequence design, and sequence design is increasingly an information problem that computational biology and artificial intelligence can accelerate.

The most ambitious application currently in clinical development is the personalized cancer vaccine. Tumors evolve under constant genetic pressure, accumulating mutations that change the protein sequences of cancer cells. Some of these mutations produce proteins that exist only in that patient's tumor and nowhere else in the body. These tumor-specific proteins are called neoantigens, a term that means new antigens not present in normal tissue. Because neoantigens are unique to the cancer, they are, in principle, ideal targets for an immune response: a therapy that trains the immune system to attack neoantigens would kill cancer cells while leaving normal cells untouched.

Moderna and Merck have developed a personalized cancer vaccine approach, designated mRNA-4157 combined with pembrolizumab, that works as follows: first, tumor tissue from the patient is sequenced to identify the mutations unique to that patient's cancer. Then a computational pipeline identifies which of those mutations produce neoantigens, that is, peptide sequences likely to be recognized by the patient's immune cells. Then an mRNA sequence is designed that encodes those neoantigens. Then an mRNA vaccine is manufactured to match that patient's tumor profile and administered. The immune system is trained to recognize the patient's specific cancer. Phase 2b clinical trial data reported in 2023 showed that the combination reduced the risk of recurrence or death in melanoma patients by 44% compared with pembrolizumab alone.

This approach inverts the traditional vaccine paradigm. A conventional vaccine is designed once, manufactured identically for millions of patients, and administered to a population. A neoantigen vaccine is designed and manufactured individually for each patient, tailored to the unique molecular profile of that patient's tumor. The platform makes this personalization economically feasible because, once the infrastructure is in place, the marginal cost of a new sequence is low. The manufacturing process is the same regardless of the sequence in which it runs. The sequence is the patient-specific variable, and the sequence is software.

Diagram 6.4 - Personalized Cancer Neoantigen Vaccine: Design-to-Treatment Pipeline

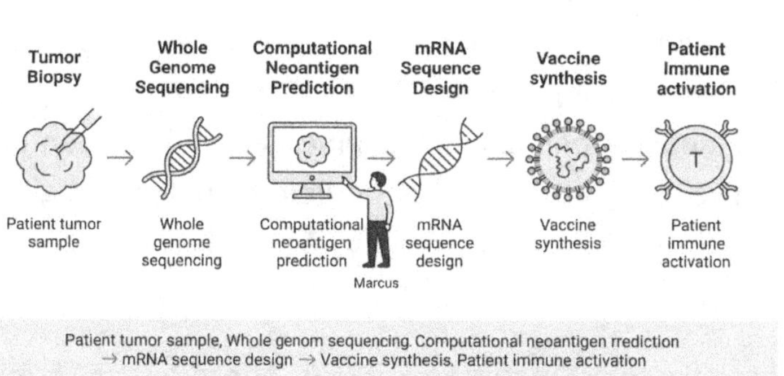

Beyond cancer vaccines, the mRNA platform is advancing across multiple therapeutic areas. In infectious diseases, mRNA-based vaccine candidates against influenza, HIV, respiratory syncytial virus, and Epstein-Barr virus are in clinical trials. The influenza application is particularly

significant because seasonal influenza vaccines must be reformulated annually based on predictions about which strains will circulate, and the manufacturing lead time has historically been six months or more, meaning that mismatches between predicted and circulating strains can reduce vaccine efficacy. An mRNA influenza vaccine can be reformulated and manufactured in weeks, not months, collapsing the manufacturing lag and improving the match to circulating strains.

In rare diseases, mRNA therapeutics offer a route to enzyme replacement that avoids some of the limitations of protein therapy. Methylmalonic acidemia and propionic acidemia, two rare metabolic disorders caused by deficiencies in enzymes involved in amino acid metabolism, are being targeted with mRNA therapies that direct the liver to produce the missing enzyme. Moderna's mRNA-3705 for methylmalonic acidemia has entered clinical trials. The same LNP technology that delivers mRNA to muscle cells for vaccine applications can be engineered to preferentially target liver cells by adjusting the lipid composition, giving the platform organ specificity as well as sequence specificity.

In cardiovascular medicine, mRNA encoding VEGF-A, a protein that stimulates the growth of new blood vessels, is in clinical trials for heart failure and peripheral arterial disease. The idea is to administer mRNA directly to cardiac muscle or to ischemic tissue, producing a local burst of VEGF-A protein that promotes angiogenesis, the formation of new blood vessels, without the systemic side effects that would accompany a continuous protein therapy. The therapeutic window is defined by the mRNA half-life, typically days to weeks, which provides a controlled duration of action.

Engineering Immune Cells to Hunt Cancer: CAR-T Cell Therapy

To understand CAR-T cell therapy, you need to understand two things about the immune system. First, T cells, which are a class of white blood cells, are the immune system's precision-guided weapons. They do not attack indiscriminately. Each T cell carries a T cell receptor, a protein complex on its surface that recognizes one specific molecular target, called an antigen. When a T cell's receptor encounters its matching antigen on the surface of an infected or malignant cell, the T cell activates, kills the target cell, and proliferates to amplify the response. The immune system's targeting precision derives entirely from this receptor-antigen recognition system.

Second, cancer frequently evades the immune system by reducing or eliminating the surface markers that would normally allow T cells to recognize it as a threat. Tumor cells, at their origin, are the patient's own cells, and they have evolved a range of mechanisms, including downregulating antigen presentation, producing immunosuppressive signals, and creating a hostile microenvironment around the tumor to avoid triggering a T cell response. Natural T cells often cannot see the cancer well enough to attack it.

CAR-T cell therapy solves both problems by engineering a new recognition capability directly into the T cell. A Chimeric Antigen Receptor, from which the therapy takes its name, is a synthetic protein designed in two functional halves. The outer half is derived from an antibody's antigen-binding domain, specifically the single-chain variable fragment (scFv), a compact version of the antibody's recognition module. The inner half is derived from the T cell receptor's intracellular signaling domain, which triggers T cell activation. The two halves are fused into a single synthetic protein and inserted into the T cell's genome so that the cell expresses it on its surface. The result is a T cell that has been given a new pair of eyes: it can now recognize a target antigen using its engineered receptor, and when it does, it activates and kills.

The first CAR-T therapies were designed against CD19, a protein expressed on the surface of B cells and on most B cell cancers, including certain leukemias and lymphomas. The anti-CD19 CAR-T cell is a precise detector: it kills any cell displaying CD19. Because normal B cells also express CD19, the therapy causes a predictable depletion of healthy B cells, necessitating long-term management. Still, the trade-off is a targeted attack on the tumor. In clinical trials and subsequent commercial use, anti-CD19 CAR-T therapies have produced complete remissions in patients with diffuse large B-cell lymphoma, acute lymphoblastic leukemia, and other B-cell malignancies who had exhausted all other options.

Diagram 6.5 - CAR-T Cell Architecture and Tumor Recognition

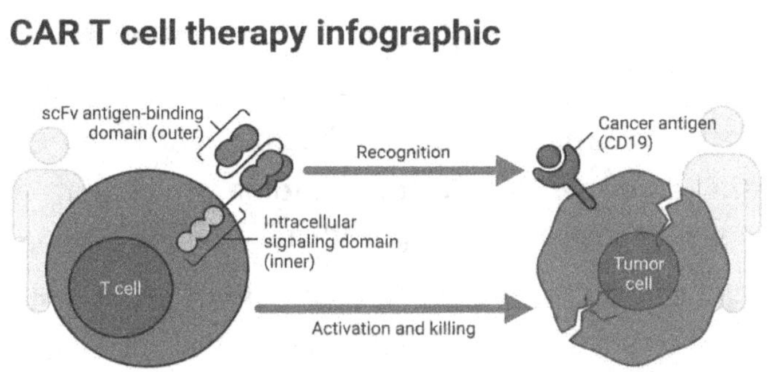

A Caption harroscape diagram infographic - an executive technical tone.

The manufacturing process for CAR-T therapy is one of the most complex in medicine. It is, in engineering terms, a personalized batch manufacturing process. The steps are as follows: a technician draws blood from the patient and isolates T cells using a process called leukapheresis. The isolated T cells are transported to a certified manufacturing facility, often in another city or state. At the facility, the T cells are activated using antibody-coated beads that stimulate them to divide, then transduced, meaning that a viral vector, typically a modified lentivirus, is used to insert the CAR gene into the T cells' genome. The engineered cells are expanded in bioreactors to hundreds of millions of cells, quality tested for potency, sterility, and correct CAR expression, cryopreserved, and shipped back to the hospital. The patient receives lymphodepleting chemotherapy to clear space in their immune system, and then the CAR-T cells are infused. The entire process takes 2 to 4 weeks, from cell collection to infusion.

The FDA has approved six CAR-T cell therapies as of 2024: Kymriah (tisagenlecleucel) from Novartis, Yescarta (axicabtagene ciloleucel) from Kite Pharma/Gilead, Tecartus (brexucabtagene autoleucel), Breyanzi (lisocabtagene maraleucel), Abecma (idecabtagene vicleucel) targeting BCMA for multiple myeloma, and Carvykti (ciltacabtagene autoleucel). The clinical outcomes in certain patient populations have been remarkable. Among patients with relapsed or refractory diffuse large B-cell lymphoma who had failed two or more prior lines of therapy, which is a population with very few remaining options, complete remission rates of thirty to forty percent have been reported in pivotal trials, and a significant fraction of those remissions have been durable, with some patients maintaining complete remission beyond five and, in longer follow-up studies, ten years.

The primary toxicities of CAR-T therapy are cytokine release syndrome (CRS) and immune effector cell-associated neurotoxicity syndrome (ICANS). Cytokine release syndrome occurs because activated CAR-T cells, upon encountering their target, release large quantities of cytokines, signaling proteins that coordinate immune responses. A large, rapid release of cytokines produces fever, low blood pressure, and, in severe cases, organ dysfunction. Neurotoxicity, which can manifest as confusion, seizures, or cerebral edema, is less well understood mechanistically but is thought to involve cytokines crossing the blood-brain barrier and triggering inflammation in the central nervous system. Both toxicities require experienced management and have limited the delivery of CAR-T therapies to academic medical centers with specialized care protocols.

Diagram 6.6 - CAR-T Cell Manufacturing: From Patient to Living Drug

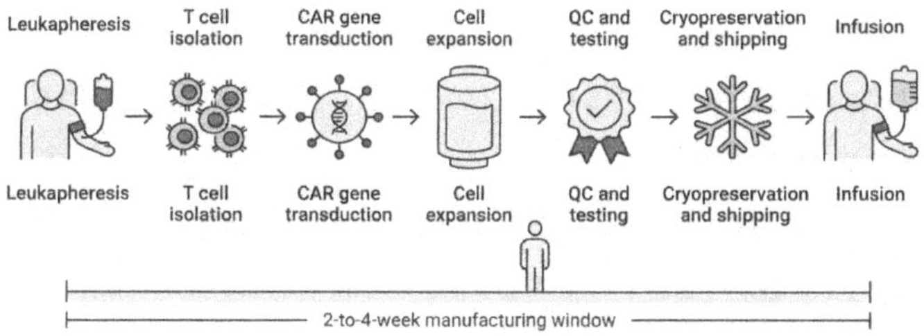

The Engineering Frontier: Automating Personalized Cell Therapy

CAR-T therapy currently costs between four hundred thousand and five hundred thousand dollars per patient treatment, a price point that reflects the labor-intensive, custom manufacturing process rather than the underlying biology. Each treatment is, in the purest sense, a batch of one: a unique biological product manufactured specifically for one patient from that patient's own cells, with no economies of scale. This is the central manufacturing engineering challenge of the field, and it is being attacked from several directions simultaneously.

The first approach is automation of the autologous manufacturing process. The current process involves dozens of manual steps, each requiring trained technicians, carefully controlled environments, and extensive documentation. Automated, closed-system bioreactors that can perform T cell activation, transduction, expansion, and formulation in a single sealed, robotically controlled device are in development. Companies including Miltenyi Biotec, Ori Biotech, and Cytovance are building platforms that compress the manufacturing process from weeks to days and from dozens of manual steps to a largely automated workflow. If the bioreactor can perform the entire manufacturing sequence autonomously, labor costs drop dramatically, and the process can be decentralized to hospitals rather than centralized at specialized manufacturing facilities.

The second approach is allogeneic, meaning off-the-shelf, CAR-T therapy. Instead of engineering each patient's own T cells, allogeneic approaches use T cells from a healthy donor, engineer them into CAR-T cells, and manufacture them in bulk batches that can be stored and administered to any patient, like a conventional drug. The challenge with allogeneic therapy is immunological: a donor T cell carries the original donor's T cell receptor alongside the engineered CAR. That original receptor could recognize the patient's tissues as foreign, a condition called graft-versus-host disease. Simultaneously, the patient's own immune system may recognize and eliminate the donor T cells before they have a chance to work. Solving these dual immunological rejection problems requires additional genetic engineering steps: knocking out the donor T cell receptor gene using CRISPR to eliminate graft-versus-host risk, and knocking out specific immune checkpoint genes to help the cells persist. Companies including Allogene Therapeutics, Fate Therapeutics, and Cellectis are advancing allogeneic CAR-T programs through clinical trials.

Marcus, looking at the manufacturing process diagram on the whiteboard during a Helix Forge design review, once asked the question that frames the engineering problem precisely: "If this were a software release pipeline, what would we need to automate to get from days to hours?" Yuki's answer was immediate. "You'd need the transduction step to be deterministic, the expansion to be closed and monitored with real-time sensors, and the quality control to be automated with machine-learning-based image analysis instead of manual cell counting. The biology is solvable. The systems integration is the bottleneck." That is a fair description of where the field stands.

A third direction, which sits at the frontier of what is currently possible, is in vivo CAR-T generation, meaning engineering T cells within the patient's body without removing them. Nanoparticles or viral vectors carrying the CAR gene are administered systemically and engineered to preferentially transduce circulating T cells. If the delivery is sufficiently specific and the CAR gene is expressed stably, the patient's own immune system generates its own CAR-T cells without any ex vivo, meaning outside-the-body, manufacturing step. Researchers at the University of Pennsylvania and several biotechnology companies have demonstrated proof of concept in preclinical models. Clinical trials are in early stages. If this approach achieves clinical efficacy, it would reduce the cost of CAR-T therapy by an order of magnitude and make it accessible to the vast majority of patients who currently cannot access it.

Diagram 6.7 - Three Paths to Scalable CAR-T: Automation, Allogeneic, In Vivo

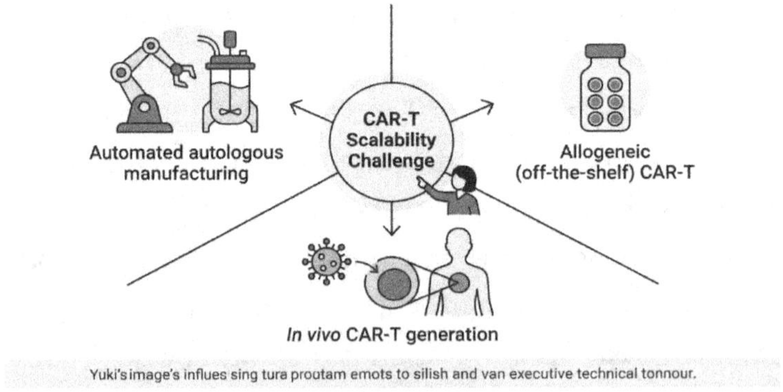

Rewriting the Code: Gene Therapy and the Age of One-Time Cures

Gene therapy, in its most direct definition, is the modification of a patient's genetic material to treat or cure a disease. The concept has been pursued since the 1970s, when the first recombinant DNA experiments established that genes could be moved between organisms. The clinical history of gene therapy has been longer, harder, and more turbulent than that of mRNA therapeutics or CAR-T, punctuated by serious adverse events, including a patient death in 1999 and the development of leukemia in patients treated in early X-linked severe combined immunodeficiency trials. But the field did not stop. It learned from each failure, improved its vectors and protocols, and has arrived in the 2020s with a pipeline of approved therapies and a clinical track record that, in certain diseases, is genuinely transformative.

The most widely used delivery vehicle for gene therapy is the adeno-associated virus, or AAV. An AAV vector is a recombinant viral particle from which all viral genes have been removed and replaced with the therapeutic gene of interest. The virus retains its ability to enter cells and deliver its cargo, but it cannot replicate or cause a viral infection. AAVs exist in multiple serotypes, which are natural variants with different surface proteins that give them different tissue tropisms, meaning preferences for infecting specific cell types. AAV9 naturally targets neurons and crosses the blood-brain barrier, making it the preferred vector for neurological diseases. AAV5 preferentially targets liver cells. This built-in tissue specificity is a significant engineering asset because it allows the therapeutic gene to be delivered preferentially to the target organ without requiring cell-type-specific engineering of the vector itself.

Luxturna (voretigene neparvovec), approved by the FDA in 2017, was the first gene therapy approved for an inherited disease in the United States. It treats RPE65 mutation-associated retinal dystrophy, a progressive condition in which a missing enzyme causes photoreceptor cells in the retina to die, leading to blindness. Luxturna delivers a functional copy of the RPE65 gene directly to retinal cells via subretinal injection. Clinical trial results showed that patients who had been legally blind recovered sufficient vision to navigate without assistance, read large print, and detect movement in very low light. The treatment is administered once. The improvement is sustained for years after the injection. This is what a one-time cure enabled by gene therapy actually looks like in a clinical setting.

Diagram 6.8 - AAV Vector: Structure and Gene Delivery

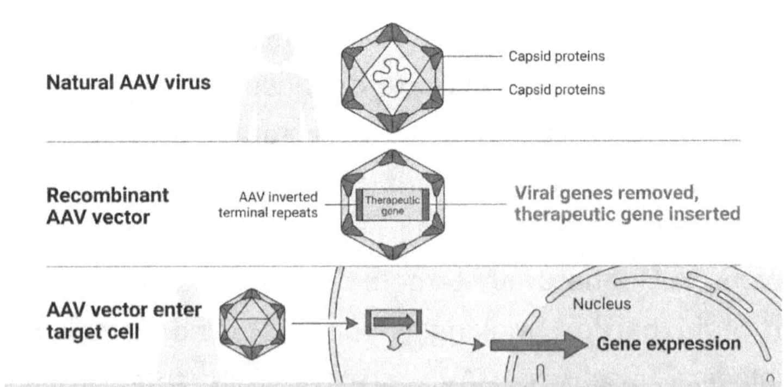

Layen/io-stack between natural AAV virus and recombinant AAV vector, therapeutic gene expression

Zolgensma (onasemnogene abeparvovec), approved by the FDA in 2019, represents a more dramatic demonstration of gene therapy's potential. Spinal muscular atrophy type 1 is caused by mutations in the SMN1 gene, which encodes a protein essential for motor neuron survival. Infants with SMA type 1 lack functional SMN1 and progressively lose motor neurons, typically losing the ability to breathe unassisted by eighteen months of age and dying within two years without ventilatory support. Zolgensma delivers a functional copy of the SMN1 gene via AAV9 in a single intravenous infusion. In clinical trials, infants treated with Zolgensma before symptom onset achieved motor milestones, including sitting without support and, in some cases, standing and walking, that had never previously been observed in the disease's natural history. Children who received Zolgensma as newborns screened positive for SMA are, in early follow-up, meeting normal developmental milestones.

The most consequential recent gene therapy approval, and arguably the one with the broadest implications for the field, is Casgevy (exagamglogene autotemcel), approved by the FDA in December 2023 for sickle cell disease and transfusion-dependent beta-thalassemia. Casgevy uses CRISPR-Cas9 to edit the patient's own hematopoietic stem cells, which are the blood-producing stem cells in bone marrow, to reactivate fetal hemoglobin production. Sickle cell disease is caused by a mutation in adult hemoglobin that causes red blood cells to adopt a rigid sickle shape, blocking small blood vessels and causing the severe, recurring pain crises and organ damage that characterize the disease. Fetal hemoglobin, the form produced by developing fetuses and switched off shortly after birth, does not carry the sickle mutation. Casgevy edits a regulatory gene, BCL11A, that normally suppresses fetal hemoglobin production, lifting that suppression and allowing the patient's cells to produce functional, non-sickling fetal hemoglobin. In the pivotal clinical trial, twenty-nine out of twenty-nine patients treated with Casgevy were free of severe vaso-occlusive crises, which are the debilitating blood-vessel-blocking episodes that define the disease, for at least twelve months post-treatment. This is, for the patients who have received it, a functional cure.

The distinction between somatic gene therapy and germline gene editing is the most important regulatory and ethical line in the field, and it is worth understanding precisely. Somatic gene therapy modifies the genes of non-reproductive cells, such as blood cells, liver cells, or retinal cells, in a living patient. The genetic changes affect only that patient and are not inherited by their children. All currently approved gene therapies are somatic. Germline editing, by contrast, modifies the cells of an embryo in ways that all future descendants of that individual would inherit. The scientific and regulatory community has drawn a clear line: somatic gene therapy is permissible with appropriate regulatory oversight; germline editing in human embryos intended for implantation is prohibited in most jurisdictions and is subject to an informal international moratorium pending resolution of the ethical questions it raises. The 2018 announcement by He Jiankui that he had implanted CRISPR-edited embryos that resulted in live births in China, an action taken without proper informed consent and outside any legitimate regulatory framework, was widely condemned by the scientific community and resulted in his criminal conviction under Chinese law.

Diagram 6.9 - Somatic Gene Therapy vs. Germline Editing: The Regulatory Boundary

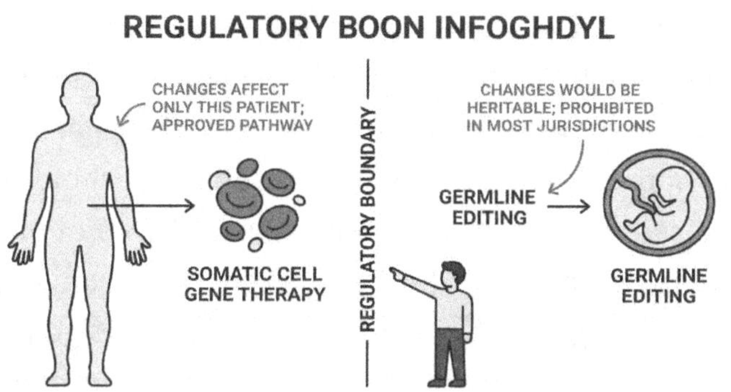

Living Medicines: Engineered Bacteria as Therapeutic Agents

The third major frontier of programmable medicine is also the most radical departure from conventional drug development. Living medicines are engineered microorganisms, most commonly bacteria, administered to patients not as inert chemical agents but as living, replicating, gene-expressing entities that sense the patient's internal biology and respond therapeutically in real time. Where an mRNA vaccine provides a cell with temporary instructions and then degrades, and where a gene therapy delivers a permanent gene to a patient's cells, a living medicine is an autonomous biological agent that operates continuously inside the patient, executing a programmed therapeutic function as a function of the local environment it encounters.

The conceptual framework for living medicines is precisely the genetic circuit framework described in Chapter 5. A living medicine is a bacterium engineered with a gene circuit comprising a sensor promoter, an input signal, a processing logic layer, and an output response. The sensor promoter is responsive to a specific molecular signal in the patient's body. When that signal crosses a threshold, the circuit activates a set of metabolic genes that produce a therapeutic compound. The circuit can be made logic-responsive: it might require two simultaneous signals, a tumor-associated hypoxia marker, and a specific metabolic waste product to activate, providing a degree of specificity that conventional drugs cannot match. The toggle switches and AND gates designed in a laboratory and described in Chapter 5 are, in living medicines, deployed inside a patient's gut or tumor as autonomous therapeutic agents.

Synlogic, a Cambridge-based biotechnology company founded on principles of synthetic biology, has been among the leaders in translating this concept into clinical applications. Their lead programs involve engineering the probiotic bacterium Escherichia coli Nissle 1917, a well-characterized, safety-tested laboratory strain, with gene circuits designed to metabolize compounds that accumulate to toxic levels in patients with specific metabolic disorders. In phenylketonuria, a condition in which the liver lacks the enzyme to process phenylalanine, an amino acid found in most dietary proteins, Synlogic's engineered bacteria are designed to consume excess phenylalanine in the gut before it can be absorbed into the bloodstream. The bacterium senses phenylalanine concentration, activates a metabolic pathway that converts it to harmless trans-cinnamic acid, and excretes the product. The gene circuit is the drug. The bacterium is the delivery vehicle that synthesizes and administers it on demand, locally, in the gut, where the problem originates.

A second Synlogic program targets hyperammonemia, a condition in which the liver's urea cycle is impaired, causing toxic ammonia accumulation in the bloodstream and, ultimately, in the brain. The engineered bacterium is designed to express genes encoding arginine biosynthesis enzymes that consume gut ammonia, thereby reducing systemic ammonia load. The circuit is sensitive to local ammonia concentration: it activates when ammonia levels are high, and its output is calibrated to the concentration, making it a genuinely feedback-responsive therapeutic agent rather than a fixed-dose drug. Phase 1 clinical trial results demonstrated that the engineered bacteria could reduce ammonia levels in healthy volunteers given a protein challenge and were generally well tolerated.

Diagram 6.10 - Living Medicine: Engineered Bacterium as Therapeutic Circuit

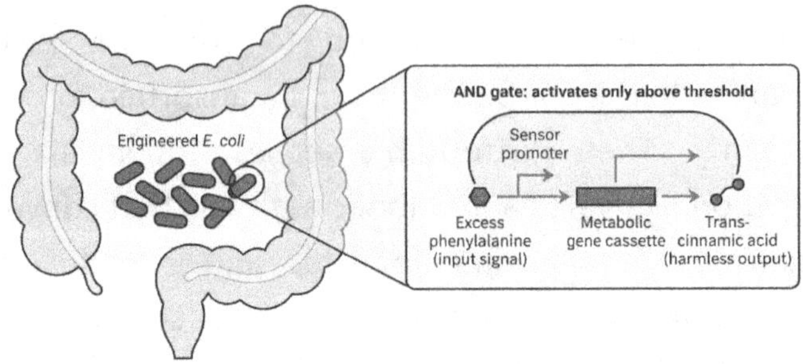

Engineered *E. coli* bacteria likeln an executive technical pattern

The most scientifically ambitious living medicine applications involve bacteria engineered to seek and act specifically within the tumor microenvironment. Solid tumors create a distinctive biochemical environment: they are hypoxic, meaning oxygen-deprived, due to the chaotic and insufficient blood vessel growth that characterizes tumor tissue. They also accumulate lactate, have a lower pH than normal tissue, and express specific surface proteins that normal tissues do not. These features collectively constitute a molecular address for the tumor. Bacteria engineered to preferentially colonize hypoxic environments, such as attenuated strains of Salmonella or Listeria, can selectively accumulate in tumors after intravenous administration because tumors provide the anaerobic conditions they prefer.

Once established in the tumor microenvironment, the bacteria serve as a local factory for therapeutic compounds. Engineered strains have been designed to produce cytotoxins, immunostimulatory signals that recruit immune cells into the tumor, checkpoint inhibitor antibody fragments that lift immunosuppression, and therapeutic RNA molecules. The gene circuit logic allows the therapeutic output to be conditioned on specific tumor signals: the bacterium only produces its therapeutic cargo when it detects the combination of hypoxia AND a tumor-specific marker, providing a specificity that a systemically administered drug cannot replicate. Clinical trials of tumor-targeting bacteria in humans are in early phase development, with initial safety and dosing data emerging from phase 1 studies at several academic medical centers.

The regulatory path for living medicines is necessarily more complex than for conventional drugs. A living therapeutic is not a molecule with a defined structure and known pharmacokinetics. It is a replicating organism whose behavior within the body depends on the complex interactions among its engineered gene circuits, the patient's microbiome, immune system, and metabolic state. The FDA's regulatory framework for living medicines is still under active development. Still, the general path runs through the Center for Biologics Evaluation and Research, which also oversees cell and gene therapies. Manufacturing controls for living medicines must address genetic stability, meaning the engineered circuits must not mutate in ways that change therapeutic function, and safety controls must address the possibility of unexpected colonization or horizontal gene transfer to other bacteria in the microbiome. These are solvable engineering problems, and the regulatory science is advancing alongside the therapeutic science.

Accelerating Discovery: Synthetic Biology Meets Pharma R and D

Beyond direct therapeutic applications, synthetic biology is transforming the earliest phases of drug discovery in ways that are less visible to the public, but that may, in aggregate, be as consequential as the therapies themselves. The central challenge of pharmaceutical drug discovery is screening: identifying, from a library of potentially millions of chemical compounds, the small subset that modulate a specific biological target, such as an enzyme, receptor, or signaling protein, in the desired way. Conventional high-throughput screening uses cell-free biochemical assays, mixtures of purified proteins and candidate compounds in microplate wells, to identify hits. These assays are fast and cheap, but they measure activity outside the complexity of a living cell, so many compounds that appear active in cell-free assays are inactive, toxic, or non-selective in living cells.

Synthetic biology enables a different approach: reporter circuits. A reporter circuit is a genetic construct engineered into a living cell that, upon activation of the target of interest, produces a measurable output signal, typically a fluorescent protein or a luminescent enzyme. If a drug candidate activates the target, the cell lights up. Automated microscopy and fluorescence plate readers can screen hundreds of thousands of cells per day, each containing the reporter circuit, against large compound libraries. The screening occurs in living cells, under physiologically relevant conditions, with all the complexity of cellular signaling intact. Hits from living-cell reporter screens have a significantly higher rate of subsequent validation in animal models than hits from cell-free assays because the cellular environment filters out many compounds that are inactive, poorly cell-permeable, or toxic.

Beyond screening, synthetic biology enables what is sometimes called target identification and validation through genetic circuit perturbation: engineering cells with tunable circuits that allow the activity of a specific gene or protein to be dialed up or down continuously, rather than in the binary on/off fashion of conventional genetic knockouts. This allows researchers to map the dose-response relationship between target activity and cellular phenotype, understanding how much target inhibition is needed to produce a therapeutic effect and how much produces toxicity. This kind of quantitative target biology was difficult before synthetic circuit design tools became available, and is now a standard part of the drug discovery toolkit at major pharmaceutical companies and biotechnology firms.

Diagram 6.11 - Reporter Circuit-Based Drug Screening: Living Cells as Drug Detectors

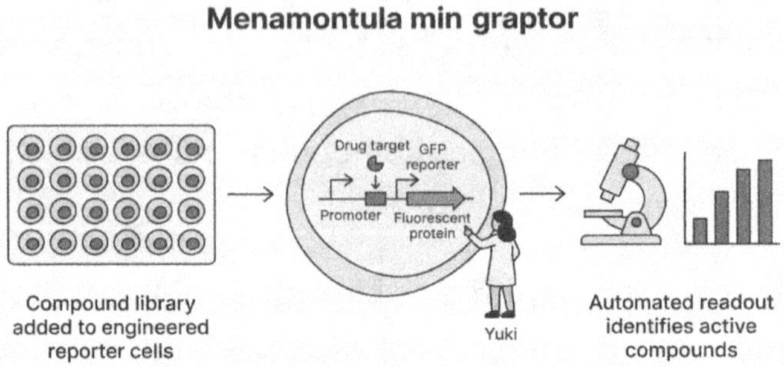

Ginkgo Bioworks has built an industrial-scale version of this approach at its Boston Foundry. Their organism engineering platform combines automated strain construction, high-throughput fermentation, and data analysis pipelines to run thousands of design-build-test cycles per week. For pharmaceutical clients, Ginkgo's Ferment division runs biosensor-based screening campaigns, using engineered yeast and bacterial strains as living detection platforms for natural product compounds, enzyme variants, and biosynthetic pathways. The throughput of Ginkgo's platform, tens of thousands of genetic constructs tested per year, would be impossible with conventional manual laboratory methods. This is drug discovery as an information-intensive engineering process, and the scale at which it operates is qualitatively different from that of a decade ago.

The Logic Gate Inside the Patient: Helix Forge's Diagnostic Circuit

Yuki pulls up the latest version of the Helix Forge diagnostic circuit schematic on the lab's shared display. The circuit, described in general terms in Chapter 5's discussion of genetic logic gates, is now in its third design iteration, and the changes from the first version are instructive. The original design used a single promoter sensing a single biomarker, a straightforward threshold detector. The problem, which Carlos identified during a regulatory review meeting, was specificity: the single biomarker was present across a wide range of conditions, not all of which required the therapeutic response the circuit was designed to trigger. The false-positive rate in the simulation was too high to consider clinical use.

The revised design implements a two-input AND gate: the circuit activates only when biomarker A, a metabolic marker elevated specifically in the disease state, AND biomarker B, a protein expressed on the surface of diseased cells, are simultaneously present above their respective threshold levels. This combinatorial logic collapses the false-positive rate by orders of magnitude, because both conditions must be satisfied simultaneously. The AND gate architecture is the same engineering pattern described in Chapter 5 for electronic logic circuits: a two-input gate that produces an output signal only when both inputs are high. The biology is different from the electronics, but the design logic is identical.

Marcus, reviewing the new schematic, nods. "So the diagnostic and the therapeutic are coupled. The circuit can activate the therapeutic response only if it has already confirmed the disease state via two independent signals. The diagnosis is built into the treatment." Yuki says yes, that is exactly right. "In conventional medicine," she says, "diagnosis and treatment are separate processes, often separated by days or weeks of testing and result interpretation. In a genetic circuit deployed as a living medicine, the diagnostic logic and therapeutic output are encoded within a single molecule. The treatment is self-diagnosing. It can only fire if the conditions for its use are confirmed in real time at the site of action." Carlos, who has been listening from across the room, says: "That is also the strongest argument for its safety profile. The circuit is its own off-switch, designed into the biology from the start."

This is the connection between Chapter 5 and Chapter 6 made concrete. The toggle switches, AND gates, and memory circuits described in the previous chapter as abstract achievements of genetic engineering are not merely academic demonstrations. They are design components for the next generation of medical devices: living diagnostic-therapeutic circuits that operate with molecular precision inside the patient's body, activating exactly when and where they are needed and remaining dormant otherwise. Helix Forge's work is a small-scale example of what an increasingly large number of biotechnology companies are pursuing. The engineering tools exist. The clinical frameworks are being built. The question of what becomes possible when a well-designed genetic circuit is deployed inside a human patient is one of the animating questions of the next decade of synthetic biology.

Diagram 6.12 - Helix Forge Diagnostic-Therapeutic AND Gate Circuit

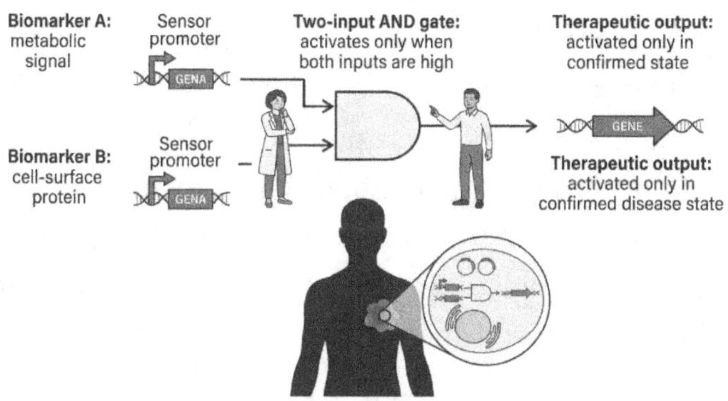

Building the Safety Net: Regulatory Pathways for Cell and Gene Therapies

The remarkable clinical achievements of CAR-T cell therapy, mRNA vaccines, and gene therapy have been enabled not only by the underlying science but by regulatory frameworks that have evolved, sometimes painfully and slowly, to handle a genuinely new category of medical product. Understanding those frameworks is not merely a compliance exercise for engineers and entrepreneurs in the field. It is essential context for evaluating the timeline, the cost structure, and the risk profile of any therapeutic development program.

The FDA evaluates cell and gene therapies primarily through the Center for Biologics Evaluation and Research (CBER), specifically its Office of Tissues and Advanced Therapies. Cell therapies, including CAR-T products, are regulated as biological products under Section 351 of the Public Health Service Act and require a Biologics License Application (BLA) for approval. Gene therapy products, including AAV-based therapies and CRISPR-based ex vivo cell modifications like Casgevy, are evaluated through the same pathway. The regulatory requirements reflect the unique characteristics of these products: they are complex biological entities, not small molecules; they may produce persistent or permanent effects; and they carry unique safety risks, including insertional mutagenesis for viral vectors and long-term immunogenicity for both cell and gene therapies.

The FDA has established two accelerated designation pathways specifically relevant to cell and gene therapies. The Breakthrough Therapy designation is available for any drug or biologic for a serious condition in which preliminary clinical evidence suggests it may demonstrate substantial improvement over existing therapies. A breakthrough designation provides more intensive FDA guidance during development and can substantially reduce the time from phase 2 data to approval. Most approved CAR-T and gene therapy products received Breakthrough designation. The Regenerative Medicine Advanced Therapy (RMAT) designation, created by the 21st Century Cures Act in 2016, is specifically for cell and gene therapies and provides the same benefits as the Breakthrough designation, plus specific provisions for using surrogate endpoints and early clinical data to support approval. The RMAT designation effectively tells a developer that the FDA will work closely with them to design a regulatory path using real-world evidence and post-approval registries rather than long-term trial follow-up, which is particularly important for gene therapies, where the durability of benefit may take years to characterize fully.

The gene therapy regulatory landscape includes a specific requirement that has no equivalent in conventional drug development: long-term follow-up. Because AAV-based gene therapies deliver a DNA cargo that integrates, at low frequency, into the patient's genome, there is a theoretical risk of insertional mutagenesis, the accidental disruption of a cancer-suppressor gene or the activation of an oncogene at the integration site. This risk has not materialized in approved AAV therapies, but it cannot be fully characterized without years of patient follow-up. The FDA, therefore, requires, as a condition of approval for most gene therapies, a minimum of 15 years of post-approval patient follow-up. This requirement fundamentally shapes the economics of gene therapy development: the regulatory commitment extends for more than a decade beyond approval, requiring ongoing patient registries, periodic reporting, and safety-monitoring infrastructure that substantially adds to the total cost of bringing a gene therapy to market.

Carlos, reviewing a draft regulatory strategy for a new Helix Forge gene circuit product at a monthly team meeting, summarizes the framework in a way that the team finds useful. "The regulatory pathway rewards transparency about what you know, rigor about what you don't know, and honesty about the irreversibility of what you're doing. For a gene therapy that makes a permanent change to a patient's genome, the standard of evidence required for approval is higher than for a drug that clears the body in forty-eight hours. That is appropriate. The safety net is designed for the stakes involved." Priya adds: "And the RMAT pathway exists because the FDA recognizes that waiting for long-term follow-up data before approving a therapy for children dying of SMA type 1 would itself be a harm. The framework is not a wall. It is a set of carefully calibrated trade-offs between known benefit and uncertain risk." That is, in the regulatory context of cell and gene therapies, a precise and fair description.

What This Means For You

If you are a software engineer or systems engineer considering a move into the biotech space, the engineering translation in this chapter is direct: mRNA therapeutics is a platform whose architecture you understand intuitively, because it separates the instruction layer from the execution layer. The mRNA sequence is the code. The lipid nanoparticle is the package manager. The ribosome is the runtime. The immune response is the output. The engineering challenges that remain, improving LNP tissue targeting, extending mRNA half-life, and reducing immunogenicity in repeat dosing, are systems optimization problems with well-defined metrics. CAR-T manufacturing is a bioprocess engineering problem at its core, and the bottlenecks, manual steps, quality-control latency, and batch-to-batch variability are exactly the kinds of problems that automation, closed-loop process control, and real-time sensor integration solve in other manufacturing domains.

If you are a biotech entrepreneur evaluating a therapeutic program, the framework in this chapter provides specific questions to guide your evaluation. For any mRNA therapeutic program: what is the tissue targeting strategy, is the LNP composition optimized for the target organ, and what is the dosing regimen for repeat administration, given the potential for anti-PEG antibody accumulation? For any CAR-T program: is the approach autologous or allogeneic, what is the manufacturing timeline and cost structure, and what is the plan for cytokine release syndrome management? For any gene therapy: what is the vector serotype and what tissue tropism does it confer, what is the integration profile, and is there long-term follow-up data on related constructs that can anchor the safety assessment? These are not abstract questions. They are the ones that distinguish an informed program evaluation from a credulous reading of a press release.

If you are a policy professional or regulatory advisor, the most important framework from this chapter is the somatic-germline distinction and its implications. Every currently approved therapeutic modifies somatic cells only, and the regulatory infrastructure for somatic therapies is mature enough to support a robust clinical pipeline. The germline editing question, which concerns modifications to embryos that would be heritable, remains categorically different: the ethical stakes, the intergenerational scope, and the irreversibility of germline changes require a level of scientific consensus and societal deliberation that has not yet been achieved, and the prohibition on clinical germline editing in human embryos in most jurisdictions reflects a considered judgment about where the line should currently be drawn. Maintaining clarity about this distinction, in public communication, in regulatory guidance, and in media coverage, is one of the most important contributions a policy professional can make to the field.

For any professional engaging with the synthetic biology industry, the unifying insight from this chapter is the platform concept. mRNA therapeutics, CAR-T manufacturing, living medicines, and reporter-circuit-based drug screening are all instances of the same underlying shift: biology as programmable infrastructure, where the platform is built once, and the specific application is a parameter change. Evaluating any individual product, company, or clinical program is easier when you understand the platform it sits on, because the platform sets the ceiling for what is possible, the floor for what it costs, and the timeline for what comes next.

Takeaway

Medicine is undergoing a platform transition. For most of human history, drugs were chemicals discovered by testing compounds against disease targets and selecting those that worked well enough to be useful. That paradigm is not disappearing, but it is being joined by something fundamentally different: programmable biological agents designed from first principles to execute a defined therapeutic function with molecular precision. The shift is architectural. The instruction layer, the mRNA sequence, the CAR gene, and the bacterial gene circuit have been separated from the execution layer, the ribosome, the T cell, and the bacterial chassis. Once that separation is achieved, developing a new therapeutic becomes, increasingly, a problem of sequence design and platform optimization rather than of discovering a new chemical entity from scratch.

The clinical outcomes that flow from this architecture are not incremental improvements on what came before. They are in a different category. A patient with sickle cell disease who has been free of vaso-occlusive crises for two years after a single treatment. A child with spinal muscular atrophy type 1 who is walking at an age when untreated children with the same diagnosis would have already required ventilation. A melanoma patient is in complete remission after a personalized vaccine trained on the unique mutational signature of their own tumor. These are not experimental curiosities. They are approved or advanced-trial outcomes available now, produced by the tools described in this chapter.

The engineering challenges that remain are real and deserve to be addressed honestly. CAR-T therapy is too expensive and too complex for most of the world's patients. Gene therapy's long-term safety profile is still being characterized in post-approval registries. Living medicines are, in the context of regulatory history, brand-new entities with frameworks that are still being constructed. mRNA repeat dosing for chronic conditions faces immunogenicity hurdles that single-dose vaccine applications do not. None of these challenges is an argument against the platform. There are arguments for the ongoing engineering work needed to fulfill the platform's potential at a population scale.

What Priya showed the Helix Forge board, and what this chapter has tried to convey, is that the speed and precision of the COVID-19 mRNA vaccine were not an accident of timing or luck. They were the consequence of decades of platform-building, from modified nucleoside chemistry to ionizable lipid nanoparticle design to mRNA synthesis infrastructure, all of which happened to be ready when the world needed it. The Helix Forge diagnostic circuit, with its two-input AND gate and its self-diagnosing therapeutic logic, is a small, current instance of the same principle: the engineering work done in advance, the circuits designed and tested and iterated, creates the capability that looks like magic when it is finally deployed at the moment of need. There is no magic. There is only infrastructure, built carefully, and biology, understood deeply. This is what medicine looks like when it is reimagined as engineering.

7 The Living Factory

Opening Scenario

Marcus Webb had been inside semiconductor fabrication plants before, and he knew what industrial precision looked like: clean rooms, machines behind glass, engineers studying wafer defect maps on enormous screens. Nothing in that experience prepared him for what he was walking through on a Tuesday morning in Boston, inside the facility that Ginkgo Bioworks calls its Foundry. The place had the same dense, purposeful energy as a chip fab, but the machines here were not printing silicon. They were growing life.

His guide, a Ginkgo process engineer named Danielle, stopped him in front of a row of stainless-steel bioreactors, each vessel sealed and humming with biological activity. Inside every unit, billions of engineered yeast cells were converting sugar into a target molecule, following metabolic instructions her team had spent months writing into the organism's genome. Sensors measured temperature, dissolved oxygen, pH, and product concentration in real time, and data from every vessel streamed to a screen that ranked each strain variant by production performance. The worst performers would be deprioritized. The best would be scaled up and run again. 'This is not a lab,' Danielle said. 'This is a programming environment. The organisms are the code. The bioreactors are the runtime.'

Marcus thought about something Priya had told him months earlier: that the petrochemical industry was built on the assumption that chemistry required heat, pressure, and fossil carbon, while biology had been doing the same chemistry at room temperature on renewable inputs for three and a half billion years. The question was never whether biology could compete with petrochemistry. The question was whether we could learn to program biology fast enough. Standing in Ginkgo's Foundry, watching fermentation data populate a screen in real time, the answer was becoming clear.

Why It Matters

The petrochemical industry converts roughly four billion metric tons of fossil carbon every year into the plastics, solvents, fertilizers, surfactants, pharmaceutical precursors, and specialty chemicals that the modern economy runs on. Those processes require high temperatures, high pressures, and petroleum feedstocks extracted at high environmental cost. The carbon released accumulates in the atmosphere. Supply chains are geopolitically fragile. And for many complex chiral molecules, those whose exact three-dimensional shape determines their function, chemical synthesis is expensive, slow, and often low-yielding.

Engineered organisms offer a different approach. A well-designed production organism takes in a renewable carbon source, glucose from sugarcane or agricultural waste. It converts it through a precisely engineered metabolic pathway into a target molecule at ambient temperature and pressure. The feedstock is renewable. The organism self-replicates. And for complex chiral molecules, biology builds them with a geometric precision that chemical synthesis struggles to match.

For engineers and entrepreneurs evaluating this sector, the question is no longer whether engineered organisms can produce useful molecules: the early commercial wins, from artemisinin to spider silk to biodegradable plastics, demonstrate that they can. The questions that matter now are which molecules, at what cost, at what scale, and on what timeline. This chapter provides that framework.

Diagram 7.1 - The Living Factory Concept

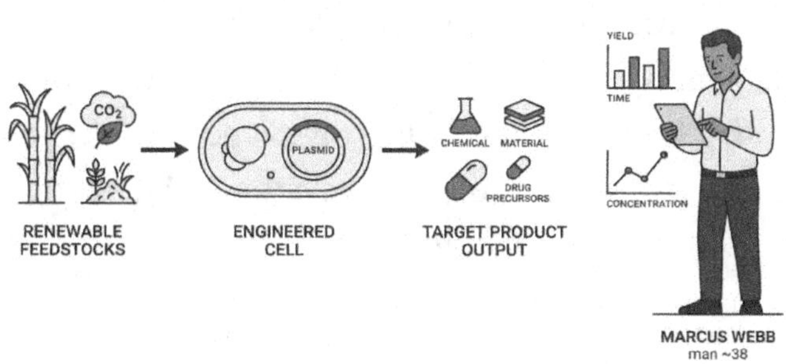

The specialty chemicals market alone, covering fragrances, cosmetic ingredients, pharmaceutical precursors, and performance materials, is worth hundreds of billions of dollars annually and is currently served almost entirely by petrochemical or solvent-extraction processes. Biomanufacturing can address this market with a combination of cost, precision, and sustainability that conventional chemistry cannot easily replicate. The remaining challenge is scaling biomanufacturing across a broader portfolio of molecules at costs competitive with conventional chemistry, and that is the engineering problem automated biological foundries are now solving.

Fermentation: The Core Process of Biomanufacturing

In an industrial biomanufacturing context, fermentation means the controlled cultivation of microorganisms, typically bacteria or yeast, inside a bioreactor, a sealed vessel with systems to supply nutrients, control the environment, and harvest the product. The organism consumes a carbon source, usually glucose, and uses metabolic machinery to convert it into the desired compound. Temperature, pH, dissolved oxygen, and nutrient levels are controlled by systems that keep the organism within its productive range.

Industrial bioreactors span a vast scale range, from bench-top vessels of a few liters used in early strain development to stainless-steel tanks of tens of thousands of liters used for commercial production. The challenge of scale-up, moving a process from a development vessel to a production tank, is one of the most demanding problems in the field. Mixing behavior, oxygen transfer, heat distribution, and concentration gradients all shift significantly with scale, and a strain that performs well in a small flask can lose productivity dramatically when the physical environment changes.

Diagram 7.2 - Inside a Bioreactor

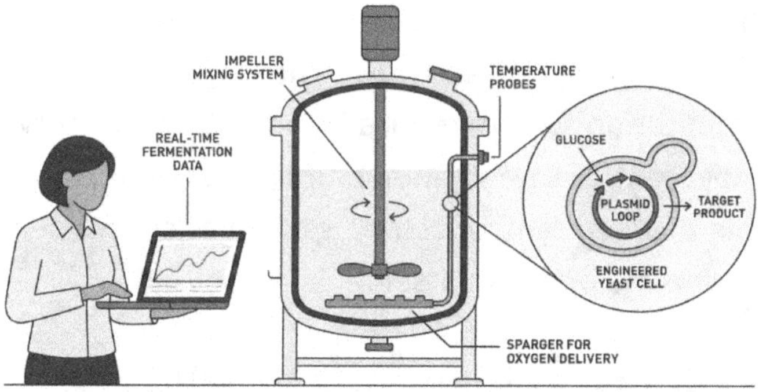

Commercial viability depends on three metrics engineers call TRY: titer, rate, and yield. Titer measures how much product accumulates per liter of broth, in grams per liter. The rate measures production speed in grams per liter per hour. Yield measures feedstock conversion efficiency, in grams of product per gram of feedstock. These three numbers together determine whether a biomanufacturing process can compete economically with conventional chemistry. High titer reduces downstream processing cost. High rate reduces the time and capital tied up per production run. High yield reduces feedstock cost, typically the largest variable expense in a large fermentation.

Improving all three simultaneously is genuinely hard. Higher titer often requires expressing more enzyme, which consumes cellular energy and reduces yield. A higher rate can require conditions that trigger stress responses, which reduce both titer and yield. Every metabolic engineering project is a search for the genetic and process combination that raises all three metrics together rather than trading one off against another. Downstream processing, the operations that separate and purify the target product from the fermentation broth, typically accounts for fifty to seventy percent of total manufacturing cost, which means improving downstream efficiency is often as consequential as improving the organism itself.

Choosing the Right Chassis Organism

A chassis organism, borrowing engineering's term for a standard frame onto which functional components are mounted, is the microbial species selected as the production host for a biomanufacturing program. The chassis determines which genetic tools are available, how fast the organism grows, which feedstocks it can consume, what product concentrations it can tolerate, and what regulatory framework governs its industrial use. Choosing the wrong chassis can add years to a development program.

Saccharomyces cerevisiae, baker's yeast, is one of the most widely used chassis organisms. Yeast is a eukaryote, meaning its cells have a nucleus and an internal membrane system that resembles that of human cells more closely than that of bacteria. This makes yeast especially well-suited for producing complex proteins that require post-translational modifications, the chemical additions that occur after a protein is synthesized and that are essential for the function of many pharmaceutical and nutraceutical compounds. Yeast also has a long history of safe industrial use, simplifying regulatory approval, and its genetic toolkit is mature enough to support rational engineering.

Diagram 7.3 - Chassis Organism Selection

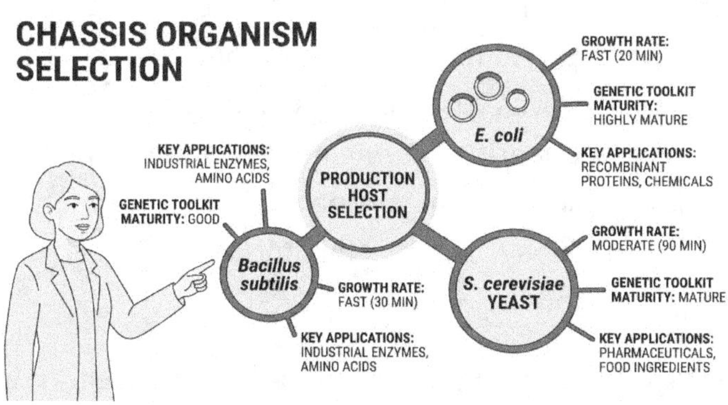

Escherichia coli is the other dominant chassis. It grows roughly twice as fast as yeast, is the most thoroughly characterized organism in biology, and has the most mature genetic toolkit in the field. For small molecules, bulk chemicals, and proteins that do not require post-translational modification, E. coli is frequently the chassis of choice. Its limitations are sensitivity to product toxicity at high concentrations, which caps titer for many molecules, and the inability to perform the eukaryotic protein modifications needed for many pharmaceutical targets. Other organisms serve specific niches: Bacillus subtilis secretes proteins into the growth medium, simplifying downstream processing; Corynebacterium glutamicum is used to produce amino acids at a commercial scale; Pseudomonas putida tolerates toxic compounds that would kill more sensitive hosts.

Pathway Engineering: Rerouting Cellular Traffic

Metabolic engineering is the systematic redesign of an organism's metabolic network to redirect carbon and energy toward a target molecule. Metabolic flux, the rate at which carbon moves through a particular biochemical pathway, is the quantity the engineer is optimizing. Every intervention is an attempt to increase flux through the production pathway while minimizing diversion to competing reactions.

The traffic routing analogy is precise rather than decorative. Think of the metabolic network as a city of interconnected roads. Glucose enters at the main gate and can flow along many routes: toward growth, energy storage, cellular biosynthesis, or the production pathway you have engineered. Your job is to widen roads leading toward the product, close roads that divert traffic away from it, and build new roads where the natural network does not connect the starting material to the target product.

Diagram 7.4 - Metabolic Flux Pathway Redesign

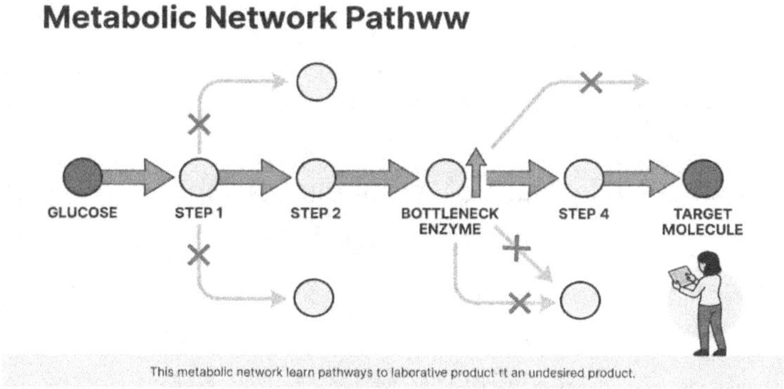

Widening roads means overexpressing enzymes at rate-limiting steps. By placing a gene encoding a limiting enzyme under a strong promoter, a genetic element that drives high-level transcription, you increase capacity at the bottleneck and push more carbon toward the product. Closing roads means knocking out competing pathways that divert carbon without contributing to the target. Identifying which pathways to close requires detailed knowledge of the metabolic network, because closing the wrong road can starve the organism of essential metabolites and reduce growth.

Building new roads means introducing heterologous enzymes, sourced from other organisms, to create reaction steps the chassis cannot perform naturally. Each borrowed enzyme must be codon-optimized, meaning its DNA sequence is rewritten to match the host organism's preferred codon usage to ensure efficient translation, and then tested for activity and compatibility with the surrounding network. Dynamic regulatory circuits add further sophistication: sensors detect the organism's internal metabolic state and adjust pathway activity in real time, temporarily reducing production flux when a precursor runs low and restoring it once levels recover.

The systems-level nature of metabolic engineering is what makes it genuinely difficult. Changing one enzyme changes the concentrations of all metabolites connected to it, which in turn affects every other enzyme that shares those metabolites. A modification that improves titer by 40% in isolation may reduce yield by 30% when combined with a second modification that appears independent. Whole-cell metabolic models help predict these interactions, but even the best models are incomplete, and experimental iteration remains essential.

Artemisinin: The Project That Changed Industry Expectations

In the early 2000s, malaria was killing more than a million people a year, most of them young children in sub-Saharan Africa. Artemisinin-based combination therapy was the most effective treatment available. Still, artemisinin itself could only be extracted from the sweet wormwood plant, Artemisia annua, which could not be grown fast enough or at a large enough scale to supply global demand reliably. Prices were volatile, and the people who needed the drug most were in the places least able to absorb price spikes.

Jay Keasling, a chemical engineer at UC Berkeley, proposed engineering yeast to produce artemisinin through a biosynthetic pathway assembled from enzymes sourced across multiple organisms. The project required inserting more than a dozen new enzymatic steps into yeast metabolism, including a key enzyme from Artemisia annua that converts a common yeast metabolite into the artemisinin precursor amorphadiene, followed by oxidation steps converting it into artemisinic acid, the immediate precursor to artemisinin. Each enzyme had to be codon-optimized for yeast, integrated into the genome, and verified for activity without disrupting essential cellular functions.

Diagram 7.5 - Artemisinin Biosynthetic Pathway in Yeast

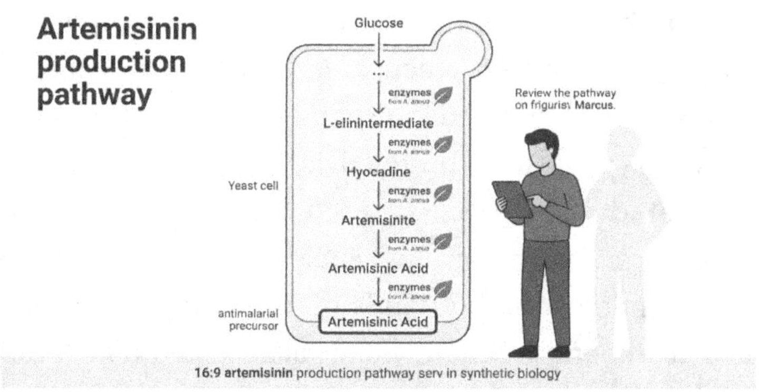

The work took nearly a decade, required advances in genetic tools and fermentation engineering that did not yet exist when the project began, and was eventually published in Nature in 2006. The pathway was licensed to Sanofi, which developed the industrial fermentation process needed for commercial supply. By 2013, semi-synthetic artemisinin from engineered yeast was entering the supply chain at a price that made treatment accessible to more patients than natural extraction had ever permitted.

The artemisinin project established three industry benchmarks. A complex multi-step pathway requiring enzymes from multiple organisms could be assembled in a single production host. Such a process could be scaled to industrial volumes without losing efficiency. And the economics could be competitive with natural extraction for a structurally complex molecule. Keasling's approach became the template for nearly every biomanufacturing program that followed.

The Ginkgo Bioworks Foundry Model

For most of the history of metabolic engineering, organism development was a craft practice. A researcher designed a modification, implemented it by hand in a small flask, grew the organism, measured productivity, revised the design, and repeated the process. Each cycle took weeks. Developing a commercially viable production strain required hundreds or thousands of such cycles, meaning years of work, and frequently still failed when bench-top strains did not maintain their productivity at an industrial scale.

Ginkgo Bioworks was founded in 2009 by MIT synthetic biologists who recognized that organism engineering was fundamentally a manufacturing problem, not a research problem, and that the right response was to build a facility designed to run the design-build-test-learn cycle at industrial throughput. The result was the Boston Foundry: a facility that applies semiconductor-industry logic to biology, standardizing inputs, automating processes, and improving continuously based on accumulated data.

Diagram 7.6 - The Ginkgo Foundry DBTL Pipeline

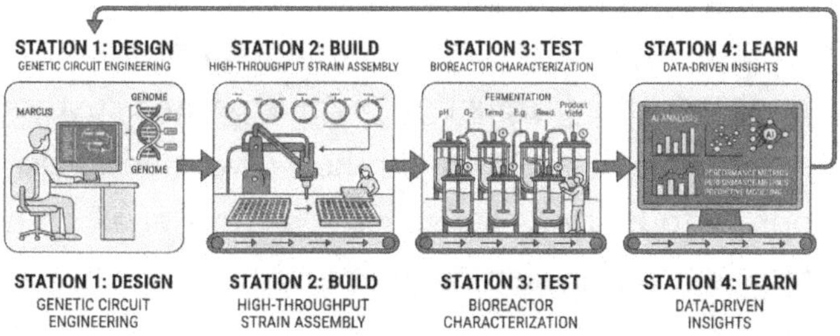

The foundry model fundamentally changes the economics of metabolic engineering. In the traditional model, the dominant cost is skilled labor: each modification requires a trained researcher, and each fermentation run requires careful manual preparation. The foundry model replaces this with capital-intensive automated systems running thousands of experiments in parallel. Cost per experiment drops dramatically, throughput increases by orders of magnitude, and the data from parallel experiments is far richer than that from sequential, hand-crafted ones.

The comparison to semiconductor fabrication is precise, not poetic. A semiconductor fab converts a circuit design into a physical chip through automated, high-throughput manufacturing steps. Ginkgo's foundry converts a genome design into a production organism through an analogous sequence: DNA synthesis, gene assembly, organism transformation, fermentation, and measurement. In both cases, power comes from standardization combined with automation, allowing continuous operation without bottlenecking on human labor. Ginkgo operates as a platform company: organizations bring their product goals, Ginkgo engineers the production organisms, and customers take the resulting strains to build their own manufacturing operations, a foundry-as-a-service structure analogous to how TSMC operates in semiconductors.

Spider Silk and Bolt Threads: Engineering Impossible Materials

Spider silk is one of nature's most extraordinary materials. Pound for pound, it is stronger than high-grade steel and tougher than Kevlar, with a combination of tensile strength and elasticity that materials scientists have spent decades trying to reproduce synthetically. Farming spiders the way silkworms are farmed is not viable: spiders are territorial and cannibalistic, and a dense population becomes a mass-extinction event for itself.

Bolt Threads, a San Francisco-based synthetic biology company, engineered yeast to produce recombinant spidroin protein, the structural protein responsible for spider silk's remarkable properties, by inserting the relevant spider silk genes into the yeast genome. Getting the yeast to produce spidroin at commercially meaningful concentrations was itself a significant engineering challenge. Spidroin proteins are among the largest and most repetitive proteins in biology, making them prone to premature aggregation inside the cell and difficult to express at high levels without errors. Solving the production challenge required extensive metabolic engineering to tune expression levels and reduce aggregation.

Diagram 7.7 - Spider Silk Protein Production in Yeast

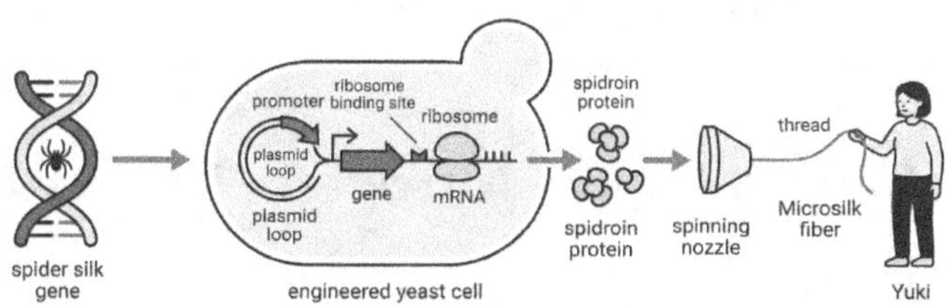

Once a production organism was established, the next challenge was to form fiber. Spider silk is not naturally soluble: the spider's silk gland concentrates the protein at a very high density. It forces it through a narrow spinneret under shear stress, which triggers the protein to fold into its characteristic crystalline fiber structure—replicating, at commercial scale, the industrially required development of proprietary spinning technology that mimics the conditions of the spider's spinneret. The resulting material, branded as Microsilk, has mechanical properties closely resembling natural spider silk and has been used in commercial fashion and materials products.

The Bolt Threads story illustrates the synthetic biology materials paradigm. Identify a material with extraordinary properties that biology produces, but that cannot be sourced at scale through any existing means; engineer a production organism that accumulates the key molecule at commercially meaningful concentrations; and develop the downstream process to convert that molecule into the commercial material. Once established, manufacturing cost depends primarily on fermentation economics, which improve predictably as the strain is optimized and the process is scaled.

Pivot Bio: Biological Nitrogen Fixation for Agriculture

Nitrogen is the most abundant element in the atmosphere, but atmospheric nitrogen, two atoms connected by a triple bond, is chemically inert: plants cannot use it in that form. To be useful, nitrogen must be converted into ammonia or nitrate through nitrogen fixation. The Haber-Bosch process does this chemically, reacting atmospheric nitrogen with hydrogen under high temperature and pressure to produce synthetic fertilizer that underwrites roughly half of global food production. But it accounts for roughly 2% of global energy consumption and contributes significantly to greenhouse gas emissions through its energy use and the nitrous oxide emitted from fertilized soils.

Diagram 7.8 - Nitrogen-Fixing Bacteria on a Corn Root

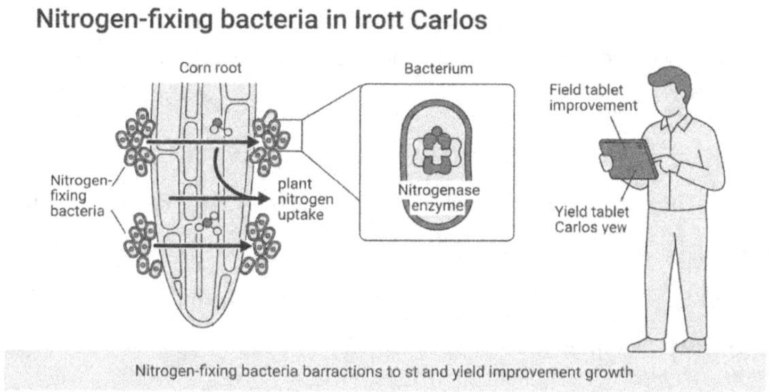

Certain bacteria fix atmospheric nitrogen biologically using an enzyme called nitrogenase, which breaks the nitrogen triple bond at ambient temperature and pressure. Legume farmers have exploited this for centuries through crop rotation. The limitation is that natural nitrogen-fixing bacteria primarily associate with legumes, not with corn, wheat, and rice, the staple crops that consume the most synthetic nitrogen fertilizer. Pivot Bio, founded in 2011, engineered nitrogen-fixing bacteria to colonize cereal crop roots by modifying the genetic circuits that suppress nitrogenase expression when synthetic fertilizer is present, creating strains that fix nitrogen consistently regardless of ambient nitrogen levels. The resulting product, applied to seeds before planting, colonizes developing root systems and delivers a portion of the plant's nitrogen requirement from the atmosphere, reducing fertilizer inputs without changing farming practices.

Biodegradable Plastics and Sustainability Opportunity

Conventional plastics are made from petrochemical feedstocks, are designed for durability, and persist in the environment for hundreds of years after disposal. The engineering challenge is producing materials with comparable performance properties from renewable feedstocks that degrade in natural environments on ecologically compatible timescales.

Polyhydroxyalkanoates, or PHAs, are polyesters produced naturally by certain bacteria as intracellular energy storage compounds, the bacterial equivalent of fat. When carbon is plentiful, but another nutrient like nitrogen or phosphorus is scarce, PHA-producing bacteria accumulate polymer granules inside their cells. PHAs are fully biodegradable in soil, freshwater, and marine environments by bacteria that produce PHA-degrading enzymes, and they can be processed into films, fibers, and rigid plastics with mechanical properties that overlap significantly with conventional petroleum-based plastics.

Diagram 7.9 - PHA Bioplastic Production

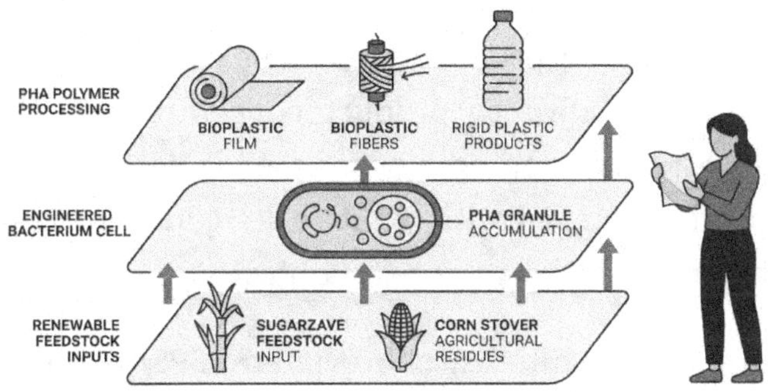

Priya asamined inerpitop with renewable feedstock hinp in an executive technical tone.

Wild-type PHA-producing bacteria grow slowly and accumulate polymer inefficiently. Metabolic engineering is used to increase production flux, improve polymer composition to target specific mechanical properties, and enable growth on low-cost feedstocks like agricultural waste. Companies, including Danimer Scientific and Full Cycle Bioplastics, are developing commercial-scale PHA production. Still, both face the same core challenge: conventional petroleum-based plastics are extraordinarily cheap, and PHA production costs have not yet dropped to fully competitive levels for most applications. The economics are moving in the right direction, driven by carbon-pricing pressure, improved strain performance, and scaling fermentation processes, but cost parity remains elusive.

Cell-Free Synthesis: Manufacturing Without the Living Cell

Every production strategy discussed so far keeps the organism alive throughout the manufacturing process. A living cell must maintain its own growth and survival, competing with the production pathway for carbon and energy. It is sensitive to product concentrations above certain thresholds, capping titer for molecules toxic to the host. And feedback circuits regulate its gene expression, which the engineer does not fully control.

Cell-free protein synthesis, abbreviated CFPS, retains the cell's molecular machinery while discarding the cell itself. In a CFPS system, a cell is lysed, the contents are extracted and partially purified, and the resulting extract, containing ribosomes, RNA polymerase, transfer RNAs, and energy regeneration systems, is used to transcribe and translate a DNA template outside any living cell. You provide the gene encoding the protein you want, and the extract produces the protein without growth requirements, feedback regulation, or metabolic competition.

Diagram 7.10 - Cell-Free Protein Synthesis Workflow

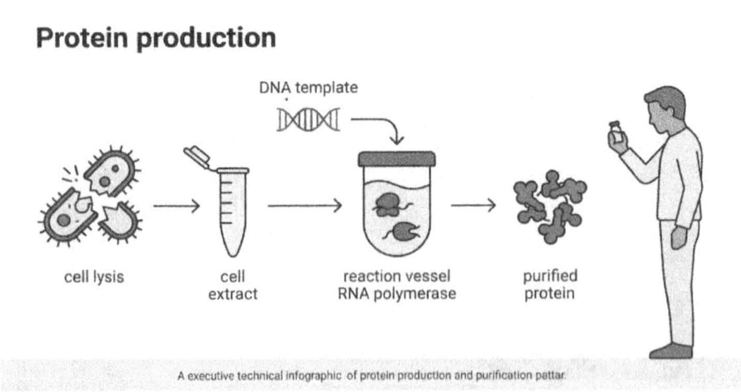

Proteins toxic to living cells can be produced in CFPS systems because there is no cell to kill. Membrane proteins, difficult to produce in vivo because they misfold or aggregate when overexpressed, can be produced in CFPS supplemented with lipid vesicles. Proteins containing non-standard amino acids can be incorporated by adding modified translation machinery. Greenlight Biosciences pioneered cell-free RNA production at commercial scale, demonstrating competitive economics for specific product categories. Cell-free metabolic engineering extends this by assembling defined sets of purified enzymes to produce small molecules without the constraints of cellular metabolism.

What This Means For You

For engineers evaluating biomanufacturing programs, the central questions are: what are the current titer, rate, and yield numbers, and what is the roadmap for improving all three simultaneously? A strong titer with poor yield means losing a large fraction of the feedstock cost to nonproductive metabolism. A strong yield with poor titer means processing enormous broth volumes per unit of product, thereby inflating downstream processing costs. Programs that have achieved competitive TRY metrics at bench scale but not yet at pilot scale face the scale-up challenge, a genuine and frequently underestimated engineering problem. These distinctions let you evaluate biomanufacturing company claims with the rigor you would apply to semiconductor yield data.

Diagram 7.11 - TRY Metrics: The Commercial Viability Triangle

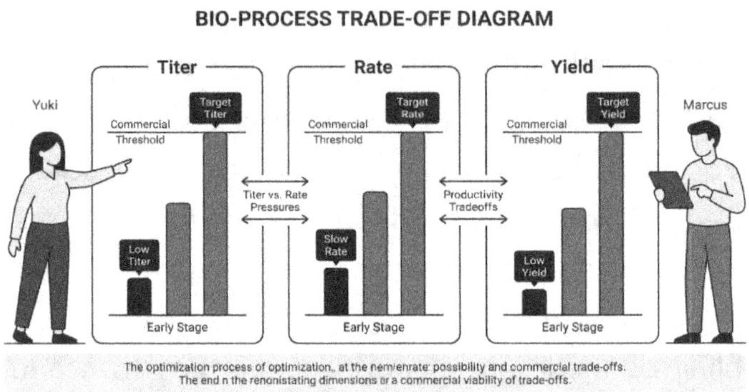

For entrepreneurs and investors, the platform-versus-product distinction is the key strategic frame. A company that has engineered one organism for one product has demonstrated scientific capability but has a narrow competitive position. A company that has built a platform, a set of tools, protocols, and automated infrastructure applicable to many molecules, has a far stronger position because each new product amortizes the same sunk cost. Evaluating foundry-model companies requires understanding not just their current portfolio but the speed and cost at which their platform can develop new production organisms.

For policy professionals, the regulatory framework for biomanufacturing is generally more mature than for therapeutic synthetic biology, because products are evaluated by their properties and safety profile rather than their biological origin. The EPA, FDA, and USDA each govern portions of this landscape depending on product type, and knowing which pathway applies to a given product is a prerequisite for evaluating its development timeline and commercial risk. For curious professionals across all fields, the most important shift this chapter asks for is from thinking about manufacturing as a chemistry problem to thinking about it as a programming problem: the atoms were always available, the reactions were always feasible, and the engineering question was always whether we could design, build, and operate a production system reliably enough and cheaply enough to make the product accessible. For an increasing list of molecules, the answer is now yes.

Takeaway

The living factory is not a metaphor for a possible future. It is an operational description of what is happening right now, in foundries and fermentation facilities across the world, producing molecules that the petrochemical industry once held a monopoly on. Artemisinin saves lives because Keasling and his team spent a decade rewriting yeast metabolism. Spider silk is used in commercial products because Bolt Threads has solved the problem of integrating fermentation engineering and fiber spinning. Nitrogen-fixing bacteria are reducing synthetic fertilizer use across millions of acres because Pivot Bio has modified bacterial circuits that suppress nitrogen fixation in fertilized soils. These are not proofs of concept. They are revenue-generating commercial operations.

Diagram 7.12 - Biomanufacturing Commercial Landscape

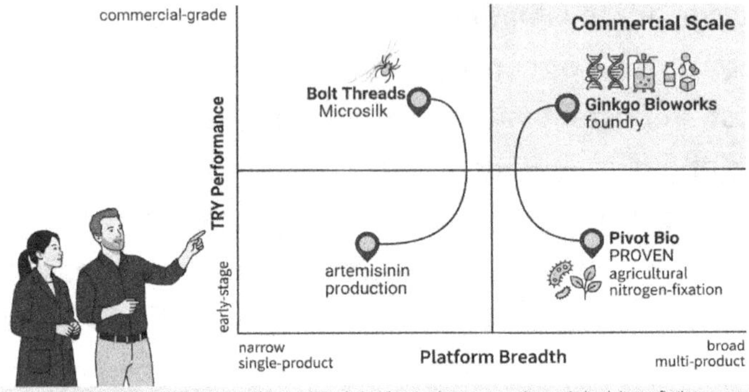

Marcus Webb (m. ~38, business-casual navy), Yuki Tanaka (n~35), study. athieoonarroys entity or agricultural nitrogen-fixation.

The engineering principles making biomanufacturing work are the same principles running through every other chapter: design the genetic instructions, build the organism that executes them, test performance against quantitative metrics, and iterate based on data. What biomanufacturing adds is the commercial reality test that production biology imposes. A production organism that achieves its TRY targets on a bench fermenter but collapses under the mixing and oxygen-transfer conditions of a fifty-thousand-liter production tank is a failed scale-up program. The discipline that industrial biomanufacturing applies to synthetic biology has made the field more rigorous, more quantitative, and more honest about the gap between what is demonstrable and what is deployable.

Metabolic engineering, pathway design, chassis selection, foundry automation, cell-free synthesis: these are the vocabulary of a manufacturing transition as significant as the shift from handcraft to machine manufacture in the first industrial revolution. That transition was not frictionless, and neither will this one be. But the organisms are running, the bioreactors are humming, and the data accumulating in foundries across the world points in only one direction.

Marcus's guide at the Ginkgo Foundry was right. The organisms are the code. The bioreactors are the runtime. And once you understand it from first principles, the program is one of the most consequential engineering projects in human history.

8 Engineering What We Eat

Opening Scenario

The lunch table at the Cambridge Synthetic Biology Food Summit looks, at first glance, like any catered conference spread. But the protein on offer is not from any farm that existed a decade ago. In the center sits a platter of golden-brown chicken breast produced by UPSIDE Foods, grown from muscle cells in a bioreactor without a single bird being slaughtered. Next to it, a row of shaker cups contains a protein shake from Perfect Day, made with whey and casein proteins molecularly identical to those in cow's milk but assembled by engineered fungi in a fermentation tank. At the far end, a stack of plant-based burgers carries a label that Priya reads aloud: 'Contains precision-fermented soy leghemoglobin for authentic beef flavor.' That ingredient, heme, the iron-containing compound that gives beef its color and taste, was produced by engineered yeast.

Carlos has been taking notes throughout the meal, and when the plates are nearly empty, he looks up and raises an eyebrow. 'The science is real,' he says. 'Every one of these products works. But who decides whether this is safe at scale? Who decides whether it needs a label indicating whether it is cultivated or fermented-derived? And who in this room has talked to the ranchers, dairy farmers, and poultry workers whose livelihoods depend on the systems these products are designed to replace?' The table goes quiet.

That silence is where this chapter begins. The engineering is extraordinary and worth understanding in full. The commercial and social context is complicated and worth being honest about. Neither truth cancels the other.

Why It Matters

Food is synthetic biology's most visible frontier. Most readers of this book have probably already encountered a headline about lab-grown meat, seen a precision-fermented ingredient on a product label, or eaten a plant-based burger seasoned with engineered heme. The concepts are in the cultural conversation. What is rarely in that conversation is how the engineering works, what the genuine constraints are, and what the distance between a regulatory milestone and a supermarket price tag looks like in practice.

That distance matters for engineers because the engineering problems in food biotechnology, bioreactor scale-up, serum-free growth media, scaffold fabrication, and fermentation yield optimization are among the most technically demanding challenges in applied biology. Understanding the specific bottlenecks in each approach is essential for evaluating a food biotech company or designing a platform to serve it. It matters for entrepreneurs because the regulatory landscape is new and jurisdiction-specific, and the entrepreneur who does not understand the distinctions between product categories is operating with incomplete information in a capital-intensive sector. And it matters to policy professionals because whether synthetic biology transforms the food system in ways that produce broadly distributed benefits depends on decisions being made right now in agencies and legislatures that are still learning what they are regulating.

Precision Fermentation: The Biological Brewery

Precision fermentation is, in one sense, the oldest biotechnology humans practice. Fermentation underpins bread, beer, wine, cheese, yogurt, and penicillin. What changes in precision fermentation are due to programming the microorganism? Instead of producing alcohol as its primary output, the engineered microbe, typically a yeast, filamentous fungus, or bacterium, executes a program the engineer specified: producing a specific protein or ingredient rather than its natural metabolic product. The tank, the nutrient feedstock, the temperature and oxygen controls, the downstream separation process, all of it resembles conventional industrial fermentation. The difference is what comes out.

Think of the fermentation tank as the brewery. The engineered microorganism is the brewer executing a genetic program. The sugar feedstock is the grain. And the product is not alcohol but the specific animal protein the engineer specified when writing the genetic program. Perfect Day produces whey protein using engineered Trichoderma reesei fungi, a filamentous organism widely used in industrial enzyme production. Their engineers inserted the gene sequences for bovine beta-lactoglobulin, the primary whey protein, into the fungal genome under the control of promoters, the genetic switches that drive high-level protein expression. The fungus grows on a sugar feedstock, secretes large quantities of beta-lactoglobulin, and the resulting powder is, at the molecular level, identical to the whey protein from a cow.

Recombinant casein refers to casein proteins, which make up roughly 80 percent of the protein in cow's milk, produced by microorganisms carrying the relevant bovine genes rather than from dairy animals. The proteins have the same amino acid sequence, molecular weight, and functional properties as conventionally sourced casein. They can be used in cheese-making, yogurt, and food formulation in the same ways. Multiple food companies have launched products using precision-fermented casein, and the FDA has issued GRAS (Generally Recognized As Safe) no-objection letters for several of these proteins.

Clara Foods, now rebranded as Every Company, applies the same approach to egg white proteins, producing ovalbumin and other egg white proteins using engineered yeast, with functional properties identical to those of conventional egg whites.

Diagram 8.1 - Precision Fermentation Tank: From Gene to Protein

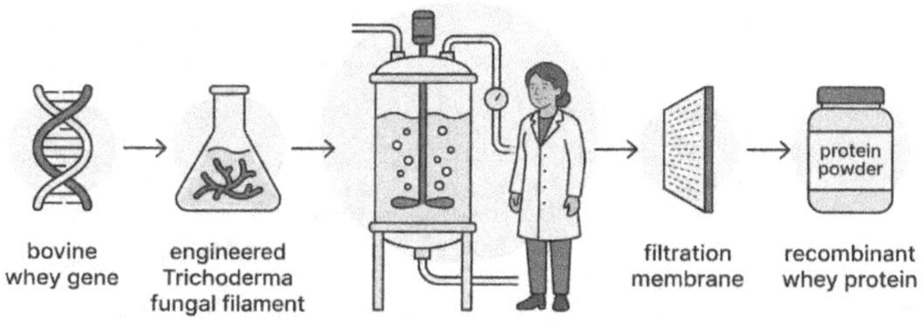

The commercial economics of precision fermentation are compelling in principle and still challenging in practice. Conventional dairy protein is produced on an enormous scale, with decades of process optimization behind it, and its per-kilogram cost is low. Precision-fermented whey protein is currently more expensive because fermentation yields are still being optimized, and the capital cost of commercial-scale fermentation must be amortized over product output. The path to price parity, the point at which precision-fermented proteins cost the same per gram as conventionally sourced proteins, runs through larger fermentation scale and continuous process improvement.

Most industry analysts project that price parity for precision-fermented dairy proteins is achievable within the current decade, though the timeline depends on continued capital investment and process development. Critically, price parity, rather than regulatory approval, is the primary commercial bottleneck for precision fermentation: regulatory approval is already in place for most major precision-fermented protein products.

Diagram 8.2 - Precision Fermentation Yield Curve: Cost vs. Scale

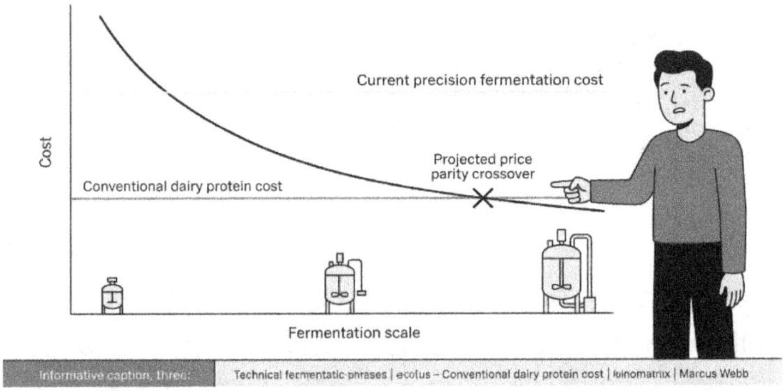

The Heme Story: Engineering the Taste of Meat

Impossible Foods took a different approach to precision fermentation, and understanding it requires understanding what makes beef taste like beef. The characteristic flavor and color of cooked beef come primarily from heme, an iron-containing molecule that binds oxygen in myoglobin (giving muscle tissue its red color) and hemoglobin (carrying oxygen in blood). When muscle tissue is cooked, heme undergoes chemical reactions that produce a specific set of flavor compounds. Those compounds are the taste of meat.

Plants contain heme too, in a form called leghemoglobin, concentrated in the root nodules of legumes like soybeans, where it regulates oxygen levels during nitrogen fixation. Impossible Foods identified soy leghemoglobin as a functionally equivalent substitute for animal heme: the same iron-containing core structure, the same flavor-generating reactions during cooking, and a nearly identical sensory experience. The challenge was supply. Extracting leghemoglobin from soy root nodules at a commercial scale would require enormous quantities of soybeans. So Impossible inserted the gene for soy leghemoglobin into Pichia pastoris, a yeast widely used in industrial protein production, and engineered that yeast to produce and secrete large quantities of the protein. The purified heme is incorporated into the burger patties, giving them the bleeding and browning behavior of beef.

The FDA regulatory review of Impossible heme is instructive for understanding how novel food ingredients navigate US oversight. When Impossible first approached the FDA, the agency declined to issue a GRAS no-objection letter in response to the first submission, citing the need for additional safety data. Impossible conducted further toxicology studies, submitted a revised application, and ultimately received FDA GRAS affirmation. The process took years and required substantial investment in regulatory science, establishing a template that subsequent precision fermentation companies have followed. The story also illustrates a regulatory distinction: soy leghemoglobin is molecularly distinct from animal heme, so the FDA treated it as a novel ingredient requiring affirmative safety demonstration. By contrast, precision-fermented bovine whey protein, which is structurally identical to a protein with millennia of safe human consumption, faces a more straightforward safety case. Knowing which category your ingredient falls into before beginning regulatory submissions is essential.

Diagram 8.3 - Heme Protein Production in Engineered Yeast

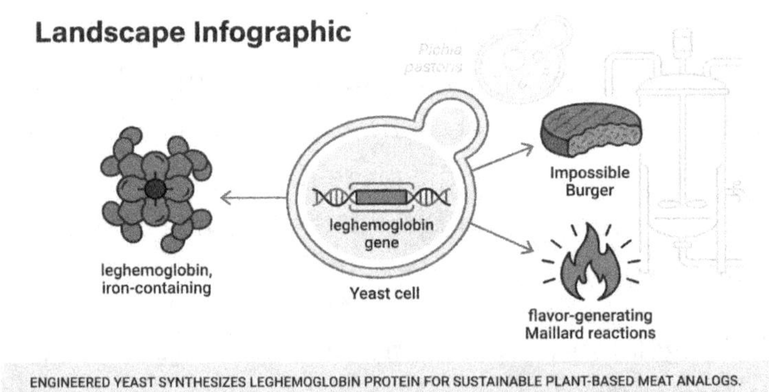

Cultivated Meat: Growing Muscle in a Bioreactor

Cultivated meat is the approach that generates the most cultural attention and the most engineering complexity. The concept is straightforward: instead of raising and slaughtering an animal to obtain its muscle tissue, you take a small biopsy from a living animal (performed without killing the animal and causing minimal discomfort), isolate the muscle stem cells from that sample, and grow those cells in a controlled environment until they multiply into enough tissue to process into food. The animal is unharmed, no slaughter occurs, and the product, at the cellular level, is genuine animal muscle tissue.

The biology of muscle stem cells, also called satellite cells, is central to understanding why this works. In a living animal, satellite cells are the repair and growth mechanism of muscle tissue. When muscle fibers are stressed or damaged, satellite cells activate, proliferate, and fuse to form new muscle fibers. They are the muscle tissue's version control system: a pool of undifferentiated cells that produce new fibers on demand. In cultivated meat, that natural behavior is exploited outside the body. The satellite cells are provided with nutrients, growth factors, and physical conditions to proliferate in a bioreactor rather than in an animal, requiring roughly 20 to 30 cell doublings from the starting biopsy sample to reach food-relevant cell mass.

Diagram 8.4 - Cultivated Meat Bioreactor with Scaffold Architecture

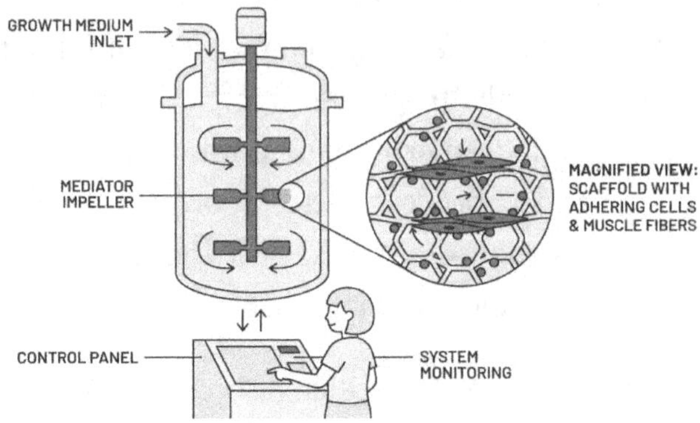

Scaffold design is the second major engineering challenge. Proliferated satellite cells do not spontaneously organize into structured muscle tissue. In a living animal, satellite cells fuse into fibers along a highly organized extracellular matrix, the protein scaffold that surrounds cells in tissue. Growth scaffolds for cultivated meat have been made from food-grade materials, including soy protein, mycoprotein (a fungal protein), plant cellulose, and edible gelatin. The scaffold must be porous enough for nutrients to diffuse throughout the tissue, strong enough to maintain structural integrity during culture, and digestible or food-safe in the final product. Getting scaffold design right at a cost that does not make the product prohibitively expensive is one of the central engineering challenges of the field.

The growth medium challenge is currently the most commercially sensitive bottleneck. Conventional cell culture media for mammalian cells contain fetal bovine serum (FBS), derived from bovine fetal blood, which provides a complex mixture of growth factors and hormones difficult to replicate with defined ingredients.

The irony is clear: a technology designed to reduce dependence on animal slaughter currently depends on a product derived from a particularly ethically fraught form of animal exploitation. Serum-free media formulations that replace FBS with defined recombinant growth factors are under active development. Progress is real, but the transition typically requires extensive optimization and often results in somewhat lower initial proliferation rates.

Diagram 8.5 - Serum-Free Media Challenge: From FBS to Defined Formulation

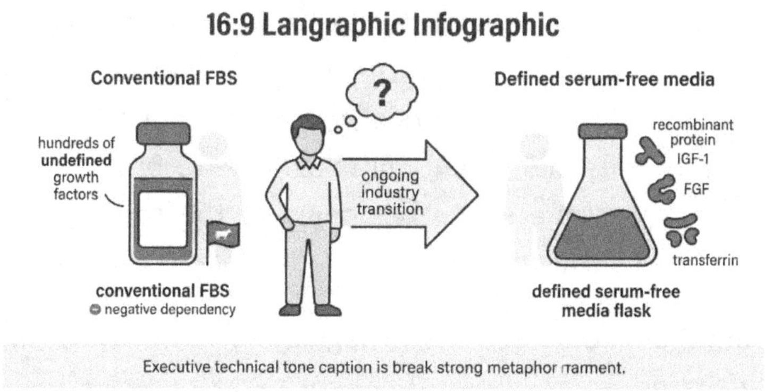

UPSIDE Foods navigated the first US regulatory pathway for cultivated meat. In November 2022, the FDA issued a no-objection letter for UPSIDE's cultivated chicken following a pre-market safety consultation. In June 2023, the USDA granted inspection authority to both UPSIDE Foods and Good Meat (the cultivated meat division of Eat Just), authorizing commercial sale. These were the first cultivated meat products legally cleared for commercial sale in the United States. Singapore had cleared Good Meat's product in 2020, making Singapore the first national market to approve cultivated meat.

The regulatory milestone deserves clear-eyed interpretation. A USDA grant of inspection is proof of regulatory pathway, historically significant because it establishes that cultivated meat can be evaluated and sold under the existing US food safety framework. It is not a proof of commercial scale or economics. At the time of the approvals, UPSIDE Foods was producing cultivated chicken at an estimated cost of hundreds of dollars per kilogram, in a facility designed for regulatory demonstration rather than commercial volume. The distance between a regulatory green light and a grocery-store-competitive product is a function of bioreactor engineering, media optimization, and capital investment that will take years to bridge. The regulatory milestone is the beginning of the commercial story, not its conclusion.

Diagram 8.6 - Cultivated Meat Regulatory Pathway in the United States

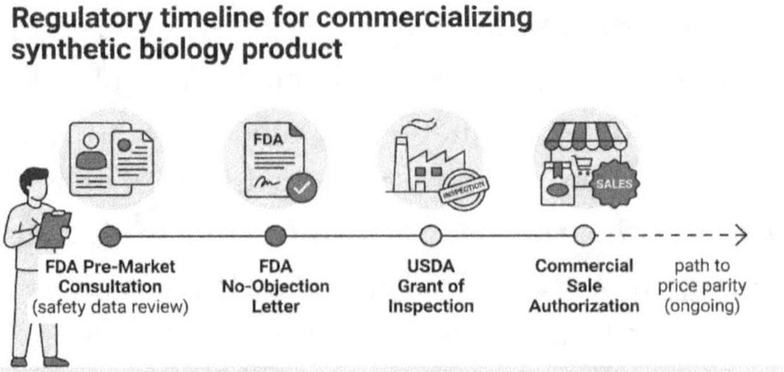

Caption– regulatory timeline for commercializing a synthetic biology product

Engineered Crops and Agricultural Synthetic Biology

Engineered crops have been part of commercial agriculture since the mid-1990s. The first generation, what most people mean when they say "GMO," involved inserting one or a few foreign genes into a crop plant's genome to confer a specific trait: insect resistance in Bt corn and herbicide tolerance in Roundup Ready soybeans. These approaches achieved enormous commercial adoption, with more than 90 percent of US corn, soybean, and cotton acreage now carrying at least one engineered trait. Synthetic biology's approach to agriculture is fundamentally different. The first-generation question is: what single-gene modification can I make to this plant? The synthetic biology question is: what is the biological system the plant and its environment constitute, and how can I engineer that system as a whole? This systems-level thinking opens a much larger design space, including engineering the soil microbiome on which the plant depends rather than modifying the plant itself.

Pivot Bio is the most commercially successful example of the synthetic biology approach in agriculture. Their product PROVEN addresses nitrogen, the single largest input cost in commodity crop production, by engineering the microbes that live on crop roots. Nitrogen fixation, converting atmospheric nitrogen gas to ammonia that plants can absorb, is one of the most important biological processes on Earth. Certain soil bacteria evolved the ability to fix atmospheric nitrogen using a complex enzyme called nitrogenase. In modern agriculture, decades of heavy synthetic fertilizer application have suppressed this natural nitrogen fixation by signaling bacteria to down-regulate the metabolically expensive nitrogenase pathway. Pivot Bio's insight was that this suppression is a genetic regulatory response that can be reversed. Their scientists identified the genetic switches in Azospirillum bacteria that sense ambient nitrogen and down-regulate nitrogenase, then used targeted modifications, including CRISPR-based edits, to alter those switches so that the bacteria maintain nitrogenase activity even in nitrogen-replete environments. Modified bacteria coated onto seeds establish themselves in the root zone at germination and provide fixed nitrogen directly to the plant throughout the growing season.

Diagram 8.7 - Pivot Bio Nitrogen Fixation: Engineered Soil Microbe at Crop Root

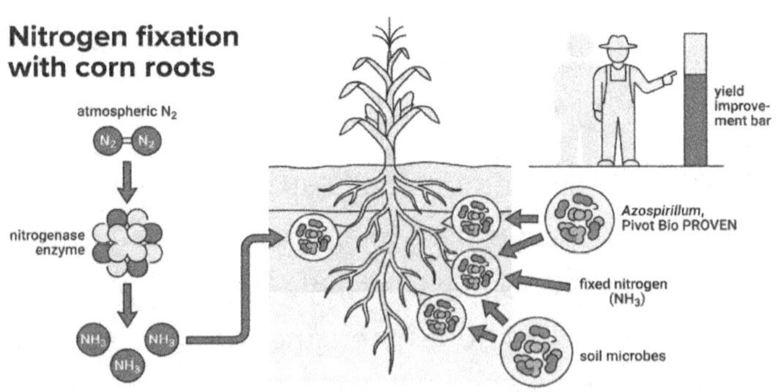

A minisist executive technical infographic & the nitrogen fixation process with corn roots

PROVEN's commercial results are documented across millions of acres of US corn farmland: a nitrogen fertilizer reduction of 15 to 25 percent without yield loss, and, in many cases, modest yield increases attributable to the consistency and timing of microbially supplied nitrogen. Because the bacteria deliver nitrogen directly at the root zone exactly when the plant needs it, the biological approach can outperform the conventional approach in nutrient delivery efficiency. Pivot Bio has deployed on over 10 million acres of US farmland and is expanding globally. Joyn Bio, a joint venture between Ginkgo Bioworks and Bayer, is pursuing a similar strategy targeting corn, wheat, and other cereals to extend the benefits of biological nitrogen fixation to the cereal crops that consume the largest share of global synthetic fertilizer production.

CRISPR-based crop improvement represents a third category. Pairwise, spun out of the Broad Institute, uses CRISPR to improve water-use efficiency by editing regulatory networks that control stomatal opening. Stomata are the microscopic pores on leaf surfaces that open to allow carbon dioxide in during photosynthesis and inevitably lose water vapor when open. Engineering more precise stomatal control reduces water loss without reducing photosynthesis, improving drought tolerance without introducing any foreign DNA into the plant. Nutritional enhancement uses similar tools: CRISPR is being used to increase lycopene content in tomatoes, omega-3 fatty acid content in soybeans, and amino acid profiles in cereal crops. The US has generally treated CRISPR-edited crops without foreign DNA as conventional plant varieties. At the same time, the EU has historically applied stricter oversight to any genetic modification of food crops, a policy currently under active review.

Diagram 8.8 - Engineered Crop Systems: Three Synthetic Biology Approaches

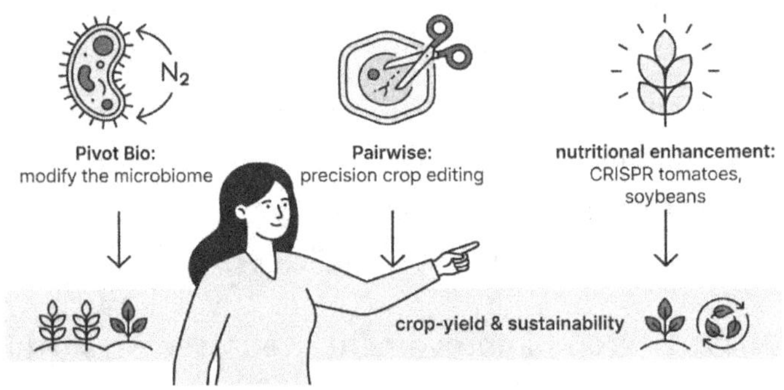

Scale-Up Bottleneck: Where Engineering Gets Hard

Honesty about scale-up is the chapter's editorial commitment. The gap between a functioning proof of concept and a commercially competitive product is large in every dimension: cost, scale, regulatory acceptance, and consumer adoption. Understanding that gap clearly is not pessimism about the technology. It is the minimum level of analytical rigor that anyone evaluating these companies should apply.

For cultivated meat, the primary bottleneck in scale-up is bioreactor economics. Mammalian cells grow slowly, are metabolically fragile, sensitive to shear forces in large bioreactors, and require complex, expensive growth media containing multiple defined growth factors. Pharmaceutical manufacturers pay tens of thousands of dollars per kilogram for mammalian cell-produced biologics because of exactly these constraints. Cultivated meat faces the same constraints but must compete with conventional meat at grocery-store prices. Techno-economic assessments suggest that at very large bioreactor scales, 10,000 liters and above, with serum-free media and high cell density culture, production costs could potentially reach ten to thirty dollars per kilogram. Whether those performance levels are achievable is an active research question in engineering, not a settled matter. Several independent analyses have noted that the cell density and media efficiency assumptions in the most optimistic projections are at or beyond the current state of the art, and that the capital cost of very large mammalian cell bioreactors is historically underestimated.

For precision fermentation, microbial fermentation at large scale is technically mature: commercial facilities that operate in the tens of thousands of liters are routine in pharmaceutical and industrial biotechnology. The challenge is whether specific production organisms and processes will perform at a commercial scale with sufficient yield to achieve target economics. Fermentation yield, measured as grams of target protein per liter of fermentation volume per unit time, is the key variable. Early-stage processes often demonstrate impressive yields at small scale but do not fully replicate when transferred to commercial-scale vessels, where different mixing and mass-transfer dynamics can alter microbial metabolism in ways that reduce yield. Solving these challenges requires years of bioprocess engineering work spanning pilot scale to commercial scale.

For engineered agricultural microbes like Pivot Bio's PROVEN, the scale-up challenge is primarily about ensuring consistent field performance. A microorganism performing well in controlled greenhouse conditions does not always perform equivalently in commercial farm fields, where soil composition, moisture, temperature, competing microbial species, and farming practices all interact. Pivot Bio has addressed this through extensive field trials across diverse geographies and soil types with consistently positive results. Still, the ecological complexity of the root zone means that performance variability across different farm environments remains an ongoing engineering and agronomic challenge.

Diagram 8.9 - Scale-Up Bottleneck Comparison Across Synbio Food Approaches

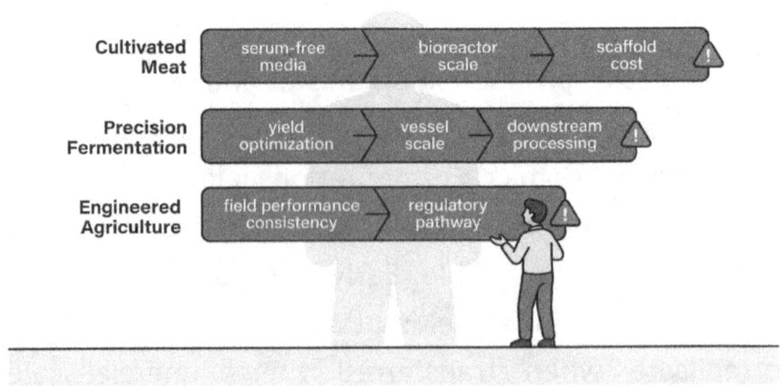

The Regulatory Pathway: Navigating Novel Foods

The US regulatory framework for synthetic biology food products divides responsibility between two agencies. The FDA (Food and Drug Administration) holds primary authority over food safety and ingredient approval, including the GRAS process used to evaluate new food ingredients. The USDA (Department of Agriculture) has authority over meat, poultry, and egg products. Cultivated meat uniquely spans both: the FDA oversees the cell culture process and the cells themselves, while the USDA oversees final product inspection and labeling. This dual-agency jurisdiction was formalized in a 2019 FDA-USDA joint agreement and operationalized through the 2023 approvals.

The FDA GRAS process is the primary regulatory mechanism for precision-fermented ingredients. GRAS status can be achieved through self-determination (company experts document the safety basis without notifying the FDA) or FDA consultation (a submitted safety dossier reviewed by the FDA, resulting in a no-objection letter). Most precision fermentation companies pursue FDA consultation because the resulting letter provides a credible, publicly defensible safety signal for brand partners and consumers. The GRAS consultation requires molecular characterization of the substance, a description of the manufacturing process, toxicology data, allergenicity assessment, and an estimate of dietary exposure based on intended uses.

The labeling debate is active, contested, and jurisdiction-specific. In the United States, the conventional meat industry successfully lobbied several states to restrict the use of 'meat' on labels for cultivated meat. At the federal level, USDA guidelines require that cultivated meat products carry a label identifying them as cell-cultivated. Whether this disclosure increases or decreases consumer acceptance is genuinely uncertain: some research suggests transparent labeling increases trust. In contrast, other research suggests that any label emphasizing the novel production method reduces purchase intent, particularly among those with lower prior exposure to food technology.

International regulatory divergence is a significant commercial factor. Singapore approved Good Meat's cultivated chicken in 2020, the first national market to do so. The EU's novel foods framework under Regulation (EU) 2015/2283 requires pre-market authorization for any food without a significant EU consumption history before May 1997, and cultivated meat approvals have not yet resulted. Israel has approved cultivated beef. China has announced national support for the development of cultivated meat. Any entrepreneur building a food biotech business needs jurisdiction-specific regulatory counsel, because approval status and labeling requirements differ substantially across major markets.

Diagram 8.10 - Regulatory Framework for Synbio Foods in the United States

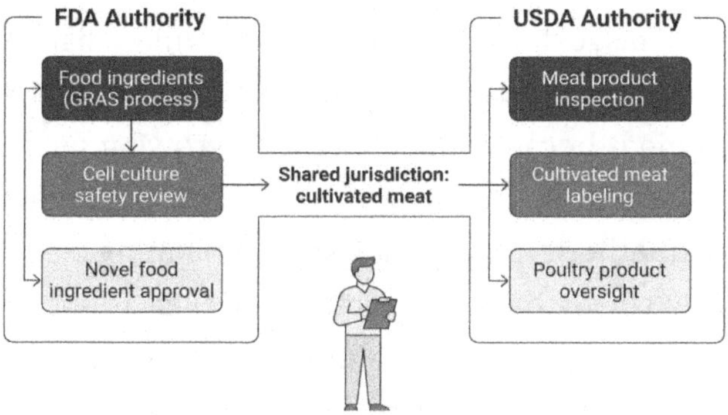

Consumer Acceptance and the Labeling Challenge

The engineering and regulatory challenges of synthetic biology food products have known solution pathways: invest capital, solve the technical problem, scale the process, and achieve the economics. Consumer acceptance is a different kind of challenge, because it is not primarily technical. It is social and psychological, shaped by culture, values, identity, risk perception, and institutional trust, none of which respond simply to better data or lower prices.

Consumer research on willingness to try cultivated meat and precision-fermented dairy consistently shows a pattern: stated willingness is reasonably high in the abstract, often above 50 percent in survey populations, but drops significantly when specific contextual factors appear. When told the likely price premium, willingness to purchase drops substantially. When told the product requires a label saying 'cell-cultivated' or 'lab-grown,' willingness drops further. 'Disgust sensitivity,' the psychological tendency to experience disgust in response to unfamiliar food preparation methods, is strongly predictive of resistance to cultivated meat because the process of growing meat in a bioreactor activates cognitive systems that flag unfamiliar processing methods as potentially contaminating. Research consistently shows that 'bioreactor' and 'lab' frames elicit higher disgust responses than descriptions that emphasize the cells' natural biological nature, even when the underlying product is identical.

The framing and labeling choices that companies and regulators make are not neutral. Describing a product as 'cultivated chicken' rather than 'lab-grown chicken' produces measurably higher purchase intent. Providing educational information about the production process before asking about purchase intent increases acceptance among certain demographic groups. The conventional meat industry's successful push to attach stigmatizing language to competitors' products through state labeling legislation was as much a consumer psychology strategy as a legal one. For the engineer or entrepreneur reading this, the practical implication is that the consumer acceptance strategy must be a parallel development track from the earliest stages of product development, not an afterthought. The companies that succeed will invest in understanding their consumer segments, develop communication strategies grounded in empirical research, and sequence market entry through channels where the consumer relationship already supports premium pricing and novel ingredients.

The Sustainability Case: Land, Water, Carbon, and Nuance

The environmental case for synthetic biology food products is frequently cited and frequently oversimplified in the direction of enthusiasm. The engineering reality is more nuanced, and understanding the nuances is important for anyone evaluating sustainability claims in this sector. The conventional livestock production numbers are genuinely large: conventional beef requires approximately 15,000 liters of water per kilogram produced, roughly 164 square meters of land, and produces approximately 60 kilograms of carbon dioxide equivalent per kilogram of beef, reflecting methane from enteric fermentation in cattle, nitrous oxide from manure, and carbon dioxide from land use change and energy inputs.

Cultivated meat life-cycle analyses project substantial land use reductions because the bioreactor footprint per kilogram of protein is dramatically smaller than the land required to raise cattle. The energy picture is more complicated: mammalian cell culture in a bioreactor is energy-intensive, and if that energy comes from fossil fuel-powered electricity, the greenhouse gas footprint of cultivated meat could be higher than or comparable to conventional chicken production, and lower than conventional beef only under low-carbon electricity scenarios. A cultivated meat facility powered by renewable energy achieves a dramatically different carbon footprint than one powered by coal. Precision fermentation has a substantially more favorable land and water footprint than conventional animal agriculture for equivalent protein, because fermentation facilities are compact and microbial organisms convert feedstock to product protein twenty to forty times more efficiently than cattle convert feed to edible protein.

Synthetic nitrogen fertilizer production via the Haber-Bosch process, which converts atmospheric nitrogen to ammonia using natural gas as both feedstock and energy source, consumes approximately 1 to 2 percent of total global energy annually and produces significant greenhouse gas emissions. Reducing synthetic nitrogen application by 15 to 25 percent across millions of US acres through Pivot Bio's engineered microbes represents a quantifiable and already-demonstrated environmental benefit. This is synthetic biology producing measurable impact at commercial scale today, not in a projected future. The methodological caveat is that life-cycle analyses of emerging technologies rely on assumptions about future production systems that may not yet be realized. The most favorable projections for cultivated meat assume bioreactor scales, media compositions, and energy sources that do not exist at a commercial scale today. The reader evaluating sustainability claims should ask: what are the assumptions about energy sources, and what is the sensitivity of the results to changes in those assumptions?

Diagram 8.11 - Environmental Footprint Comparison: Conventional vs. Synbio Food Pathways

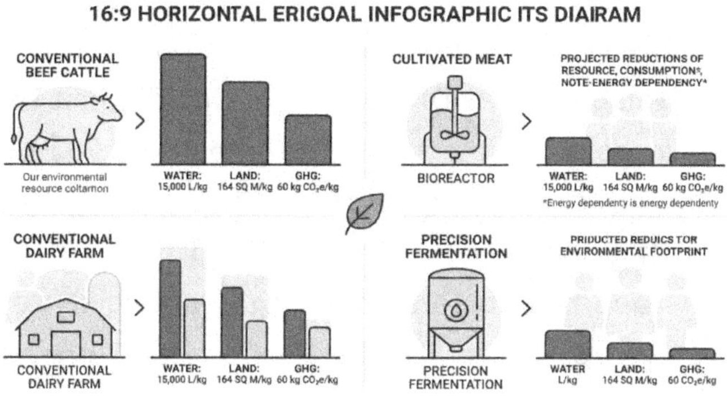

What This Means For You

If you are an engineer evaluating a synthetic biology food company, the framework for evaluation is more specific than Is the science real?' The science is genuinely real across all three major approaches. The questions that distinguish strong from weak investment cases concern the scale-up pathway. For precision fermentation: what is the current fermentation yield, what yield is needed to achieve target economics, and what is the company's track record of improving yield through strain engineering? For cultivated meat: what is the current production cost per kilogram, what percentage is attributable to growth media versus bioreactor capital versus energy, and does the company have a serum-free media formulation in production? For engineered agricultural microbes: what is the breadth and consistency of field performance data across geographies and soil types, and how does regulatory treatment vary across the company's target markets?

If you are an entrepreneur, the most important insight may be the distinction between regulatory approval and commercial viability. UPSIDE Foods achieved the first USDA grant of inspection for cultivated meat in 2023, an extraordinary regulatory milestone. But the price of their product at that point was hundreds of dollars per kilogram. Regulatory approval creates the legal possibility of a business; it does not create the economics of one. The entrepreneur who enters this space with a clear-eyed understanding of the scale-up engineering required, and who designs their company to address specific bottlenecks in that pathway, will be in a fundamentally different position than one who treats regulatory approval as the primary milestone to reach.

If you are a policy professional, the most actionable insight is the jurisdiction-specific regulatory divergence: the US has approved cultivated chicken, Singapore did so in 2020, the EU has a distinct novel foods framework that has not yet produced a cultivated meat approval, Israel has approved cultivated beef, and China is actively supporting development. A food technology that is legal in one jurisdiction may be entirely unapproved in another, with different labeling and safety data requirements. Understanding this map is a direct contribution a well-informed policy professional can make to the quality of regulatory decision-making in this sector.

Takeaway

Synthetic biology has entered the food system through three distinct doors. Precision fermentation is producing animal proteins without animals, using genetically engineered microorganisms as biological factories that are molecularly precise and scalable using existing industrial fermentation infrastructure. Cultivated meat is growing genuine animal muscle tissue in bioreactors from a small biopsy, having cleared the first regulatory hurdle in the United States, and now facing the harder commercial challenge of reducing production cost by one to two orders of magnitude to compete with conventional meat on price. Engineered agricultural biology is modifying the microbial ecosystems that crops depend on, producing measurable reductions in synthetic fertilizer use and greenhouse gas emissions at a commercial scale right now, even if it generates less cultural attention than the proteins and patties on the summit lunch table.

The engineering reality across all three approaches is more nuanced than either the most enthusiastic coverage or the most skeptical coverage suggests. The scale-up challenges are real and specific. The regulatory pathways are established and navigable, but not uniform across products or jurisdictions. Consumer acceptance barriers are psychological and cultural as well as economic, and they will not be dissolved simply by making products cheaper or providing more safety data. The sustainability advantages are genuine but depend on assumptions about energy sources and production efficiencies that have not yet been realized at a commercial scale.

What is not in question is that these technologies work at the molecular level. Perfect Day's whey protein is structurally identical to bovine whey. Impossible heme activates the same flavor chemistry as animal heme in cooked food. UPSIDE's cultivated chicken is chicken produced from chicken cells and approved by the FDA and USDA for human consumption. Pivot Bio's engineered nitrogen-fixing bacteria are reducing synthetic fertilizer use on millions of acres of American farmland. The proof-of-concept phase of synthetic biology food is complete. The phase that follows, scaling these technologies to the volumes and prices required to genuinely transform global food systems, is the engineering and commercial challenge of the current decade.

Carlos's question at the summit table was the right question. The science is real. The regulatory pathways have been opened. Commercial economics is hard but not impossible. And the conversation about what this transition means for the farmers, workers, and communities embedded in the food systems these technologies are designed to change is not a distraction from the engineering. It is part of the engineering problem because no food technology achieves its potential at scale without the trust and participation of the people who grow, process, and eat the food it produces. Synthetic biology has the tools to transform what we eat. Whether it does so in a way that produces broadly shared benefits is a question that engineers, entrepreneurs, and policy professionals will answer together, one product, one field deployment, and one honest conversation at a time.

Diagram 8.12 - Synbio Food Landscape: Commercial Maturity vs. Consumer Visibility

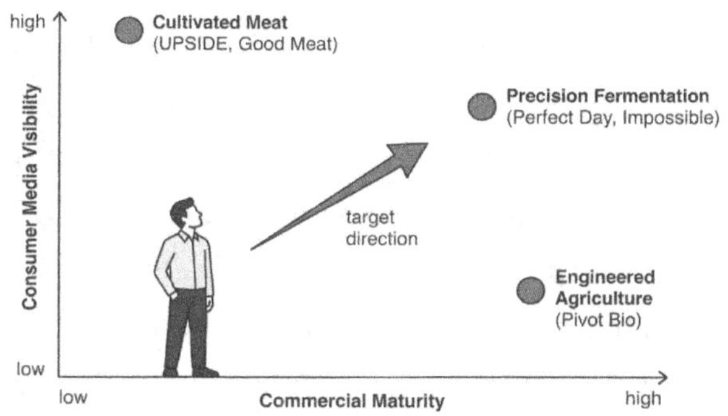

9 Biology That Listens

Opening Scenario

The lab at Helix Forge is quiet except for the low hum of the incubator and the sound of Yuki tapping notes into her tablet. It is past seven in the evening, but nobody has left. On the bench in front of her sits a petri dish that, from a distance, looks like any other piece of laboratory equipment: a shallow glass circle, a thin film of gel, the faint smell of warm growth medium. Then the overhead light dims, a blue-filtered lamp clicks on, and the dish begins to glow. A soft green luminescence rises from the center of the gel, steady and precise, marking the exact boundary between the tumor sample and the surrounding medium. Yuki photographs the result on her phone, sets the print on the conference table, and slides it across to Marcus.

"We didn't build a test," she says. "We built a cell that knows it's in the presence of cancer."

Marcus stares at the photograph. He has spent his career in software, a domain where the sensor and the signal are separate things, where the motion detector and the alarm are two different boxes wired together by copper and code. What he is looking at now is something different: a living system that simultaneously detects a condition and reports it, with no wire between the detection and the output, no laboratory instrument reading the result. The cell is both the sensor and the readout. Priya sets her coffee down and leans over to look. "The circuit is clean," she says. "Three inputs, one output. It glows only when all three microRNAs are present. False positives are essentially zero." Carlos, sitting across the table, looks up from the regulatory brief he has been drafting. "Which means we need to decide which approval pathway we are aiming for," he says, "because the path for a diagnostic is very different from the path for a therapeutic." The team is quiet for a moment, and then Marcus says the thing he always says when the engineering is working: "Explain that again from first principles. I want to understand exactly how it decides."

Why It Matters

Most of the applications of synthetic biology covered in earlier chapters involve making something: a medicine, a material, a modified crop, a living factory. Biosensors represent a distinct category of engineered biology, one concerned not with production but with perception. A biosensor is a biological system engineered to detect a specific molecule or combination of molecules and produce a measurable output signal when it finds what it is looking for. The output can be optical, turning a fluorescent protein on or producing a visible color change in a strip of paper. It can be electrical, generating a change in conductance that a small electrode reads. Or it can be biological, triggering downstream changes in gene expression that set off a cascade of cellular responses. What all biosensors share is the same basic engineering logic: input, processing, output. Target molecule present; circuit activates; signal produced.

That logic matters for reasons that extend far beyond any single application. Diagnostics is the most visible market, and the stakes are enormous. Infectious disease kills millions of people every year in settings where laboratory testing is expensive, slow, or simply unavailable. Cancer detected at stage one is often curable; cancer detected at stage four is often not. Agricultural contamination caught early can be remediated before it spreads; contamination discovered months later is a catastrophe. In every one of these situations, the difference between a good outcome and a bad outcome is how fast you can reliably detect the thing you are looking for. Biosensors designed with synthetic biology tools are changing the speed, cost, and deployability of detection in ways that no other technology currently matches.

There is a second reason biosensors matter that goes deeper than their applications. Every other part of synthetic biology depends on the ability to measure. The design-build-test-learn cycle that is the engineering backbone of the field requires, at a minimum, a test step, and the quality of the entire cycle is bounded by the quality of what you can measure. Biosensors are the measurement infrastructure of synthetic biology. Advances in biosensor sensitivity and specificity are not just advances in diagnostics; they are advances in the speed at which every other part of the field can iterate. When Helix Forge builds a better biosensor, they are not just building a better diagnostic product. They are building a better test infrastructure for everything else they want to build next.

The Architecture of a Biosensor

The alarm system analogy is the cleanest way into the engineering architecture of a biosensor. Every modern building alarm has three components: a sensor (the motion detector, the smoke particle counter, the glass-break microphone), a processing circuit (the control panel that decides whether the sensor signal is real and consequential), and a readout (the siren, the notification to the monitoring center, the flashing light over the door). Remove any one of those three components, and the system fails. A sensor with no processing circuit produces false alarms every time a pigeon lands on a windowsill. A processing circuit with no sensor has nothing to process. A readout with no connection to the processing circuit communicates nothing.

A biosensor has the same three-component structure. The recognition element is the biological equivalent of the motion detector: a protein, a nucleic acid strand, or an entire genetic circuit that specifically binds or responds to the target molecule. The transducer is the mechanism that converts the molecular recognition event into a form on which a signal can be built. The readout is the output that communicates the detection to whoever or whatever is listening. In the simplest biosensors, all three components are elegantly compact. In more sophisticated designs, each component is itself an engineered system with multiple layers of processing.

The recognition element is where the biological innovation lives. Engineering a recognition element for a specific target molecule is the synthetic biology equivalent of writing a lock that matches exactly one key. Antibodies are natural recognition elements, and many early biosensors used antibody-antigen binding as their detection mechanism. But antibodies are expensive to produce, require cold storage, and can lose activity over time. Synthetic biology has opened up a much wider toolkit: transcription factors, proteins that bind DNA, can be engineered to bind a small-molecule target instead, thereby activating or repressing a connected gene. Aptamers, short strands of DNA or RNA that fold into three-dimensional shapes, can be selected to bind almost any target with high specificity. CRISPR guide RNAs, as this chapter will cover in detail, can direct a CRISPR protein to any specific nucleic acid sequence with extraordinary precision.

Diagram 9.1 - Three-Component Biosensor Architecture

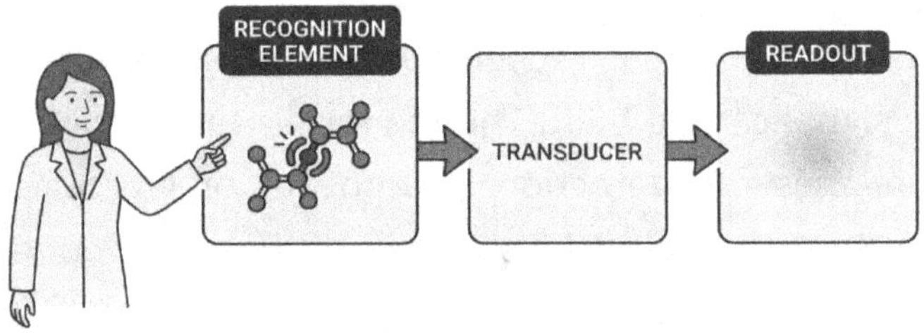

The transducer is the link between recognition and signal. In a genetic biosensor, the transducer is almost always a change in gene expression: when the recognition element (a transcription factor, an aptamer, a CRISPR protein) detects the target molecule, the resulting molecular event is connected, by genetic circuit design, to a change in the production of a reporter protein. That reporter protein is the readout. If it is a fluorescent protein, it glows. If it is an enzyme that cleaves a colored substrate, it changes the color of a solution or a paper strip. If it is a protein that affects conductance at an electrode surface, it generates an electrical signal. In this architecture, the transducer is the genetic circuit that wires the recognition event to the reporter gene.

The design parameters that engineers optimize in a biosensor are sensitivity, specificity, and dynamic range. Sensitivity is the lowest target concentration that produces a detectable signal, typically expressed as the limit of detection (LOD). Specificity is the ability to distinguish the target from closely related molecules that might trigger a false positive. Dynamic range is the concentration range over which the signal scales in a reliable, predictable relationship with the target concentration. A biosensor optimized purely for sensitivity may sacrifice specificity, producing false positives when a similar molecule is present. A biosensor optimized for specificity may be too slow or require target concentrations found only in advanced disease states, thereby missing early-stage cases. The engineering challenge is to optimize all three parameters simultaneously while meeting the constraints of the deployment context.

Diagram 9.2 - Sensitivity, Specificity, and Dynamic Range

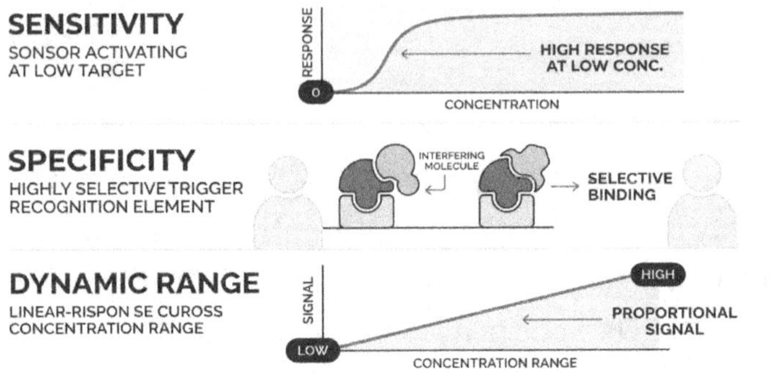

Concontsation is an a conn ielt, of target concentrations loost the 16:9 image.

The Promoter-Repressor Circuit as a Detector

Chapter 3 introduced the promoter-repressor system as a core regulatory mechanism in genetic circuit design. A promoter, recall, is the DNA sequence that marks the start of a gene and acts as the binding site for the molecular machinery that reads and copies the gene into messenger RNA. A repressor is a protein that binds to the promoter and physically blocks transcription, keeping the gene switched off until the repressor is removed. Toggle switches, oscillators, and logic gates in synthetic biology all use promoter-repressor pairs as their computational building blocks. Biosensors are, at their core, a direct application of that same circuit architecture, redirected from computation to detection.

The most common design logic works like this. An engineer selects a transcription factor, a protein whose natural or engineered function is to bind specifically to a small molecule of interest. This is the ligand-binding property of the transcription factor: it changes its shape, and therefore its behavior, when the target molecule is present. In the absence of the target molecule, the transcription factor binds to the promoter region of a reporter gene and acts as a repressor, keeping the reporter gene switched off. When the target molecule appears and binds to the transcription factor, the transcription factor changes shape and releases the promoter. The gene is now free to be expressed. The reporter protein is produced, and the signal appears. The biosensor has fired.

This is not a metaphor for how the circuit works. It is a literal description of the molecular mechanism. The transcription factor is a physical protein that either occupies the promoter binding site or does not, depending on whether it is carrying the target molecule. The promoter is a physical DNA sequence that either has an obstruction on it or does not. The gene downstream of the promoter is either being read or it is not. The entire detection event is a molecular-scale physical event: a protein changing shape and releasing a DNA strand. Signal amplification arises because a single molecular recognition event can trigger the production of thousands of copies of the reporter protein, since transcription and translation are themselves amplifying processes.

Diagram 9.3 - Promoter-Repressor Detection Circuit

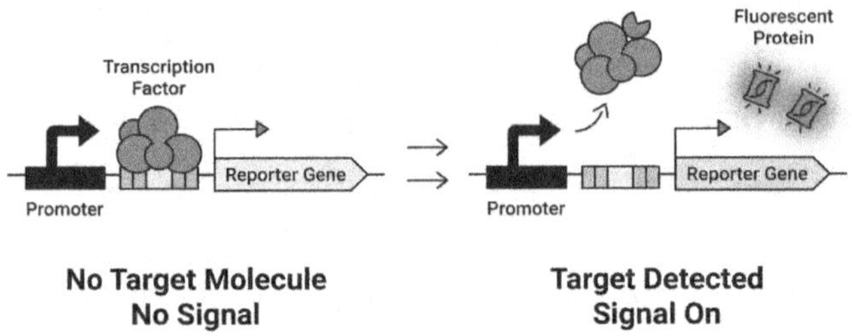

The inverse design is equally useful: a transcription factor that acts as an activator rather than a repressor will keep the reporter gene off until the target molecule appears, causing the transcription factor to bind the promoter and activate expression. In either case, the fundamental detection logic is the same. The transcription factor is the molecular sensor. The promoter is the processing circuit. The reporter gene is the readout. What makes synthetic biology powerful in this context is the ability to engineer transcription factors to bind targets they do not naturally recognize, to tune the affinity and kinetics of the binding interaction, and to connect multiple detection events in series or in parallel using the same genetic circuit design tools that build logic gates.

A riboswitch is a related but distinct detection mechanism that operates not at the level of transcription but at the level of translation, the second step in gene expression, where messenger RNA is decoded into protein. A riboswitch is a structural element built into the messenger RNA itself. In the absence of the target molecule, the RNA folds into a shape that either blocks the ribosome from binding and starting translation or promotes premature termination of the RNA strand before it is completed. When the target molecule binds to the riboswitch, the RNA refolds into a different shape, allowing translation to proceed. The result is the same as the transcription factor design: target molecule present, reporter protein produced, signal appears. But the riboswitch works at a different point in the expression process, which gives it different kinetics and different engineering properties. Riboswitches are particularly attractive for cell-free biosensor systems, because they can function in a simplified biochemical environment that does not require the full complexity of a living cell.

CRISPR-Based Diagnostics: SHERLOCK and DETECTR

CRISPR, introduced in Chapter 4 as a precision genome editing tool, has a second life in diagnostics that is arguably as consequential as its editing applications. The insight that enabled CRISPR diagnostics was the discovery that certain CRISPR proteins exhibit what researchers call collateral cleavage activity. When the CRISPR protein finds and binds its target nucleic acid sequence, it does not simply cut that one specific target and stop. It enters a state of non-specific activation and begins cutting other nearby nucleic acid strands indiscriminately, including any specially designed reporter molecules that the engineer has added to the reaction.

This collateral cleavage behavior, which initially seemed like an undesirable side effect of the CRISPR mechanism, turned out to be an extraordinary signal amplification engine. Here is why: a single CRISPR protein that finds its target sequence can cleave thousands of reporter molecules in the minutes that follow. Each cleaved reporter molecule produces a detectable signal. The result is that one copy of the target sequence can produce a signal large enough to detect without any additional amplification step, giving CRISPR-based diagnostics sensitivity that matches or exceeds polymerase chain reaction (or PCR, the laboratory gold standard for nucleic acid detection, while operating in a format that does not require thermocycling equipment or a trained laboratory technician.

SHERLOCK, which stands for Specific High Sensitivity Enzymatic Reporter unLOCKing, was developed at the Broad Institute by Feng Zhang's team and uses the Cas13 protein. This CRISPR variant targets RNA rather than DNA. DETECTR, developed at UC Berkeley by Jennifer Doudna's group, uses the Cas12a protein, which targets DNA. Both platforms follow the same diagnostic workflow: a patient sample is collected; any nucleic acid from the target pathogen (or biomarker of interest) is optionally pre-amplified using a simple isothermal amplification step that does not require specialized equipment; the CRISPR detection reaction is added; and the reporter molecules, if cleaved, produce a signal on a lateral flow strip, the same paper-strip format used in home pregnancy tests, that can be read by eye in about thirty minutes. No centrifuge. No PCR machine. No laboratory infrastructure.

Diagram 9.4 - SHERLOCK Collateral Cleavage Mechanism

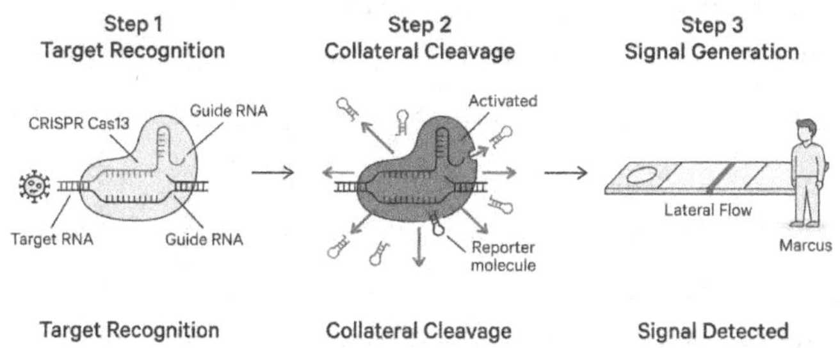

The performance of SHERLOCK and DETECTR in the COVID-19 pandemic demonstrated what CRISPR diagnostics could do in a real-world deployment under intense pressure and time constraints. Both platforms were adapted to detect SARS-CoV-2 within weeks of the pathogen's genome being sequenced and published. SHERLOCK-based tests achieved sensitivity in the attomolar range, meaning they could detect target RNA at concentrations of one hundred attomolar or less, which translates to detecting just a few copies of viral RNA in a sample. The SHERLOCK-based SARS-CoV-2 test received Emergency Use Authorization from the US Food and Drug Administration in 2020, establishing the first regulatory precedent for a CRISPR-based diagnostic and demonstrating that the regulatory pathway existed for these platforms to reach clinical deployment.

The broader implication of CRISPR diagnostics goes beyond COVID-19 or any single pathogen. The guide RNA in a CRISPR diagnostic is essentially a software module: a 20-nucleotide sequence that tells the CRISPR protein what to look for. Changing the guide RNA changes the target. Designing a new CRISPR diagnostic for a new pathogen takes days to weeks, not months, because the underlying detection platform remains the same. The hardware, to use the software analogy, is constant. Only the search query changes. This programmability is the feature that makes CRISPR diagnostics uniquely powerful for responding to new and emerging pathogens, for expanding access to testing in low-resource settings, and for building multiplex diagnostics that can test for multiple targets simultaneously in a single reaction.

Diagram 9.5 - CRISPR Diagnostic Workflow from Sample to Result

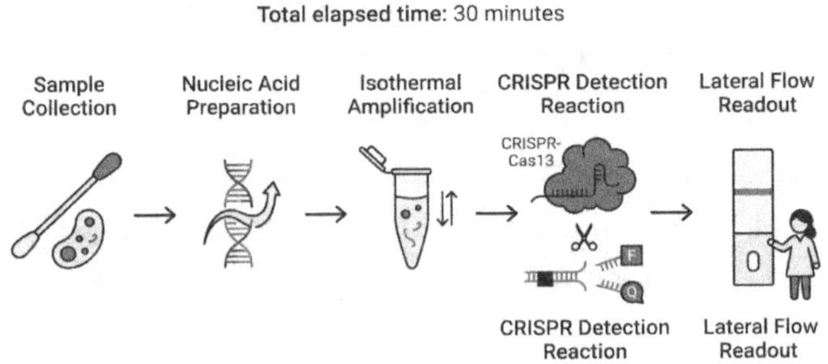

Point-of-Care Diagnostics: Bringing the Lab to Patient

Point-of-care diagnostics, often abbreviated POC, are diagnostic tests designed to be performed outside a clinical laboratory, at or near the patient's location: a rural health clinic, a remote field site, a home, or an emergency room bed. The category sounds straightforward, but it imposes a set of engineering constraints that are significantly more demanding than those for a laboratory test. A laboratory diagnostic can assume access to refrigeration, centrifuges, thermocyclers, trained technicians, and stable electrical power. A point-of-care diagnostic assumes none of those things. It must work at ambient temperature. It must produce a result that an untrained user can interpret correctly. It must be manufacturable at a low enough cost to be deployed in large quantities in low-resource settings. And it must remain stable during storage and transport without a cold chain.

Synthetic biology is enabling a new generation of point-of-care biosensors that meet these constraints in ways that earlier generations of diagnostic technology could not. The most powerful platform for POC biosensors based on synthetic biology is the cell-free system. A cell-free system is exactly what the name suggests: the protein-production machinery of a cell, specifically the ribosomes, transfer RNA molecules, amino acids, energy molecules, and regulatory proteins that carry out transcription and translation, extracted from cells and concentrated into a solution that can carry out gene expression without any living cells present. This cellular machinery can be freeze-dried, pressed into a paper strip, and stored at room temperature for months. When a liquid sample is applied to the strip, the freeze-dried machinery rehydrates; the genetic circuit in the strip activates, depending on whether the target molecule is present; and the reporter protein is produced, creating a visible signal.

The cell-free paper-based biosensor is one of the most elegant applications of synthetic biology to real-world constraints. It combines the programmability and specificity of a genetic circuit with the simplicity and cost-effectiveness of a paper-strip format. The paper strip is the same basic format as a home pregnancy test or a COVID-19 antigen test, a technology that hundreds of millions of people already know how to use. But where a pregnancy test detects a single hormone using antibodies embedded in the strip, a cell-free synthetic biology biosensor can, in principle, detect any molecule for which an appropriate transcription factor or riboswitch can be engineered, and it can implement logic-gate processing in the circuit so that the signal only appears when multiple conditions are simultaneously met. The cell-free paper biosensor has been demonstrated for Zika virus detection, lead contamination, drug metabolite monitoring, and various other applications, in each case achieving laboratory-quality sensitivity and specificity in a format that a health worker with minimal training can operate in the field.

Diagram 9.6 - Cell-Free Paper-Based Biosensor Strip

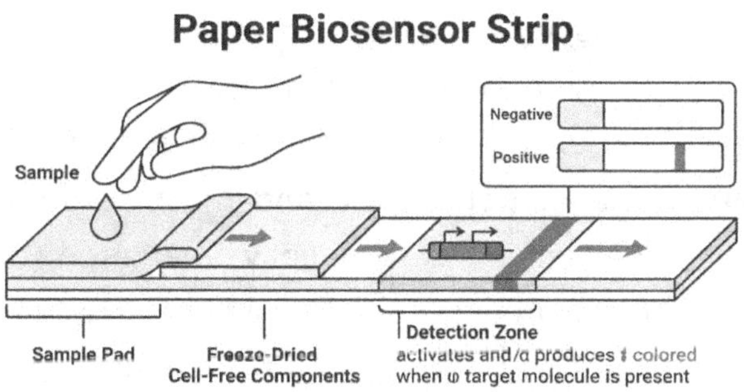

Cross-sectional view a paper biosensor strip, 16:9 hclzortal landscape

Wearable biosensors represent a second category of point-of-care deployment that is at an earlier stage of development but advancing rapidly. The concept is straightforward: genetic circuits or biosensor components incorporated into a material that can be worn on the skin or embedded in clothing, continuously monitoring biomarkers in sweat, interstitial fluid, or the immediate environment. The challenge is that genetic circuits require some biological machinery to function, which means the wearable biosensor must either use cell-free components that have a limited lifespan before they exhaust their biochemical energy, or it must house living engineered cells in a biocompatible material that protects them from the environment while allowing them to sense and respond. Several research groups have demonstrated prototype wearable biosensors capable of detecting markers of inflammation, hydration status, and glucose concentration. However, commercial deployment of fully genetic wearable biosensors remains several years away.

The regulatory pathway for point-of-care synthetic biology diagnostics follows the framework that governs all in vitro diagnostics, or IVDs, in the United States. The FDA classifies IVDs into three risk categories. Class I devices are low risk and are generally exempt from premarket review. Class II devices present a moderate risk and must demonstrate substantial equivalence to a legally marketed device through the 510(k) process. Class III devices are high-risk and require Premarket Approval (PMA), which involves submitting clinical performance data demonstrating safety and effectiveness. Most POC diagnostics for infectious diseases fall into Class II, while novel diagnostic platforms for cancer biomarkers or other high-stakes applications typically require Class III review. Carlos has spent considerable time mapping the Helix Forge biosensor through this framework, and his conclusion is clear: the FDA's Emergency Use Authorization pathway, which was substantially clarified during the COVID-19 response, provides a precedent-backed route for novel CRISPR-based diagnostics to reach clinical use when public health urgency justifies accelerated review.

Cancer Biomarker Detection: The AND Gate Approach

The problem of detecting cancer early is one of the hardest problems in diagnostic medicine, and it illustrates with particular clarity both the power and the engineering difficulty of genetic biosensors. The challenge has two parts. First, cancer biomarkers, the molecular signals that a tumor releases into the bloodstream or other accessible bodily fluids, are present at extremely low concentrations, especially in early-stage disease when the tumor mass is small, and the biomarker signal is faint. The sensitivity requirements for cancer liquid biopsies, tests that detect cancer from blood samples rather than tissue biopsies, push up against the fundamental limits of molecular detection. Second, no single biomarker known today is perfectly specific to cancer. Most cancer-associated proteins and nucleic acid fragments are also present at low levels in healthy individuals, and the distributions overlap in ways that make single-biomarker thresholds unreliable for clinical decision-making. A test that is sensitive enough to catch early cancer will also flag many healthy people as positive. A test specific enough to avoid false positives will miss many early cancers.

The AND gate biosensor design addresses the second problem directly and elegantly. In digital electronics, an AND gate is a logic circuit that produces an output only when all of its inputs are simultaneously active. In a two-input AND gate, input A must be present, and input B must be present for the output to be on. In a genetic AND-gate biosensor, the reporter gene is expressed only when two or more specific biomarker molecules are simultaneously present and detected by their respective recognition elements. The probability that two unrelated biomarkers are both elevated in a healthy individual is much lower than the probability that either is elevated alone. A three-input AND gate, requiring three biomarkers to be simultaneously elevated, can achieve specificity approaching clinical utility for early cancer detection.

The Helix Forge prototype that Yuki validated in the opening scene of this chapter is exactly this design: a three-input AND gate genetic circuit that activates only when three specific microRNAs, short non-coding RNA molecules that regulate gene expression and are known to be co-elevated in early-stage pancreatic cancer, are simultaneously present in the sample. MicroRNAs, often abbreviated miRNAs, are a class of regulatory RNA molecules, each about twenty to twenty-two nucleotides in length, that fine-tune gene expression by binding to messenger RNA strands and either blocking their translation or marking them for degradation. Certain miRNA combinations are consistently dysregulated in specific cancers, elevated in tumor cells, and detectable in blood plasma. The Helix Forge circuit uses three transcription-factor-based detection arms, each responsive to a specific miRNA, wired in series so that the reporter gene activates only when all three arms simultaneously detect their respective targets.

Diagram 9.7 - Three-Input AND Gate Cancer Biosensor Circuit

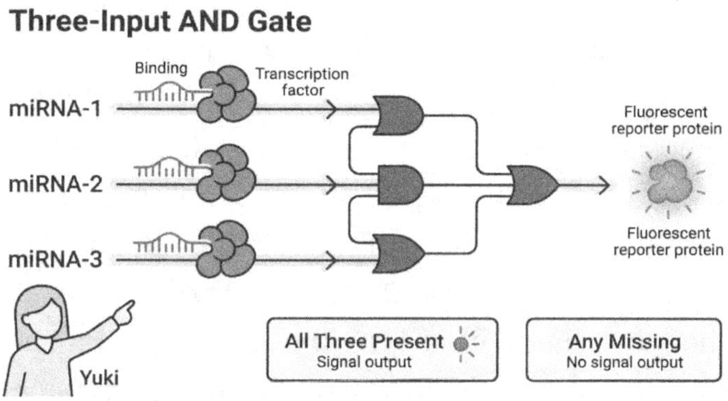

The choice of pancreatic cancer as the target application for the Helix Forge prototype is deliberate. Pancreatic cancer has one of the lowest five-year survival rates of any major cancer, not because it is intrinsically more lethal once detected than other cancers, but because it is rarely detected early. The pancreas is a deep abdominal organ with no reliable early symptoms, and by the time patients present with clinical signs, the cancer has typically spread beyond surgical resectability. An accurate liquid biopsy test capable of detecting pancreatic cancer at stage one or stage two, when surgery can still be curative, would represent one of the most significant advances in oncology in decades. The sensitivity and specificity requirements are demanding but not out of reach for a well-engineered genetic AND gate biosensor, and the Helix Forge team is not alone in pursuing this direction. Several academic groups and diagnostic companies are developing multi-biomarker detection strategies for pancreatic and other high-mortality cancers.

The engineering roadmap for the next generation of cancer biosensors includes not only more input channels, extending from three to five or more simultaneous biomarker inputs, but also integration with CRISPR-based amplification to achieve the attomolar sensitivity required for early-stage detection of circulating tumor DNA. Circulating tumor DNA, or ctDNA, consists of fragments of DNA shed by tumor cells into the bloodstream. These fragments carry mutations characteristic of the tumor's genome, and detecting them provides a direct molecular signature of the tumor's presence. The concentrations of ctDNA in early-stage cancer are often below the sensitivity of transcription-factor-based biosensors. Still, CRISPR collateral-cleavage amplification, combined with AND-gate specificity logic, may bridge that gap. This is an active area of development, and the convergence of genetic circuit design with CRISPR amplification chemistry represents one of the most promising technical trajectories in the field.

Diagram 9.8 - Liquid Biopsy Biosensor Workflow

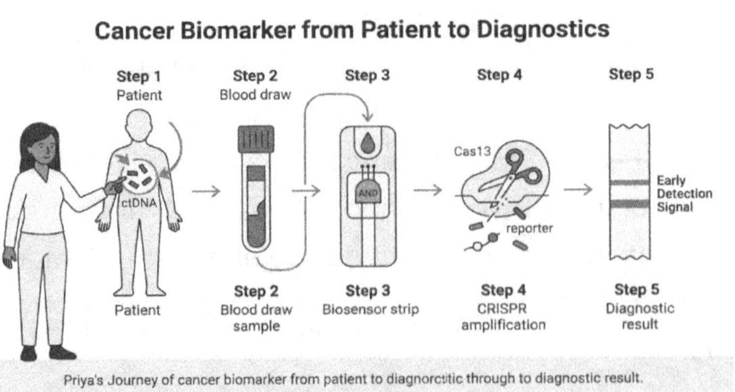

Priya's Journey of cancer biomarker from patient to diagnorctitic through to diagnostic result.

Environmental Biosensors: Bacteria That Read the Water

The most long-standing and well-demonstrated application of whole-cell biosensors outside medicine is environmental monitoring, specifically the detection of heavy-metal contamination in water supplies. The field's classic example is the arsenic biosensor. Arsenic contamination of groundwater is a public health crisis affecting hundreds of millions of people globally, concentrated in South and Southeast Asia, parts of South America, and Africa. In Bangladesh and Cambodia, where tens of millions of people depend on tube wells for drinking water, arsenic concentrations above the World Health Organization's guideline of 10 micrograms per liter are common. Still, systematic laboratory testing of individual wells is expensive, logistically difficult, and intermittent. The testing gap is the problem. Contamination that is not detected is contamination that is not acted on.

The arsenic biosensor addresses this gap with engineering that, at its core, is a straightforward application of the promoter-repressor logic covered earlier. Bacteria carry a natural genetic system for responding to arsenic stress: the ArsR protein. Under normal conditions, this transcription factor binds to and represses a set of arsenic-resistance genes. When arsenic enters the cell and binds to ArsR, the protein changes shape, releases the DNA, and the arsenic-resistance genes are expressed. This is the organism's natural alarm and response system for arsenic exposure.

Synthetic biologists have repurposed this natural circuit by replacing the arsenic-resistance genes downstream of the ArsR-controlled promoter with reporter genes, typically a fluorescent protein or a color-producing enzyme. The result is a bacterium that emits a visible signal specifically in response to arsenic at concentrations calibrated to the relevant public health threshold.

The performance characteristics of engineered arsenic biosensors have been validated in field settings with genuine rigor. Strains designed to produce a green fluorescent signal above 10 micrograms per liter of arsenic and no signal below that threshold have been tested on Bangladeshi and Cambodian field water samples and shown to correlate well with laboratory inductively coupled plasma mass spectrometry measurements, the analytical gold standard for arsenic quantification. Field workers using a simple visual readout, no equipment required beyond the biosensor culture itself, a small incubation period, and a portable blue light, can assess a water sample in a few hours. The biosensor is not a replacement for laboratory confirmation of positive results. Still, it is a screening tool that is orders of magnitude cheaper, faster, and more deployable than laboratory testing for every sample.

Diagram 9.9 - Arsenic Whole-Cell Biosensor in a Water Sample

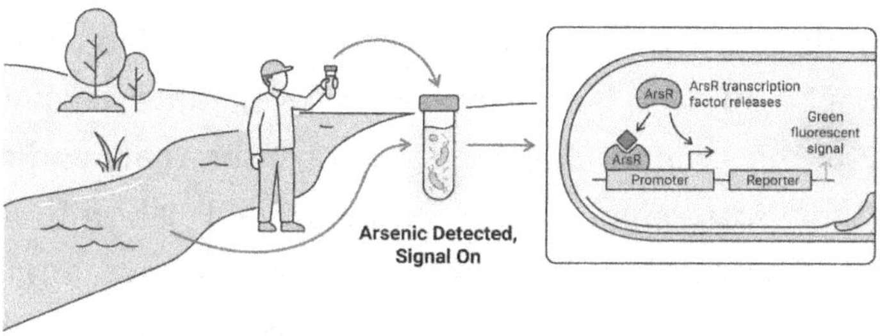

Beyond arsenic, whole-cell biosensors have been developed or are under development for lead, mercury, cadmium, and other heavy metals using metal-responsive transcription factors analogous to ArsR. Agricultural applications include biosensors for monitoring soil nitrogen levels, helping farmers apply fertilizer with far greater precision than current blanket-application practices allow, and reducing both costs and the environmental damage caused by nitrogen runoff into waterways. A whole-cell nitrogen biosensor deployed in an agricultural field could provide continuous, spatially resolved data on soil nitrogen levels at a per-data-point cost that is orders of magnitude lower than periodic laboratory soil testing, enabling precision agriculture practices that are currently economically out of reach for smallholder farmers in low-income countries.

The deployment of whole-cell biosensors in the environment poses engineering challenges that do not arise in clinical or laboratory settings. Cell viability is the first challenge: engineered bacteria deployed in real-world environments encounter variable temperature, pH, salinity, nutrient availability, and competition with native microbial communities, all of which can reduce the viability and performance of the biosensor strain over time. Signal stability is the second challenge: a biosensor that works reliably for forty-eight hours in controlled laboratory conditions may drift significantly in signal output after weeks in a field environment. Containment is the third challenge, and in many ways the most important from a regulatory and governance standpoint: releasing engineered organisms into an open environment, even organisms with no apparent fitness advantage over native strains, raises questions about ecological impact and horizontal gene transfer that regulatory frameworks are only beginning to address. This containment question is a direct prelude to the environmental governance discussions in Chapter 10, where the challenges of intentional release of engineered organisms at scale are examined in full.

Biosensors in Industrial Fermentation: The Test in the DBTL Loop

Chapter 7 covered the biomanufacturing applications of synthetic biology: engineered microorganisms producing pharmaceuticals, specialty chemicals, materials, and food ingredients in industrial fermenters at scales ranging from a few hundred liters to hundreds of thousands of liters. A consistent theme in that chapter was the iterative nature of strain engineering, the design-build-test-learn cycle that refines a production organism's performance across dozens or hundreds of rounds of design and testing. The test step in that cycle limits iteration speed because the quality of a test step depends entirely on the ability to measure what is happening inside the fermenter, and measuring the internal state of a complex fermentation in real time is genuinely hard.

Traditional fermentation monitoring measures the external observables: dissolved oxygen, pH, temperature, carbon dioxide production rate, and optical density as a proxy for cell density. These external measurements are informative but indirect. They tell you that something is happening inside the fermenter, but not specifically what. The production of the target molecule, the accumulation of toxic byproducts, the metabolic flux through specific pathways, and the organism's stress responses are all invisible to external sensors. A batch that is going off-target, accumulating a pathway intermediate that will eventually crash productivity or kill cells, may look perfectly normal by external measurements until the problem is too advanced to correct. By then, a multi-thousand-liter batch worth tens or hundreds of thousands of dollars is lost.

Whole-cell biosensors integrated into the production organism, or deployed as co-culture sensor strains alongside the production organism, address this gap directly. A biosensor strain engineered to produce a fluorescent signal when a specific metabolic intermediate exceeds a threshold concentration, or when a stress-response gene is activated, gives the fermentation control system a real-time window into the internal state of the fermentation that no external sensor can provide. Automated control systems can use this signal to adjust dissolved oxygen levels, nutrient feeding rates, temperature, or pH in real time, keeping the fermentation within the productive operating range that strain engineering has defined as optimal.

Diagram 9.10 - Whole-Cell Biosensor in an Industrial Fermenter

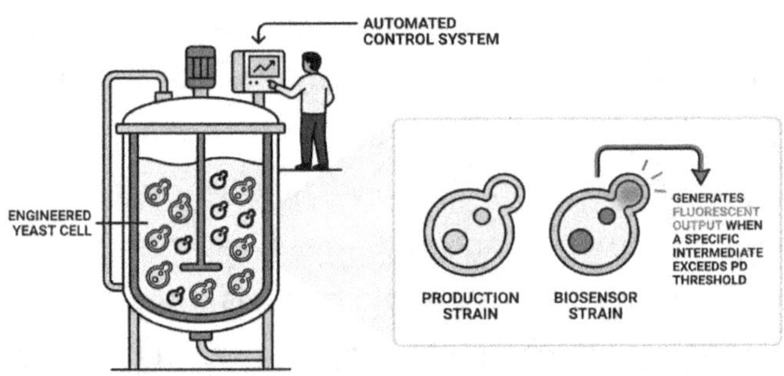

Engineered yeast cell tanks herhonics cell generate a specific metabolic intermediate as a predefined threshold

The convergence of biosensor technology and the DBTL cycle is more than an incremental improvement in fermentation control. It represents a qualitative change in the type of feedback available to the engineer. Without biosensors, the test step in the DBTL cycle for a metabolic engineering project requires sampling the fermentation, processing the sample through analytical chemistry, waiting for laboratory results, and then interpreting those results in the context of a process that may have moved on significantly in the hours since the sample was taken. With a biosensor providing a continuous real-time signal from inside the fermenter, the test step becomes instantaneous and continuous. The DBTL cycle accelerates because the feedback loop tightens. This is not a theoretical benefit: research groups and industrial biotech companies that have integrated biosensor-based monitoring into their fermentation platforms report measurably faster strain optimization timelines and lower rates of batch failure.

There is a deeper point about biosensors and the DBTL cycle that extends beyond fermentation monitoring. The design-build-test-learn framework, as Marcus understands it from software engineering, is only as good as the test step. In software, the test step is fast, cheap, and deterministic: you run the code, check whether it works, and get a precise error message telling you where it failed. In early synthetic biology, the test step was slow, expensive, and often uninformative: you built a genetic circuit, you grew cells, you took samples, you sent them to an analytical instrument, and days later, you learned that something was not working but not quite why. Better biosensors are making biological testing faster, cheaper, and more informative, bringing it closer to the experience of debugging software than to that of running a classical biochemistry experiment. This is one of the structural reasons that the pace of progress in synthetic biology has accelerated so sharply in the past decade, and it will continue to accelerate as biosensor technology matures.

Cell-Free Systems: Gene Circuits Without the Cell

Cell-free biosensors deserve their own section because they represent a distinct engineering paradigm that solves several fundamental problems associated with whole-cell biosensor deployment, while introducing a different set of constraints and trade-offs. In a whole-cell biosensor, the genetic circuit operates inside a living organism. The organism provides the transcription and translation machinery, the energy metabolism, and the cellular infrastructure that the circuit needs to function. It also provides everything that makes a living organism difficult to deploy in uncontrolled environments: it grows, it evolves, it responds to environmental stress in ways that may alter circuit performance, and it raises containment concerns when deployed outside a laboratory.

A cell-free system decouples the genetic circuit from the living cell by extracting the protein-production machinery and running the circuit in solution or on a solid support, without any living cells. The extract typically contains ribosomes, transfer RNA molecules loaded with amino acids, RNA polymerases, transcription factors, energy-regenerating enzymes, and the small molecules required to run transcription and translation. This extract is added to a reaction mix containing the DNA template encoding the circuit and the target-responsive components, and the circuit runs in the tube or on the paper substrate until the biochemical components are exhausted. Because no living cells are present, the cell-free biosensor cannot reproduce, cannot evolve, cannot colonize an environment, and does not raise the regulatory concerns associated with the release of a living engineered organism.

The freeze-drying capability of cell-free systems is their most practically transformative property for point-of-care and field deployment. Cell-free extracts that would normally require cold storage to maintain activity can be freeze-dried, a gentle dehydration process that removes water while preserving the structural integrity of the proteins and nucleic acids, and stored as a dry pellet at room temperature for months to years. When a sample is applied to the dried extract, it rehydrates and begins functioning within minutes. This cold-chain-free storage capability removes one of the largest logistical barriers to deploying sophisticated molecular diagnostics in low-resource settings, where reliable refrigeration is often unavailable between manufacturing and the point of use.

Diagram 9.11 - Cell-Free Biosensor Reaction in a Test Tube

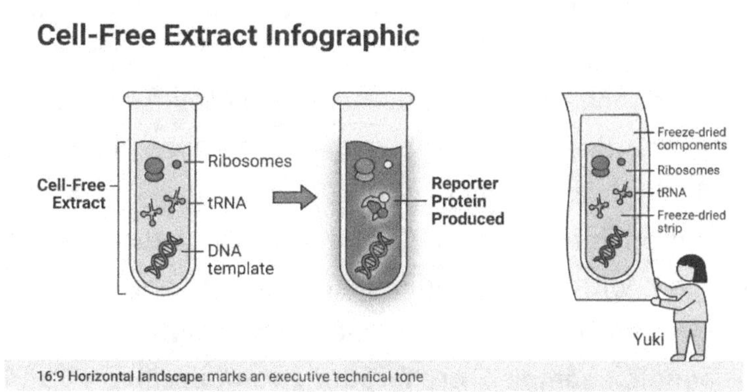

The trade-offs of cell-free systems relative to whole-cell biosensors are real and worth understanding clearly. The biochemical lifetime of a cell-free reaction is finite, typically hours to a day or two, even in the freeze-dried format, once rehydrated, because the energy-regenerating enzymes eventually exhaust their substrates and the machinery slows. A whole-cell biosensor, by contrast, can in principle remain active indefinitely as long as the cells are viable, because the cells regenerate their own energy supply. For single-use diagnostic applications, the finite lifetime of a cell-free reaction is not a limitation, because the test is run once and the result is read immediately. For continuous environmental monitoring, where the sensor must remain active and responsive for days or weeks, the finite lifetime of a cell-free system is a significant constraint, and whole-cell biosensors or conventional chemical sensors may be more appropriate.

The research frontier in cell-free biosensors is advancing in several directions simultaneously. One direction is extending the operational lifetime of cell-free reactions by improving energy regeneration systems and developing more stable enzyme formulations. A second direction is to expand the range of targets detectable by cell-free circuits by incorporating aptamer-based recognition elements, riboswitch designs, and CRISPR collateral cleavage amplification into cell-free formats. A third direction is integration with microfluidic platforms, where cell-free reactions are carried out in miniaturized channel networks that handle sample preparation, amplification, and detection in a single compact device. The combination of cell-free genetic circuits with microfluidics is moving toward a future where a credit-card-sized device can perform laboratory-quality molecular diagnostics on a finger prick of blood in twenty minutes, with no equipment, no cold chain, and no trained personnel required beyond the ability to follow a simple printed instruction.

Navigating Regulatory Pathways for Synthetic Biology Diagnostics

Carlos Rivera joined Helix Forge precisely because the regulatory landscape for synthetic biology-based diagnostics is both complex and consequential. A diagnostic test that reaches clinical use through an appropriate regulatory pathway can change patient outcomes at scale. A diagnostic test that bypasses regulatory scrutiny and performs poorly in clinical use can harm patients and set back the entire field's credibility. Carlos's perspective on the FDA framework for diagnostics is not bureaucratic caution; it is recognition that the regulatory pathway is part of the engineering problem, and that designing a product for its regulatory pathway from the beginning is far more efficient than retrofitting regulatory compliance onto a product designed without that constraint.

The FDA's framework for in vitro diagnostics, which covers all synthetic biology-based diagnostic tests, essentially classifies devices into three risk tiers. Class I devices are low risk, generally well understood, and are either exempt from premarket review or subject only to general controls, such as labeling requirements. A simple pH test strip is Class I. Class II devices pose a moderate risk to patients and must be cleared through the 510(k) process, which requires demonstrating that the new device is substantially equivalent to a legally marketed predicate device in terms of intended use and technological characteristics. Most POC infectious disease diagnostics seek Class II clearance. Class III devices are the highest-risk category, encompassing tests intended to diagnose life-threatening conditions or whose results directly drive high-stakes clinical decisions, and they require Premarket Approval. This more rigorous standard demands clinical validation data demonstrating safety and effectiveness.

The distinction between laboratory-developed tests and commercially marketed test kits is a second important dimension of the regulatory landscape. A laboratory-developed test (LDT) is a diagnostic test designed, manufactured, and used within a single laboratory, typically a hospital or academic medical center clinical laboratory. Historically, the FDA has exercised enforcement discretion over LDTs, meaning it did not actively require premarket review or clearance for tests in this category, on the theory that single-laboratory tests posed limited public health risk and that laboratory professionals were capable of validating their own tests. This has allowed academic medical centers to deploy novel genetic tests, including CRISPR-based research assays, without formal FDA clearance. However, the FDA has been moving toward a more active oversight posture for LDTs since 2024, recognizing that many LDTs are effectively commercial products used across broad patient populations, and the distinction between an LDT and a commercially marketed kit has been narrowing in practical regulatory terms.

Diagram 9.12 - FDA In Vitro Diagnostic Regulatory Pathway Overview

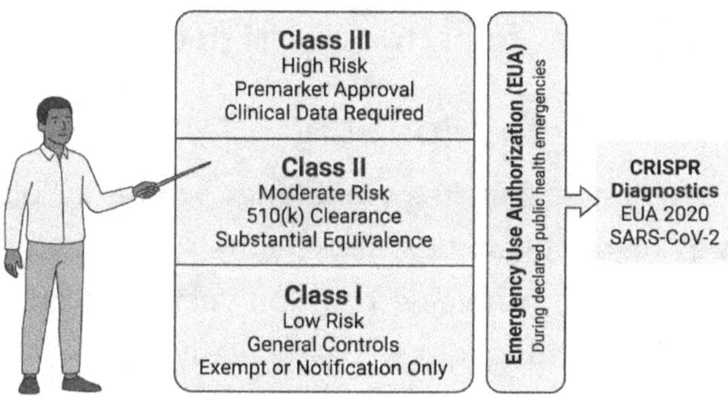

For Helix Forge and companies building CRISPR-based diagnostics, the Emergency Use Authorization pathway established during COVID-19 represents both a precedent and a cautionary note. The EUA pathway allows the FDA to authorize medical products for use during declared public health emergencies without requiring the same evidence base as full approval or clearance, balancing speed against the normal standards of rigor. The SHERLOCK-based SARS-CoV-2 test and multiple DETECTR-based tests received EUAs in 2020, establishing that the FDA could and would move quickly on CRISPR diagnostic platforms when the evidence of analytical performance was strong and the public health need was clear. But EUAs are temporary, conditional on the continuation of the declared emergency, and do not substitute for the long-term process of seeking full clearance or approval for a diagnostic platform intended for routine clinical use. In Carlos's framework, the Helix Forge team's regulatory strategy is to use EUA precedents as evidence of the FDA's familiarity with CRISPR diagnostic technology, while building the clinical validation dataset required for 510(k) clearance of the cancer biosensor platform through a prospective clinical study.

What This Means For You

If you are an engineer evaluating synthetic biology companies or opportunities, biosensors represent one of the clearest near-term value creation vectors in the field. The technical foundations, particularly CRISPR-based detection and cell-free paper biosensor platforms, are sufficiently mature that the engineering risk has shifted from whether these systems work to how well they work in deployment conditions and whether they can be manufactured at cost. The diagnostic market is large, the point-of-care segment is growing rapidly, and the programmability advantage of CRISPR diagnostics, the ability to redirect a detection platform to a new target by changing a twenty-nucleotide guide RNA, gives companies with robust platform technology a compounding advantage over time. The key technical questions to evaluate in a biosensor company are the limits of detection, the false-positive and false-negative rates in clinical samples (not just in controlled laboratory buffer conditions), and the regulatory pathway and its timeline.

If you are an entrepreneur building in this space, the most important strategic insight from this chapter is the platform-versus-product distinction. A company built around a single biosensor target is a product company with a limited addressable market and no compounding advantage. A company built around a biosensor platform, with demonstrated ability to redirect detection to new targets and deploy in point-of-care formats without specialized equipment, is a platform company with a large and growing addressable market and a technology moat that competitors must rebuild from scratch. The cell-free paper biosensor and CRISPR collateral cleavage platforms both have strong platform characteristics, and the companies that have invested in manufacturing scale, cold-chain-free deployment capability, and regulatory precedent will have durable advantages over later entrants.

If you work in policy, public health, or regulation, the biosensor landscape raises governance questions that deserve proactive attention. The deployment of whole-cell biosensors in environmental settings, even for beneficial applications like arsenic monitoring in drinking water, requires regulatory frameworks that did not exist when the technology was a laboratory curiosity. The revision of the FDA's LDT oversight policy affects millions of patients who rely on laboratory tests developed outside the commercial regulatory framework. The international harmonization of diagnostic approval standards, particularly for point-of-care tests deployed in low-income countries, determines whether the access benefits of inexpensive synthetic biology diagnostics actually reach the populations that need them most. These are engineering-adjacent governance questions, and the quality of the governance will depend on the quality of the technical understanding that policymakers bring to them.

For anyone thinking about where the next platform-scale opportunities in synthetic biology are concentrated, biosensors and diagnostics deserve more attention than they typically receive. The public imagination of synthetic biology tends toward the dramatic: CRISPR cures, lab-grown organs, microbes that eat pollution. Biosensors are less dramatic but in some ways more foundational, because they are the measurement layer that makes all the other applications work. Every new drug needs a companion diagnostic. Every engineered metabolic pathway needs a sensor to monitor it. Every environmental release of a biological agent needs a detection system that can confirm its behavior in the field. The field that builds biology that listens is building the infrastructure that all of synthetic biology runs on.

Takeaway

Biology can be engineered not just to make things but to sense them. A biosensor is a genetic circuit with an alarm-system architecture: a recognition element that detects the target molecule with specificity, a transducer that converts molecular recognition into a gene-expression event, and a readout that produces a measurable signal. The promoter-repressor system from Chapter 3, the same circuit architecture that underlies genetic logic gates and toggle switches, is the core detection mechanism for the vast majority of engineered biosensors. When that circuit is connected to a fluorescent reporter, a color-changing enzyme, or a CRISPR collateral cleavage cascade, it becomes an extraordinarily sensitive and precise detector.

CRISPR-based diagnostics, specifically SHERLOCK and DETECTR, have demonstrated that the molecular recognition precision of CRISPR guide RNAs can be used for detection, achieving attomolar sensitivity and lateral-flow readout, delivering laboratory-quality performance in a point-of-care format that requires no specialized equipment. The COVID-19 pandemic accelerated the regulatory precedent for these platforms, and the Emergency Use Authorizations granted to CRISPR-based SARS-CoV-2 tests in 2020 established the first formal regulatory recognition of CRISPR diagnostics in the United States. Cell-free biosensors built on freeze-dried genetic circuits extend this capability to cold-chain-free field deployment, removing the logistical barriers that have historically limited access to molecular diagnostics in low-resource settings.

Beyond medicine, biosensors are solving environmental monitoring and industrial fermentation problems that no other technology addresses with the same combination of sensitivity, specificity, and deployability. Whole-cell arsenic biosensors have been validated in field water samples in Bangladesh and Cambodia. Fermentation biosensors provide real-time data on internal state, accelerating the DBTL cycle in metabolic engineering. AND gate cancer biosensor circuits are approaching the specificity required for clinical liquid biopsy applications. In each case, the technology is the same core circuit architecture applied to a different context, with different recognition elements tuned to different target molecules.

The deepest point of this chapter is the one that connects biosensors to every other application in this book. The design-build-test-learn cycle is the engine of synthetic biology. The test step is what limits the engine's speed. Biosensors are the test step infrastructure, and every advance in biosensor sensitivity, specificity, and deployability directly accelerates every other part of the field. When Yuki's petri dish glows, and Priya says the circuit is clean, they are not just validating a diagnostic product. They are closing a feedback loop that makes the next design iteration possible. Biology that listens is biology that learns.

10 Biology as Planetary Engineer

Opening Scenario

The conference room at Helix Forge smelled of cold coffee and fresh anxiety. Carlos Rivera stood at the whiteboard with a briefing document he had spent three evenings writing. Behind him, a satellite photograph showed monitoring wells drilled into a patch of New Jersey landscape. Below the surface, invisible and essentially permanent, sat a plume of chlorinated solvents left behind by a dry-cleaning operation that had closed in 1987. The plume had been monitored for decades. It had barely moved.

Their potential partner company had spent four years developing an engineered bacterial consortium designed to degrade the solvents in place, converting them stepwise from trichloroethylene to harmless end products. The laboratory mesocosm trials looked remarkable: greater than 90% degradation within six weeks. The bacteria carried a genetic kill switch that would shut down the population if organisms drifted beyond the contamination plume. Carlos had reviewed the data three times, and the science was compelling.

"The moment we release a living, self-replicating organism into an open environment," Carlos said, "we have crossed a line that we cannot uncross. The question is not whether the science works. The question is who is responsible for the answer if it works in a way we did not expect." Priya tapped her pen against her notepad. Marcus studied the satellite photograph. Yuki had sketched the kill switch circuit on her scratch pad and was looking for the flaw she hoped she would not find. That question is what this chapter is about.

Why It Matters

The environmental problems synthetic biology can address are measurable and severe. More than 1,300 Superfund sites in the United States contain persistent chemical contamination that conventional approaches have spent decades failing to resolve fully. The global oceans contain an estimated 170 trillion pieces of plastic. Atmospheric carbon dioxide has reached concentrations not seen since before the advent of human civilization. Synthetic nitrogen fertilizer accounts for approximately 2% of the global energy supply.

These are engineering problems. Engineering problems have definable target states, measurable gaps, and design processes that can identify interventions. Living systems are already the most powerful environmental engineers on Earth: microorganisms have metabolized hydrocarbons, fixed nitrogen, and cycled carbon for billions of years. Cyanobacteria oxygenated Earth's atmosphere. Natural wetlands remove more nitrogen from agricultural runoff than any constructed treatment system.

Synthetic biology's contribution is not to replace natural biological processes but to augment them: to take what evolution prototyped and make it faster, more specific, more controllable, and more deployable. A bacterium that naturally degrades a hydrocarbon over six months can, with metabolic engineering, complete that task in six days. A nitrogen-fixing symbiosis restricted to legumes can be extended through engineering of the nif gene cluster to associate with wheat and rice. Getting this engineering right, including containment and governance, is one of the most consequential applied science challenges of this century.

Diagram 10.1 - Environmental Synthetic Biology Application Landscape

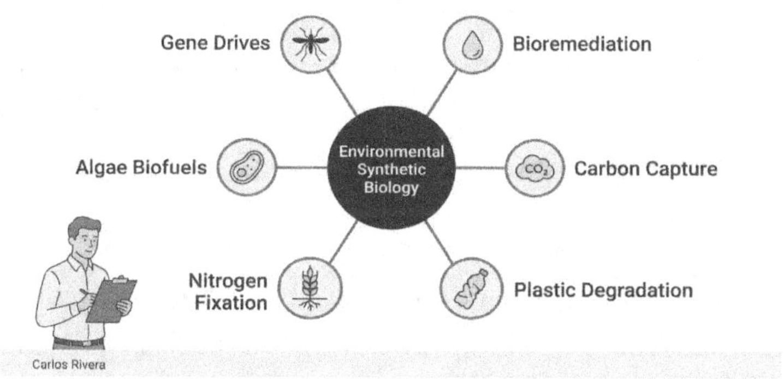

Bioremediation: The Biological Cleanup Crew

Bioremediation is the use of living organisms, most commonly bacteria, fungi, or algae, to metabolize, sequester, or transform environmental contaminants into less toxic forms. Many persistent contaminants are organic molecules, meaning they contain carbon, and organic carbon is food. Microorganisms have evolved to degrade almost any organic molecule, including ones humans have synthesized. The engineering challenge is getting the right organisms to the right place at the required rate and with the required specificity.

Practitioners distinguish three approaches. Natural attenuation relies on organisms already present to degrade contaminants without adding anything: measurable but typically slow, years to decades for persistent compounds. Biostimulation adds nutrients or growth factors to accelerate the growth of indigenous microorganisms; if nitrogen or phosphorus limits degradation, adding those nutrients can substantially increase degradation rates. Bioaugmentation, the synthetic biology approach, adds engineered or specifically selected organisms to provide metabolic capabilities the indigenous community lacks or to accelerate degradation beyond what biostimulation achieves.

Metabolic engineering can optimize degradation pathways in hydrocarbon-degrading bacteria, increasing enzyme expression and removing metabolic bottlenecks. Genetic circuit engineering can make degradation conditional: bacteria produce maximum enzyme levels only when the target contaminant is present, reducing metabolic cost when concentrations are low. This sensing-and-responding design is the same AND gate logic pattern described in Chapter 5, applied here to an environmental context.

The chlorinated solvent case from the opening scenario illustrates the complexity. Trichloroethylene and perchloroethylene, widespread industrial contaminants, can be degraded by bacteria in the genus Dehalococcoides through reductive dechlorination, a process in which the bacteria breathe the chlorinated compound, as other organisms breathe oxygen. Dehalococcoides is strictly anaerobic, requires specific cofactors including vitamin B12, and often depends on hydrogen produced by companion bacteria in a syntrophic community. Effective deployment requires engineering the whole metabolic community, not just the target organism.

Diagram 10.2 - Three Bioremediation Strategies Compared

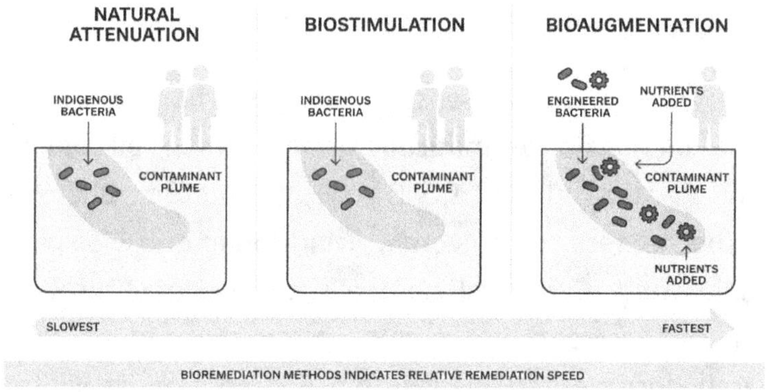

Diagram 10.3 - Reductive Dechlorination Pathway in Engineered Bacteria

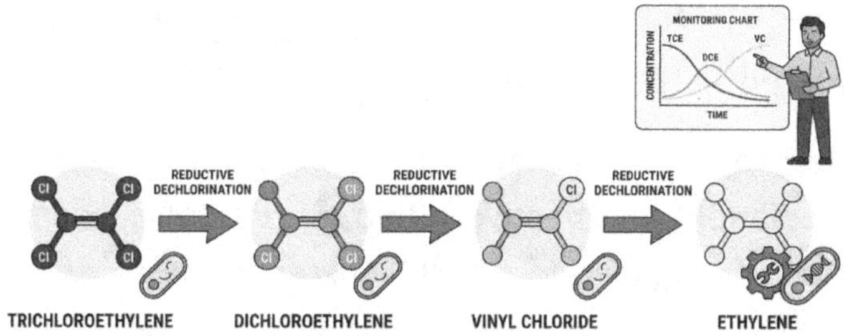

Engineered Oil-Eating Bacteria: Lessons from Deepwater Horizon

On April 20, 2010, the Deepwater Horizon drilling platform exploded in the Gulf of Mexico, triggering the largest accidental marine oil spill in history. Before the well was capped 87 days later, approximately 4.9 million barrels of crude oil had been released. The biological response triggered became one of the most thoroughly documented natural bioremediation events ever studied.

Within weeks, populations of hydrocarbon-degrading bacteria increased dramatically in the deep oil plume suspended at depths of 1,000 to 1,300 meters. Bacteria from the genera Alcanivorax, Marinobacter, Oleispira, Colwellia, and Cycloclasticus collectively constituted a natural bioaugmentation event on an enormous scale. Research documented measurable degradation of lighter alkane and monoaromatic fractions over weeks to months, while heavier polycyclic aromatic hydrocarbons persisted. At multiple sampling sites, the rate-limiting factor for bacterial degradation was not organism availability but the supply of nitrogen and phosphorus.

The lesson of synthetic biology is that natural bioremediation was effective within specific limits, and that systematic engineering could extend those limits. Engineered bacteria that co-optimize hydrocarbon degradation with internal nutrient cycling could operate more robustly in nutrient-limited marine environments. Enhanced expression of degradation enzymes for the most persistent heavy polycyclic aromatic hydrocarbons would substantially improve outcomes for the most toxic oil components.

Open-environment deployment of purpose-built synthetic biology organisms for oil spill remediation remains a research objective, constrained by both the engineering challenge and the regulatory framework. What Deepwater Horizon provided was an exceptionally detailed natural experiment: which fractions degrade preferentially, what nutrient conditions constrain degradation, and how quickly natural populations recover. That dataset directly informs current metabolic engineering targets.

Diagram 10.4 - Natural vs. Engineered Hydrocarbon Degradation in Marine Environments

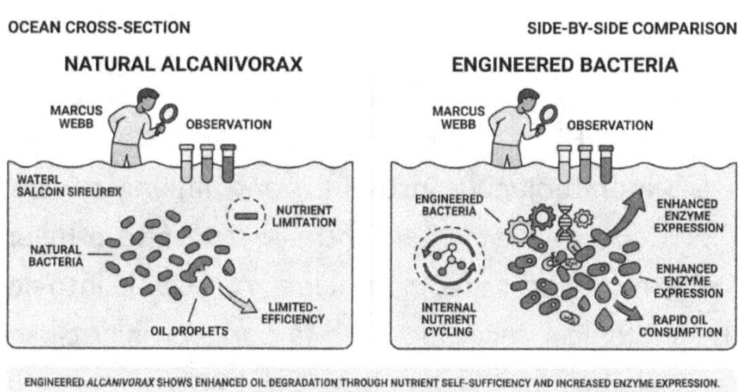

Plastic-Degrading Enzymes: PETase and Enzymatic Recycling

Plastic pollution is fundamentally different from a hydrocarbon spill. Oil spills are localized in space and time.

Plastic pollution is cumulative and effectively global: the estimated 8 million metric tons of plastic entering the oceans each year adds to a stock that has been building since the 1950s. The chemical stability that makes plastics useful for packaging and textiles is precisely what makes them persistent environmental contaminants.

In 2016, Japanese researchers discovered Ideonella sakaiensis, a bacterium isolated from a plastic-sorting facility that could degrade PET, the polyethylene terephthalate plastic used in beverage bottles and polyester fibers. The bacterium produced an enzyme they named PETase, for PET-degrading enzyme, that broke the ester bonds linking PET monomers into polymer chains. PET is one of the world's most widely produced plastics, and Ideonella sakaiensis could use it as its primary carbon source, making this discovery directly relevant to plastic waste management.

PETase cleaves PET by hydrolyzing ester bonds: the enzyme inserts a water molecule into the bond linking adjacent monomer units, releasing terephthalic acid and ethylene glycol. Both monomers are, in principle, recyclable into new PET. The biological recycling loop is conceptually closed. The practical challenge is speed: natural PETase operating at room temperature works far too slowly for industrial plastic processing volumes.

Researchers at the National Renewable Energy Laboratory, working with the University of Portsmouth, examined PETase's crystal structure and introduced amino acid substitutions predicted to improve PET binding and catalytic efficiency, yielding a variant with approximately 20% greater activity. The same group later developed FAST-PETase, a fusion enzyme combining PETase with MHETase, a second enzyme that converts an intermediate degradation product into the final recyclable monomer. FAST-PETase operates at room temperature with substantially higher overall efficiency than wild-type PETase.

Even so, enzymatic PET degradation currently takes days to weeks per batch, while mechanical and chemical recycling operate in hours. The engineering pathway to scale runs through protein engineering to increase thermal stability, immobilized enzyme systems in which the enzyme is bound to a solid support and reused across many batches, and metabolic engineering to enable bacteria to both degrade PET and metabolize the resulting monomers as a carbon source. Each step has proof of concept at laboratory scale; commercial viability is an optimization problem rather than a scientific uncertainty.

Diagram 10.5 - PETase Enzyme Cleaving a PET Polymer Chain

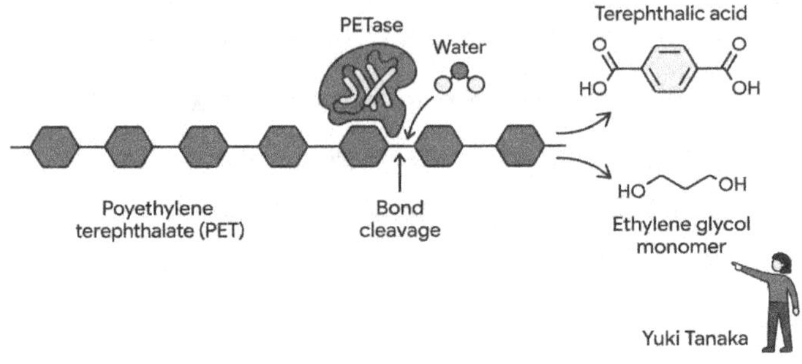

Diagram 10.6 - Engineering Pathway to Scalable Enzymatic PET Recycling

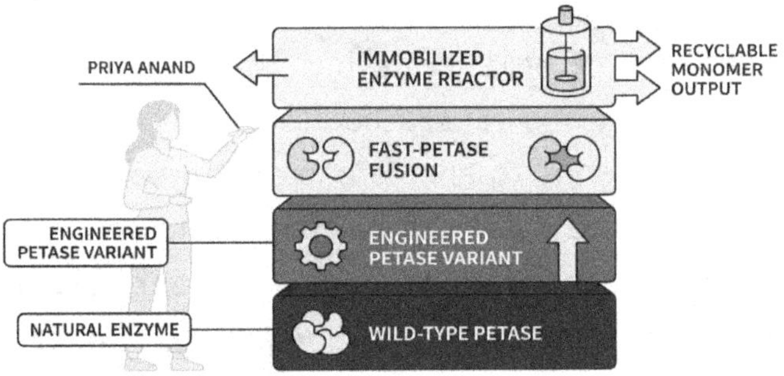

Engineered Cyanobacteria: Making Photosynthesis Work Harder

Cyanobacteria are among the oldest and most consequential organisms in Earth's history. These single-celled photosynthetic bacteria, appearing approximately 2.7 billion years ago, transformed Earth's atmosphere from one devoid of oxygen into the oxygen-rich environment all complex life now depends on. They did this through photosynthesis alone: capturing light energy, pulling carbon dioxide from the atmosphere, and releasing oxygen as a byproduct. Modern cyanobacteria still perform this carbon fixation at a planetary scale.

The primary carbon-fixing enzyme in most photosynthetic organisms is RuBisCO, short for ribulose-1,5-bisphosphate carboxylase/oxygenase. RuBisCO processes only about 3 carbon dioxide molecules per second and cannot perfectly distinguish between carbon dioxide and oxygen. In high-oxygen environments, it sometimes incorporates oxygen instead of carbon dioxide, triggering a wasteful side reaction called photorespiration that releases carbon that was just fixed. Most crop plants achieve only one to two percent of the theoretical maximum photosynthetic efficiency under field conditions.

Cyanobacteria have partially solved the photorespiration problem through a structural innovation called the carboxysome, a protein-shell organelle that concentrates carbon dioxide around RuBisCO, reducing competition from oxygen. This carbon-concentrating mechanism (CCM) is why cyanobacteria grow productively in environments where CO2 would otherwise limit photosynthesis. Synthetic biologists have been working to engineer the cyanobacterial CCM into crop plants, where it could reduce photorespiration and substantially increase carbon fixation efficiency.

Diagram 10.7 - Engineered Cyanobacteria Carbon Capture System

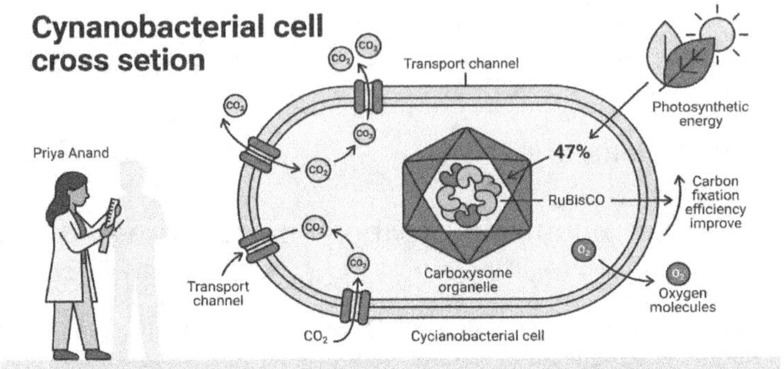

Priya Anand of Ccianobacterial cell in RuBisCO enzyme and clumonaterial cell

The RIPE project (Realizing Increased Photosynthetic Efficiency), an international research collaboration, demonstrated that introducing components of the cyanobacterial carbon-concentrating mechanism into tobacco model plants increases biomass accumulation by approximately forty percent under field conditions. Translating this to food crops is the next phase. Carboxysomes require the coordinated expression of at least eight to twelve structural proteins, and integrating them into a plant chloroplast requires those proteins to assemble correctly in the right organelle. The mechanistic pathway is now understood well enough that systematic engineering is actively proceeding.

Researchers at the Max Planck Institute for Terrestrial Microbiology designed a synthetic carbon fixation cycle called the CETCH cycle, demonstrated in a cell-free system, that operates approximately five times more efficiently than the natural Calvin cycle in terms of ATP consumed per carbon fixed. Implementing this in a living organism is a harder engineering problem. Still, the thermodynamic data establishes a compelling target for metabolic engineers and a clear pathway to substantially improved carbon capture at scale.

Diagram 10.8 - Photosynthetic Efficiency Comparison Across Systems

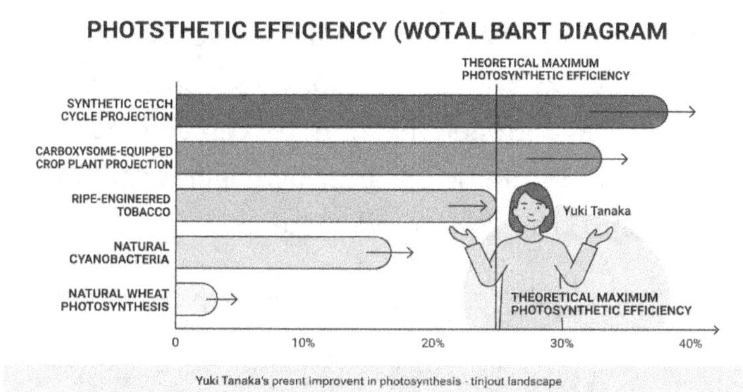

Engineering Nitrogen Fixation: Feeding the World with Less Chemistry

Nitrogen is the most abundant gas in Earth's atmosphere at approximately 78 percent, yet it is one of the most common limiting nutrients for plant growth. Atmospheric nitrogen is two atoms bonded in a triple bond of exceptional stability that most organisms cannot break. Biological nitrogen fixation occurs in nature primarily by Rhizobium and related bacteria that form symbiotic relationships with legume plants within root nodules, using an enzyme complex called nitrogenase to convert atmospheric nitrogen into ammonia. The plant provides carbon and a low-oxygen microenvironment; nitrogenase is irreversibly destroyed by oxygen.

The industrial replacement for biological nitrogen fixation is the Haber-Bosch process, which converts atmospheric nitrogen to ammonia under extreme heat and pressure. It enables intensive agriculture for roughly half the global population but consumes one to two percent of the world's total energy supply. Synthetic biology's approach is to extend biological nitrogen fixation to cereal crops that currently require synthetic fertilizer by engineering the nif gene cluster into crop-associated bacteria.

Diagram 10.9 - Biological Nitrogen Fixation Extended to Cereal Crops

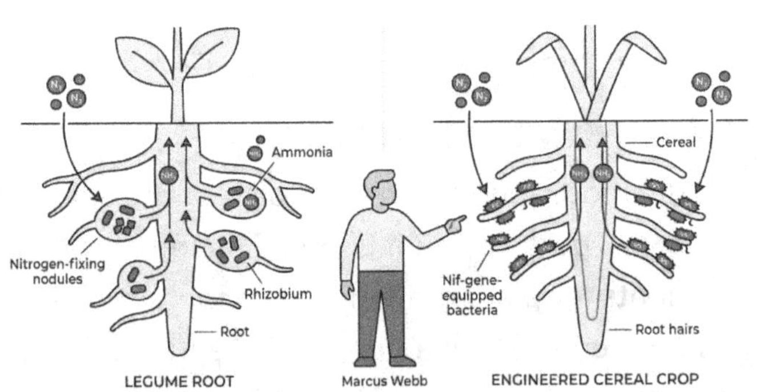

ENGINEERED NITROGEN FIXATION IN CEREAL CROPS FOR SUSTAINABLE AGRICULTURE

The engineering challenge is that nitrogenase is oxygen-sensitive: even brief exposure permanently destroys its activity. Recreating the low-oxygen nodule environment for bacteria colonizing cereal root surfaces is not yet commercially solved. Pivot Bio has engineered soil bacteria to fix more nitrogen than wild-type counterparts on cereal crop roots. Joyn Bio develops nitrogen-fixing microbes for specific cereal varieties and soil environments. Azotic Technologies offers a nitrogen-fixing bacterium that colonizes plant tissues, including cereals. A twenty to thirty percent reduction in synthetic nitrogen requirements for cereal crops globally would meaningfully reduce agricultural emissions and input costs.

Diagram 10.10 - Algae Biofuel Production: Natural vs. Engineered Secretion Approach

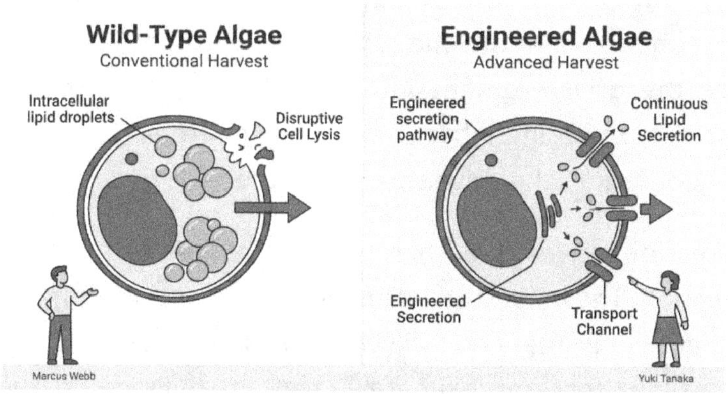

Gene Drives: Engineering Populations at Scale

Every tool described so far involves engineering microorganisms or enzymes to perform useful chemistry in the environment. Gene drives are a fundamentally different category: heritable genetic elements that spread through a wild animal population, potentially affecting every individual across a wide geographic area. A gene drive biases inheritance so that it passes to offspring at a higher rate than the standard fifty percent predicted by Mendelian genetics, allowing any linked trait to spread through an entire wild population.

The practical demonstration came in 2015, when Ethan Bier and Valentino Gantz showed that CRISPR-based gene drives could propagate through Drosophila fruit fly populations at rates approaching 100% inheritance. In a standard CRISPR gene drive, the Cas9 machinery and guide RNA are encoded at the target site in the genome. When a drive organism mates with a wild-type individual, Cas9 cuts the corresponding site on the wild-type chromosome and copies the drive element in through homology-directed repair. The offspring inherits two copies rather than one. Each generation, the drive spreads further.

Suppression drives aim to reduce or eliminate a target population. The most studied application targets Anopheles gambiae, the primary malaria vector in sub-Saharan Africa, responsible for approximately half a million deaths annually. The Target Malaria consortium has spent over a decade developing gene drive constructs in contained laboratory populations of Anopheles gambiae. Modification drives spread a desirable trait without eliminating the population: making mosquitoes refractory to Plasmodium, the malaria parasite, would eliminate disease transmission without eliminating the mosquito, a less ecologically disruptive intervention.

Gene drives for invasive species management present additional applications. Rats and mice introduced to island ecosystems have driven dozens of seabird species toward extinction. Conventional rodent eradication with poison baiting carries non-target toxicity risks at large scales. A gene drive that suppresses invasive rodent populations in island ecosystems could allow native seabird populations to recover without repeated poison applications. New Zealand's Predator Free 2050 initiative has explored gene drive approaches alongside conventional trapping.

Diagram 10.11 - CRISPR Gene Drive Propagation Through a Mosquito Population

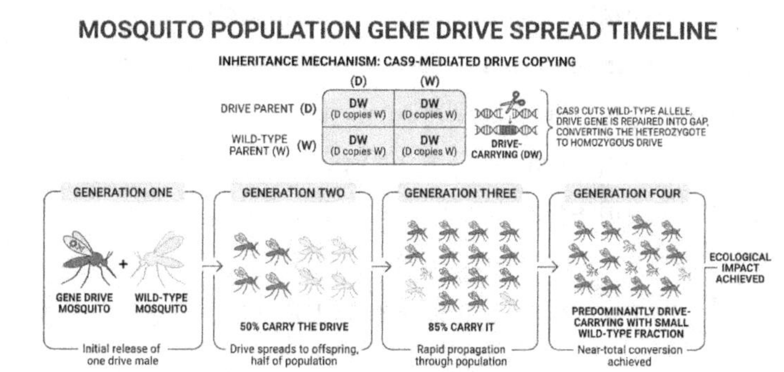

MOSQUITO POPULATION GENE DRIVE SPREAD TIMELINE

The technical limitations of current gene drives are real. Any mutation disrupting the drive mechanism creates a resistance allele that spreads in parallel, eventually reducing the drive's effectiveness, a problem documented in laboratory Anopheles gambiae populations. More sophisticated architectures address it: split drives separate the Cas9 and guide RNA onto different chromosomes, limiting persistence after introduction. Daisy-chain drives limit propagation to a defined number of generations. Self-limiting drives diminish in frequency after a set number of generations.

Biocontainment and Kill Switches: Engineering the Off Switch

Every environmental application in this chapter involves organisms operating outside a contained bioreactor. Bacteria used for bioremediation are released into contaminated soil. Nitrogen-fixing bacteria colonize open-field plant roots. Cyanobacteria at scale would operate in open ponds or the ocean. Gene drives are designed to propagate through wild populations. In each case, Carlos's question applies: once a self-replicating organism has been released into an open environment, how do you take it back? The honest answer is that you cannot, for the most part. Biocontainment, the design of genetic systems that limit the survival, spread, and persistence of organisms under defined conditions, addresses this challenge directly.

A kill switch, sometimes called a genetic containment circuit, is a synthetic gene circuit that causes cell death when the organism encounters conditions outside its intended deployment environment. The concept is analogous to a circuit breaker: a sensor linked to an effector that terminates activity when an out-of-bounds condition is detected. Kill switch designs fall into three main categories based on the sensing mechanism they use.

Auxotrophic kill switches engineer the organism to require a synthetic molecule, typically a non-natural amino acid not found in nature, for survival. A critical cellular component is made non-functional unless the synthetic amino acid is incorporated at a specific sequence position. In the deployment environment, the synthetic amino acid is supplied. Outside it, the organism cannot make the critical protein and dies. Engineered Escherichia coli strains with synthetic amino acid dependencies showed essentially zero survival in environments lacking the supplement.

Temperature-sensitive kill switches program cell death outside a defined temperature range, making the organism viable only within the thermal window of its deployment site. Quorum-sensing kill switches use population density as the signal for containment. If the organism's population density falls below the threshold expected at the deployment site, indicating it has drifted away from the dense local population, a low-density signal triggers cell death. This approach is particularly relevant for soil bioremediation, where the engineered organism should persist in the contamination plume but not spread into adjacent clean soil.

Diagram 10.12 - Kill Switch Genetic Circuit Architecture

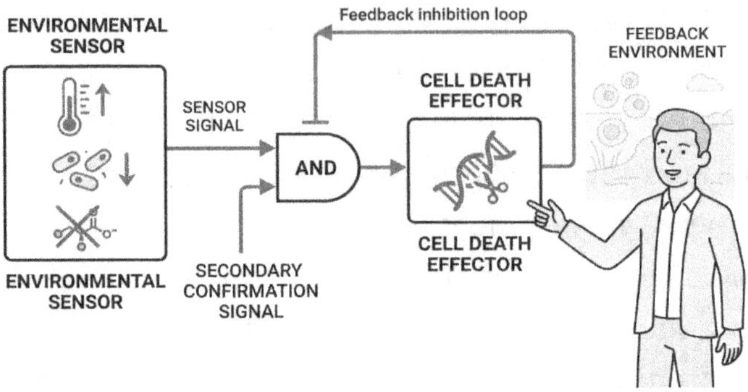

Kill switches are necessary but not sufficient for open-environment release decisions. A population of billions of bacteria under strong selection will generate, through random mutation, individuals in which the kill switch has been disabled. Because the kill switch represents a metabolic cost, escape mutants often have a growth advantage and spread. The field's response is layered biocontainment: combining multiple independent mechanisms so that escape requires simultaneously disabling each one. Layered biocontainment, combined with physical containment and regulatory monitoring, is the current best practice.

In the United States, regulatory authority over environmental releases is divided among the EPA (microbial commercial applications under TSCA, microbial pesticides under FIFRA), the USDA (engineered organisms that could pose as plant pests), and the FDA (food-contact applications). Internationally, the Cartagena Protocol on Biosafety governs the transboundary movement of living modified organisms. The regulatory gap Carlos's briefing identified is real: the framework was designed for first-generation agricultural GMOs and lacks clear guidelines for synthetic biology organisms with multiple engineered traits, integrated kill switches, and self-limiting designs.

What This Means For You

For the engineer, environmental synthetic biology is a precision discipline with measurable performance targets, well-defined failure modes, and a design-build-test-learn cycle operating in increasingly realistic conditions. Bioremediation engineers optimize metabolic flux, protein stability, and sensing-circuit responsiveness with the same systematic methodology that semiconductor engineers apply to transistor design. The question is: where could biological components, engineered enzymes, or microbial consortia improve on the abiotic approaches you currently use?

For the entrepreneur, environmental synthetic biology is at a stage comparable to where consumer synthetic biology was roughly a decade ago: the science is ahead of the business models, but enabling technologies are reaching commercial viability. PETase-based plastic recycling is one to two engineering generations from industrial-scale feasibility. Nitrogen-fixing microbial products are already commercially available for row crops. Go-to-market timelines are longer than for contained biomanufacturing because regulatory approval for environmental release requires more extensive safety data.

For the policy professional, the central regulatory challenge is that the current framework was built for first-generation GMOs with single introduced traits in agricultural containment. Synthetic biology organisms for environmental applications often have multiple engineered traits, function outside containment, and have effects that propagate over long timescales. The EPA's 2020 synthetic biology guidance and the National Academies reports on genetically engineered organisms are the current authoritative starting points.

For the curious professional, the most important takeaway is the distinction between containment in principle and containment in practice. Every environmental application here has a technical biocontainment component, a kill switch, a nutritional dependency, or a self-limiting genetic design. These mechanisms provide risk reduction, not absolute risk elimination. The regulatory question is how much risk reduction is sufficient for a given application in a given environment. That framing allows intelligent engagement with the governance debates that Chapter 11 addresses in full.

Takeaway

The problems that environmental synthetic biology is designed to address are real and measurable. Chlorinated solvent plumes have persisted for forty years in industrial groundwater. A global ocean carrying 170 trillion pieces of plastic. Atmospheric carbon dioxide is rising faster than any natural feedback mechanism can match. Synthetic nitrogen fertilizer production accounts for a significant fraction of global energy consumption. These are engineering failures: cases where human industrial activity has released consequences into natural systems that natural systems alone cannot resolve at the required speed.

The tools are more powerful than most people outside the field realize, and more limited than some advocates have claimed. PETase can degrade plastic, but not yet at an industrial scale. Engineered bacteria can improve on natural attenuation rates, but have not been deployed commercially in open environments. Carboxysome engineering increases crop biomass by 40% under controlled conditions but faces challenges in field translation. Gene drives face resistance evolution, which limits their long-term effectiveness in wild populations. In every case, the distance between laboratory demonstration and open-environment deployment is significant.

What Carlos's briefing captured precisely is that the limiting factor for environmental synthetic biology is no longer scientific feasibility. It is the development of governance frameworks, regulatory standards, monitoring protocols, and public engagement processes that support responsible environmental release decisions. Kill switches are necessary but not sufficient. Regulatory frameworks designed for first-generation GMOs are necessary but not sufficient. The field needs institutional capacity to make environmental release decisions with explicit acknowledgment of uncertainty and genuine accountability for outcomes.

Biology has been engineering planetary systems for 3.8 billion years. Bacteria fixed the nitrogen in your proteins. Cyanobacteria produced the oxygen in your lungs. The fossil fuels that powered the Industrial Revolution were accumulated from the carbon fixation of ancient marine organisms. Synthetic biology brings human design intentionality to processes that have always been fundamentally biological. That intentionality, applied carefully and well governed, is one of the most powerful tools available to address the environmental consequences of the past two centuries. Chapter 11 takes up the ethical dimensions of that intentionality in full.

11 The Ethics of Engineering Life

Opening Scenario

The meeting was Carlos Rivera's idea. The email had gone out the previous night: all hands, conference room, nine in the morning. When the Helix Forge team filed in, Carlos was already standing at the whiteboard with a printed NIH letter in one hand and a highlighter in the other. The letter flagged a biosensor manuscript co-authored by one of Helix Forge's researchers under the NIH Dual Use Research of Concern (DURC) policy. The reviewers noted that the tool, designed to detect pathogen virulence markers at low concentrations, could, in principle, inform efforts to engineer a pathogen that expressed those markers more reliably. The science was sound. The dual-use inference was real.

Carlos set the letter on the table. 'The science is not the question,' he said. 'The line between a diagnostic tool that detects a pathogen and a design guide for engineering one is not always visible from inside the lab. Our job is to know where that line is before we submit.' Priya asked: 'What does flagged mean in practice?' Carlos answered: The Institutional Biosafety Committee at the partner university would review the full protocol. The NSABB might weigh in. Publication could be delayed, or methods redacted. Marcus looked at the letter. 'So a paper about detecting a threat could be held up because it might help someone build the threat.' Carlos nodded. 'That is the DURC problem in one sentence. Welcome to bioethics.'

The rest of that meeting became the foundation for Helix Forge's formal responsible innovation protocol. Carlos walked the team through the DURC review process, then turned to the broader landscape: germline editing controversies, the regulatory patchwork of FDA, EPA, and USDA authorities, and the equity problem of who actually benefits from the field's most advanced therapeutics. By the end, the team had a shared vocabulary for questions that engineers in synthetic biology cannot afford to treat as someone else's department.

Why It Matters

Ethics in synthetic biology is not a chapter at the end of the textbook that the professor skips when the semester runs short. It is a design parameter, as concrete and consequential as titer, yield, or regulatory pathway. Every synthetic biology project that reaches the real world has passed through institutional, regulatory, and ethical filters, and the quality of those filters shapes whether the field's promise is realized safely and equitably or creates new categories of harm.

The stakes are genuine on both sides of every question this chapter covers. Gain-of-function research on dangerous pathogens has produced knowledge that informs vaccine design and pandemic preparedness; it has also, in the case of H5N1 influenza, produced a laboratory-generated, airborne-transmissible strain of the virus with an estimated case-fatality rate of nearly 60 percent. CRISPR tools that could eliminate heritable diseases were used by He Jiankui in 2018 to edit human embryos without adequate scientific justification or regulatory oversight. The bioremediation tools being developed to clean contaminated environments are primarily built by companies in wealthy countries for communities that had no voice in the risk calculations.

Ethical judgment about synthetic biology is only as good as the technical understanding underneath it. When the science is fuzzy, the ethics become a set of competing intuitions. When the science is clear, the ethical questions become tractable and specific, even when the answers remain contested. The reader who understands the biology can engage the ethics with the precision the questions deserve.

Diagram 11.1 - The Dual-Use Inference Chain

Dual-Use Research of Concern: The Foundational Governance Challenge

Dual-use research of concern, DURC, is research conducted for legitimate scientific purposes that could be misapplied to pose a biological threat with mass casualty potential. Under current US policy, research involving any of fifteen listed select agents triggers DURC review if it meets one of seven criteria: enhancing a pathogen's harmful consequences; disrupting immunity or vaccination effectiveness; increasing pathogen resistance to treatment; increasing human-to-human transmissibility; increasing animal-to-human transmissibility; enhancing evasion of diagnostic detection; or enabling weaponization of biological agents. These criteria were written in direct response to the H5N1 controversy of 2011 and 2012.

Synthetic biology makes the DURC problem structurally harder in two ways. First, it has democratized capability. DNA synthesis costs have dropped from roughly ten dollars per base pair in 2000 to fractions of a cent today. Experiments that once required major institutional infrastructure are now accessible to small teams. The barrier that confined dual-use capability to well-resourced state actors no longer exists in the same form. Second, synthetic biology's modularity means that the same standardized parts, promoters, ribosome binding sites, and genetic circuits that accelerate beneficial applications also accelerate reasoning about assembling pathogen-relevant functions from components.

Diagram 11.2 - DURC Review Trigger Criteria

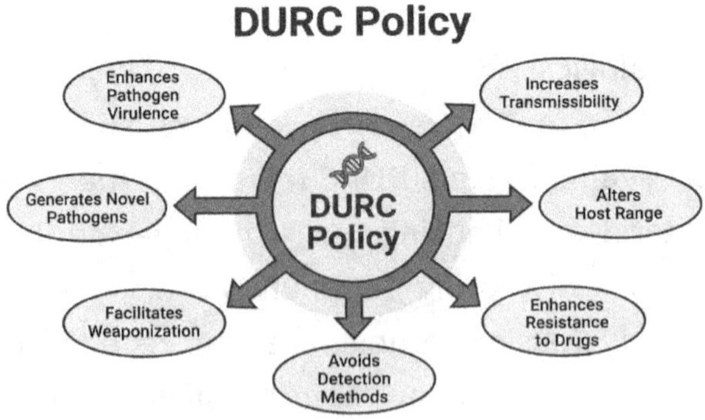

The DURC review process operates at two levels. Institutionally, every federally funded research organization must maintain an Institutional Biosafety Committee, or IBC, that screens proposals against DURC criteria before federal submission. The IBC reviews protocols, assesses dual-use risk, and may require modifications to experimental design; IBC quality varies across institutions and is not consistently applied everywhere. At the federal level, the NIH DURC Policy of 2012 requires funding agencies to review flagged research, and the NSABB handles the most sensitive cases. NSABB recommendations are advisory, not binding, but carry substantial weight with journals and institutions.

The publication debate is where the governance structure faces its sharpest tension. Science operates on a norm of openness: methods, data, and results are published in sufficient detail to allow independent replication. Biosecurity governance operates on a competing norm: information with high potential for misuse should be restricted. These norms are genuinely in conflict. The scientific community's openness norm is not carelessness; it is what makes science self-correcting and trustworthy. The security community's restriction norm is not censorship; it is recognition that some information, if released to the wrong parties, could cause irreversible harm. The H5N1 controversy exposed this conflict in real time, and it remains unresolved.

Diagram 11.3 - Institutional and Federal DURC Review Levels

Levels of Review for Dual-use Research of Concern (DURC)

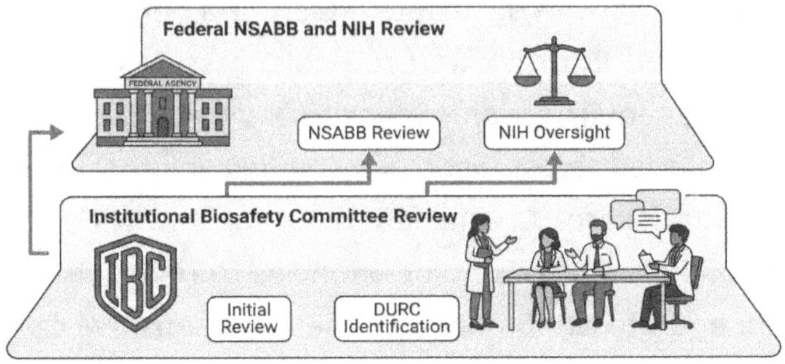

Gain-of-Function Research and the H5N1 Controversy

Gain-of-function research, GOF, refers to experiments that confer on a pathogen a new or enhanced property: transmissibility, virulence, host range, treatment resistance, or immune evasion. The scientific rationale is legitimate: understanding how a pathogen might acquire pandemic potential allows researchers to design vaccines and surveillance systems before a natural variant emerges. The risk is equally real: producing an enhanced pathogen in a laboratory creates it, and the history of laboratory accidents involving dangerous organisms provides no basis for assuming that containment is always guaranteed.

The controversy that made GOF a public governance problem began in 2011. Two independent research groups, one led by Ron Fouchier at Erasmus Medical Center and the other by Yoshihiro Kawaoka at the University of Wisconsin-Madison, independently created H5N1 influenza strains that were transmissible between ferrets via respiratory droplets. Ferret respiratory transmission is the standard predictive model for human-to-human influenza spread. H5N1 in its natural form has an estimated case-fatality rate of about 60 percent in confirmed human cases; it does not transmit efficiently between humans. The laboratory strains did transmit by the respiratory route. Both groups submitted their results for publication in late 2011.

Diagram 11.4 - H5N1 Gain-of-Function Timeline

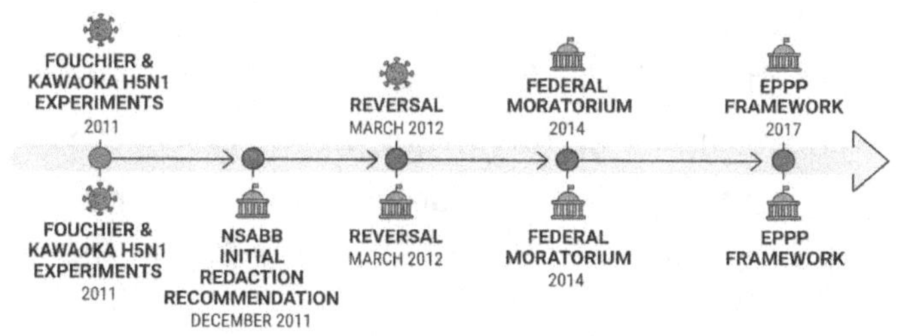

Chart significant risk events and governance responses regarding gain-of-function research

The NSABB recommended in December 2011 that both journals publish redacted versions, describing the findings but withholding the specific methods that would allow replication. The recommendation was unprecedented and immediately contested. Arguments against redaction included: the methods were necessary for independent scientific evaluation; restricting the papers would not prevent a determined state actor from replicating the work; and the benefits of full publication to vaccine developers and surveillance systems outweighed the risks. The NSABB reversed its recommendation in March 2012 after reviewing additional information from the research teams. Both papers were published in 2012 with full methods.

The US government responded with a series of policy steps. In 2014, the Obama administration announced a moratorium on federal funding for new GOF experiments with influenza, MERS, and SARS that could enhance transmissibility or pathogenicity. In 2017, it was replaced by a framework governing enhanced potential pandemic pathogen research (ePPP), subjecting proposed work to multi-agency pre-funding review. The honest assessment is that the ePPP framework is better than what preceded it, but remains incomplete: the definition of GOF research is inconsistently applied, the framework binds only to federally funded US research, and international coordination through the BWC and WHO lacks enforcement mechanisms.

Human Germline Editing and the He Jiankui Case

The somatic-versus-germline distinction is the most consequential technical boundary in the ethics of engineering life. Somatic cells are non-reproductive body cells: liver cells, T cells, skin cells. An edit to a somatic cell affects only that individual. CAR-T cell therapy, the most commercially advanced CRISPR application, is a form of somatic editing: the patient's T cells are edited outside the body and reinfused. If the patient has children, those children inherit nothing. The modification is contained within one lifetime. Germline edits are heritable: they pass to every cell in the resulting individual and, if that individual reproduces, to all subsequent descendants. Germline editing means editing the human evolutionary lineage.

The scientific community held an informal but broadly respected consensus against human germline editing long before CRISPR made it technically practical. The consensus rested on three grounds: the irreversibility of heritable changes; the risk that off-target edits at unintended genomic locations would propagate through the germline; and the absence of any therapeutic justification strong enough to outweigh those risks, because somatic therapy was available for every condition for which germline editing had been proposed. None of that changed in 2018. What changed was that a researcher in China acted anyway.

Diagram 11.5 - Somatic Versus Germline Editing: Heritability Comparison

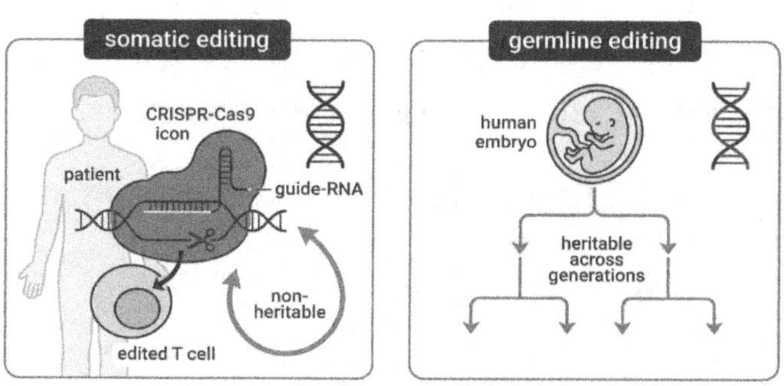

Captortion: presiaffect offspring, onour elect ation trars

In November 2018, He Jiankui announced at the Second International Summit on Human Genome Editing in Hong

Kong that he had used CRISPR to edit the germline of human embryos that had been implanted, resulting in twin girls. The girls had been given a designed deletion in the CCR5 gene, a co-receptor that HIV uses to enter certain immune cells. A naturally occurring deletion variant of CCR5 confers high resistance to HIV in carriers of two copies. His stated rationale was to protect the twins from HIV, as their father was HIV positive.

The scientific and ethical objections were immediate and unequivocal on four grounds. The therapeutic justification was inadequate: the father's HIV status did not put the embryos at meaningful risk of infection, and standard antiretroviral protocols for perinatal transmission prevention were available. The consent process was deficient: the couples were potentially vulnerable to coercive framing, and the materials minimized the experimental nature and risks. The off-target risk assessment was insufficient to establish safety for germline use. He had obtained no approval from any regulatory body with jurisdiction over human germline research.

Diagram 11.6 - He Jiankui Case: Four Governance Failures

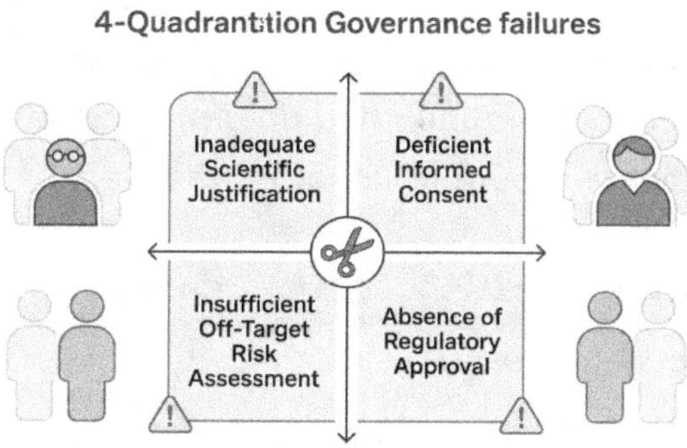

He Jiankui was convicted of illegal medical practice by a Chinese court in December 2019 and sentenced to three years in prison. The scientific community's response was unified: this was a violation of standards repeatedly articulated by international bodies, not a disagreement at a contested frontier. The International Commission on the Clinical Use of Human Germline Genome Editing published a 2020 framework with preconditions for responsible clinical use: reliable editing without off-target effects, a compelling medical indication with no reasonable alternative, verifiable patient selection criteria, a robust oversight system, and broad societal consensus. None have been met.

What the He Jiankui case exposed was not primarily a gap in Chinese law, though those gaps existed. It exposed the absence of operational enforcement across national jurisdictions. The consensus against heritable human genome editing was real and well-articulated before He acted; it had no enforcement mechanism. International advisory bodies can issue guidance but cannot compel compliance. A sufficiently motivated researcher in a jurisdiction with inadequate oversight could cross the line the international community had drawn, and the tools for preventing it were reputational rather than legal.

Access and Equity: Who Benefits, Who Bears the Risk

The equity dimensions of synthetic biology are structural, not incidental. They arise from who funds the research, where the biofoundries are built, who holds the patents, who serves on regulatory bodies, and what the commercial incentive structure rewards. Understanding equity in synthetic biology means examining the actual distribution of benefits and risks, not stated intentions.

The most commercially advanced synthetic biology therapeutics are among the most expensive treatments in the history of medicine. CAR-T cell therapies for blood cancers carry list prices of 400,000 to 500,000 US dollars per treatment course; gene therapies using CRISPR or related tools have carried prices of one million to three million dollars per patient. These prices reflect genuine costs: manufacturing personalized cell therapies at a clinical scale is extraordinarily expensive. The consequence is that these treatments are accessible only to patients in well-resourced healthcare systems, excluding patients in low-income countries and many in wealthy countries without adequate coverage.

Diagram 11.7 - Synthetic Biology Benefit and Risk Distribution by Region

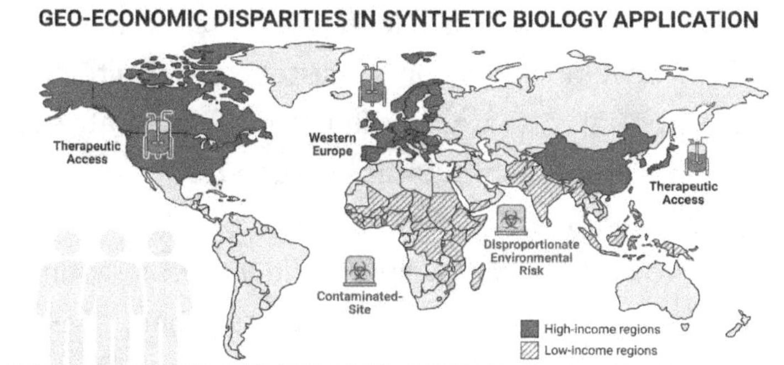

Caption: Geographical and economic ratitorrs application distraut to synthetic biology retrepens his con:miic risk..

On the risk side, synthetic biology applications that involve environmental release pose risks borne disproportionately by communities with little role in designing or approving them. The communities most in need of bioremediation, because they carry the highest burden of legacy chemical contamination and heavy metal exposure, are frequently low-income communities globally. Those same communities are typically underrepresented on the regulatory bodies that review environmental release applications. The pattern is consistent: technologies designed primarily by and for well-resourced populations, with environmental risks borne by less-resourced populations, and governance structures that do not systematically correct for it.

The patent landscape reinforces the concentration of benefit. MIT, the Broad Institute, Harvard, and UC Berkeley hold foundational CRISPR-Cas9 patents. Companies commercializing CRISPR-based medicines typically license from Broad's portfolio on workable terms for high-income country markets. For low-income country agricultural applications, access is less clear, and the commercial incentive to develop tools for subsistence agriculture or neglected tropical diseases is limited by market size. Equitable governance requires structural responses: diverse representation on regulatory bodies, funding directed toward high-value, low-income-country applications, and licensing frameworks that provide affordable access to foundational tools.

Diagram 11.8 - CRISPR Patent Landscape and Access Pathways

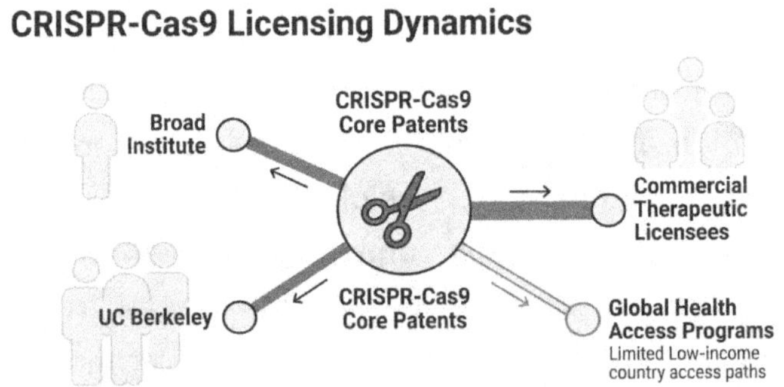

The Regulatory Landscape: Overlapping Jurisdictions and the Governance Gap

The regulatory framework governing synthetic biology in the United States is not a coherent system designed for the field's current capabilities. It is a collection of overlapping jurisdictions built from statutes developed primarily in the 1970s through the 1990s, applied with varying degrees of consistency to technologies that those statutes did not anticipate. Mapping it accurately requires neither overclaiming a coherence it does not have nor dismissing the genuine protections it provides.

The Food and Drug Administration governs drugs, biologics, and medical devices under the Federal Food, Drug, and Cosmetic Act and the Public Health Service Act. In practice, the FDA reviews and approves CAR-T cell therapies, mRNA vaccines, CRISPR-based medicines, gene therapies, and synthetic biology diagnostic tests. The FDA's Center for Biologics Evaluation and Research, CBER, handles cell and gene therapy products. The pathway requires preclinical safety data, clinical trial evidence, and manufacturing quality documentation; it is rigorous, slow, and expensive. Carlos spent two years at the FDA reviewing cell and gene therapy applications before joining Helix Forge. His assessment: the FDA's rigor is genuinely protective, even when the timeline is frustrating.

Diagram 11.9 - US Regulatory Jurisdiction Map for Synthetic Biology Products

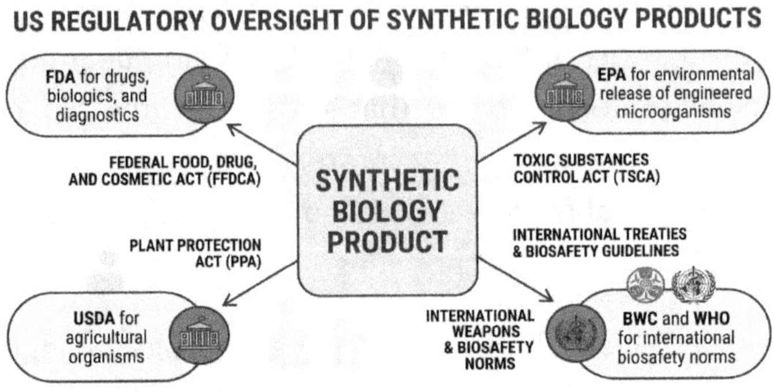

US regulatory oversight of synthetic biology products · Landscape 16:9 composition

The Environmental Protection Agency governs environmental release of engineered microorganisms under two statutes: the Toxic Substances Control Act (TSCA) and the Federal Insecticide, Fungicide, and Rodenticide Act (FIFRA. Under TSCA, an engineered organism requires pre-manufacture notification before commercial release; the developer submits identity, uses, hazards, and environmental fate information, and the EPA may impose restrictions or prohibit use. The USDA's APHIS governs engineered crop plants and animals; the USDA updated its gene-edited plant framework in 2020, creating cleaner pathways for CRISPR-edited crops with targeted edits.

Internationally, the Biological Weapons Convention, in force since 1975 with 183 states parties, prohibits the development, production, and use of biological weapons. Its prohibition is comprehensive in text but limited in practice: it lacks a verification mechanism comparable to the IAEA's role in nuclear nonproliferation, and its original text does not explicitly address engineered pathogens created with contemporary synthetic biology tools. WHO biosafety guidance is advisory, not binding. The governance gap is simply the gap between the pace of synthetic biology's capabilities and the pace of regulatory update; the frameworks were built for late-twentieth-century biotechnology, and the stretch marks show.

Diagram 11.10 - Regulatory Framework Coverage Versus Synthetic Biology Capability Growth

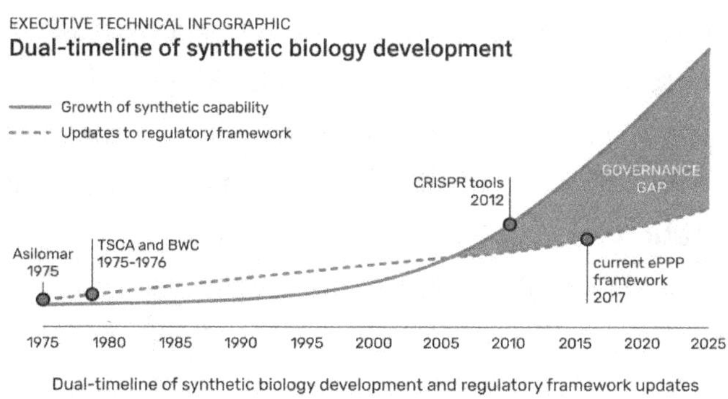

Responsible Innovation in Practice: The Carlos Rivera Framework

Abstract ethical principles become real when they are translated into operating procedures. Carlos Rivera's job at Helix Forge is to translate the abstract governance landscape into a set of processes that the team follows on every project: before experiments are designed, before papers are submitted, and before commercial applications are pursued. The framework he has built is not aspirational; it is operational. It treats ethical constraints as design parameters that must be verified before a project proceeds, not as concerns to be addressed only if they come up.

The first component is DURC screening at the proposal stage. Every Helix Forge research proposal is reviewed against the seven DURC criteria before submission to the federal government. The review involves Priya for the scientific context and Yuki, whose circuit design work frequently involves pathogen-relevant detection mechanisms. The output is a documented assessment: either the proposal does not meet any DURC criterion, with the reasoning recorded, or it meets one or more and requires IBC consultation and a modified design. Documentation is kept regardless of outcome; if the research is later questioned, the prior DURC review record is the essential first line of defense.

The second component is the standing IBC consultation. Helix Forge uses an external IBC through a consortium arrangement with several Boston-area biotechnology companies, a standard structure for early-stage companies that cannot support full internal biosafety infrastructure. The IBC reviews all protocols involving select agents, engineered organisms with novel properties, or experiments with any plausible dual-use inference chain. Carlos's approach is to bring the IBC into substantive scientific conversations when the dual-use question is genuinely difficult, which it sometimes is. The goal is to have the IBC's judgment integrated into experimental design, not appended to it after the fact.

Diagram 11.11 - Helix Forge Responsible Innovation Operating Framework

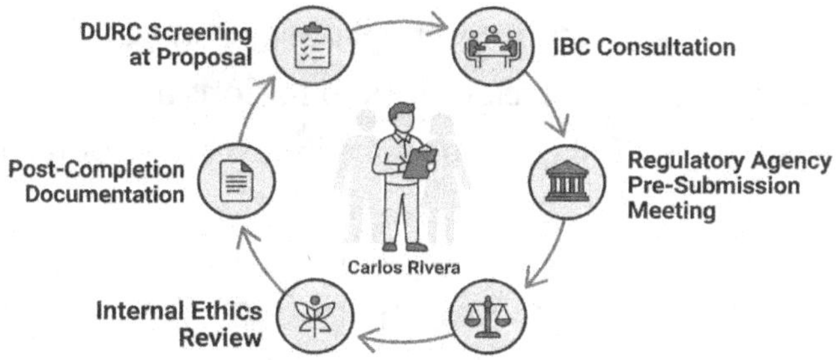

Caption: Doortician process flow uiit In-made infogram an executive technical

The third component is proactive engagement with regulatory agencies before formal submissions. Both the FDA and the EPA offer pre-submission meetings: pre-IND meetings for FDA drug applications and early engagement meetings for EPA TSCA submissions. Developers present their proposed strategy to agency staff and receive guidance before filing a formal application. These meetings do not guarantee a shorter timeline. Still, they reliably improve application quality by surfacing questions early, when they can be addressed in research design rather than in a response to an information request. Carlos considers pre-submission meetings one of the highest-return investments in the company's regulatory strategy.

The fourth component is internal ethics review for commercial applications. When a Helix Forge project moves to commercial evaluation, Carlos conducts a structured review across three dimensions: dual-use risk in the commercial context; equity implications, including who has access and who bears risks; and environmental release considerations if the application involves organisms that could persist outside a contained facility. The review is not a veto; Helix Forge has commercial obligations, and Carlos's role is to ensure commercialization decisions are made with a clear view of the full consequence landscape, not to block them.

The Bioethics of Engineering Life: Moral Status and the Enhancement Line

The ethical questions that synthetic biology raises are downstream of specific technical capabilities, and their clarity depends on technical precision. The question of the moral status of synthetic organisms is a useful starting point. Moral status refers to the property that makes an entity morally significant, meaning we owe it direct consideration. The dominant bioethics framework grounds moral status in sentience, the capacity to have experiences or feel pain. A bacterium engineered to produce a drug lacks moral status; it lacks the neurological complexity required for sentience. Whether we should engineer it is answered by reference to consequences for entities that do have moral status, the humans who benefit from the drug, and the humans who bear any risks.

The question becomes more complex as synthetic biology produces more complex organisms. Gene drive projects to suppress malaria mosquito populations, organisms engineered for aquaculture, and organoids grown from human stem cells all involve entities with nervous systems, ecological roles, and welfare considerations that the simple sentience framework does not cleanly address. Synthetic biologists working in these areas are well-served by engaging directly with these questions because the regulatory frameworks governing these applications increasingly reflect bioethical principles, and understanding those principles makes the regulatory landscape more navigable.

The treatment-versus-enhancement distinction is the axis along which the most consequential debates in human genetic modification are organized. Treatment addresses a clear harm: correcting a mutation that causes severe disease, repairing a chromosomal deletion, or conferring disease resistance for a documented vulnerability. Enhancement improves traits beyond the normal range, including height, cognitive performance, and traits associated with competitive advantage. The distinction is widely accepted as morally relevant, and most bioethical frameworks and regulatory bodies find treatment applications more defensible because treatment addresses a documented harm. In contrast, enhancement raises questions about fairness, consent, and the social dynamics of genetic advantage.

The challenge for governance is that biological boundaries are not sharp. The CCR5 deletion engineered by He Jiankui was framed as a treatment. Still, in populations with low HIV exposure, the same edit is more accurately characterized as a precautionary enhancement of a healthy genome. Genetic variants associated with reduced Alzheimer's risk, reduced cardiovascular risk, and enhanced immune function represent genuine health benefits and are technically editable. Still, the line between preventing a disease and optimizing a healthy genome is drawn by biology, and the biology is not always clear. Governance frameworks need precision about where treatment ends, and enhancement begins, and that precision must come from the technical community.

Diagram 11.12 - The Treatment-Enhancement Spectrum and Governance Zones

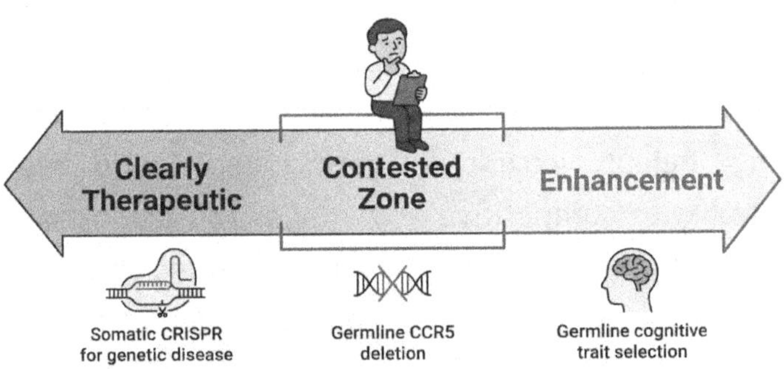

What This Means For You

If you are an engineer or scientist working in synthetic biology, the ethical framework in this chapter is part of your professional competence. DURC screening is a federal requirement for research meeting the criteria in this chapter, and your institution's IBC is the mechanism through which that requirement operates. Knowing the seven DURC criteria, being able to evaluate your own research design against them, and knowing when to escalate to IBC consultation are competencies every synthetic biologist in the United States needs. The opening meeting in this chapter is a realistic description of what happens when that competency is absent: a review letter, a delay, and a retroactive conversation that should have happened before submission.

If you are an entrepreneur evaluating or building a synthetic biology company, the regulatory landscape in this chapter defines the operating environment for your company. The overlapping FDA, EPA, and USDA jurisdictions are structures you need to understand deeply, because your regulatory pathway, timeline, and evidence requirements are determined by which agencies have jurisdiction and what their standards require. Engaging regulatory agencies early, before formal submissions, costs modest time and returns substantial clarity. Companies that treat regulatory engagement as an adversarial last step consistently face longer timelines and more extensive information requests than companies that treat it as a collaborative process from the beginning.

If you are a policy professional or science communicator, technical precision is the foundation of effective governance work. The regulatory frameworks for gain-of-function research, human germline editing, environmental release, and access equity are being actively developed and revised by people with widely varying levels of technical expertise. The NSABB members who debated the H5N1 publication question were not primarily philosophers; they were scientists, security experts, and public health professionals applying technical judgment to a governance question with real consequences. The technically grounded ethical reasoning this chapter supports is exactly what that kind of work requires.

Takeaway

Synthetic biology's ethical questions are technically difficult, not just morally complex. The dual-use problem is hard because the same molecular knowledge that enables better diagnostics also enables reasoning about pathogen enhancement. The germline debate is hard because heritability is a biological fact, and the treatment-enhancement boundary is drawn by molecular facts that are not always clean. The access and equity problem is hard because the structural concentrations of intellectual property, manufacturing capability, and regulatory expertise embedded in the field's innovation economics cannot be corrected by good intentions. The technical details are the starting point.

The governance framework for synthetic biology is under active construction. The DURC policy and NSABB review process are functional, even if inconsistently applied and limited to federally funded US research. The FDA, EPA, and USDA frameworks provide genuine protections for the applications they cover. The international frameworks, including the Biological Weapons Convention and the WHO biosafety standards, provide normative foundations without enforcement mechanisms. These structures represent accumulated learning from decades of governing recombinant DNA research, gain-of-function studies, and gene therapy applications. Building on them is the practical path toward better governance.

Carlos Rivera's operating framework at Helix Forge is a template for responsible innovation: DURC screening at the proposal stage, standing IBC consultation, proactive regulatory engagement, and internal ethics review for commercial applications. The costs are real: time, expertise, and the willingness to redesign an experiment or delay a submission when the ethics review identifies a problem. Those costs are substantially smaller than the costs of getting it wrong: regulatory delays, reputational damage, restrictions on legitimate research, or harm that cannot be undone. Ethics in synthetic biology is a design parameter, subject to the same discipline and accountability as any other design parameter.

This chapter has covered four domains: dual-use research, germline editing, access and equity, and the regulatory landscape, because those four represent the primary ethical surfaces where choices will matter most in the coming decade. They are not the only ethical questions the field will face. As synthetic biology produces more complex organisms and environmental engineering scales from laboratory to ecosystem, new questions will emerge that current frameworks are not equipped to answer. The reader who completes this chapter is equipped to engage those questions from a position of genuine technical understanding, which is the only foundation for ethical judgment adequate to the field as it is becoming.

12 The Road Ahead

Opening Scenario

The farmhouse sits at the end of a dirt road outside Concord, New Hampshire, surrounded by maple trees beginning their turn toward orange. Marcus books it every year: one weekend, no investor calls, no pitch decks. Just the four of them, a whiteboard propped against the kitchen wall, and the question Marcus asks at the start of every annual retreat: what does this field look like in ten years?

Priya goes first, as she always does. She pulls the cap off a marker and writes two words: protein design. Not protein prediction, she says. Design. There is a difference, and the difference matters. AlphaFold told us what proteins look like. The new generation of tools tells us what proteins we can build. She draws a quick arrow from sequence to structure to function, then circles function. That circle, she says, is where synthetic biology lives, and it's getting much easier to reach. Yuki adds a branch: xenobiology. If you can design proteins with non-natural amino acids, she says, you are not just expanding the design space. You are building organisms that nature has no template for. Carlos uncaps his marker and writes "governance" above Priya's drawing, underlining it twice. The frameworks being written right now, he says, will define what is permitted for the next generation. This year, for the first time in four retreats, none of their answers felt speculative. They feel operational. The future has gotten very close.

Marcus listens to all of it. He thinks about the day he first walked into Priya's lab at MIT, convinced that his software background would give him enough footing to understand what she was doing. He remembers the genuine confusion when she explained that a promoter was not a metaphor for a power switch but an actual molecular mechanism with kinetics, affinities, and noise characteristics that could be modeled but never fully controlled. He was right that the design-build-test-learn cycle rhymes with software development. What he underestimated was everything else. Sitting in this kitchen with the smell of coffee and autumn through the window screen, he thinks the gap between what synthetic biologists can design today and what they could design when he joined the field is larger than any ten-year gap he saw in software. The road ahead, he thinks, is very short.

Why It Matters

Every field has a moment when the tools catch up with the vision. Software engineering had it in the 1990s, when the internet made distribution free and the barrier to building a global product collapsed. Genomics had it in the early 2000s, when the cost of sequencing a human genome fell from $3 billion to under $1,000, and the information density of biology became legible at scale. Synthetic biology is experiencing its version of that moment right now, driven by a convergence of forces that no single discipline could have produced on its own.

The reason this matters to you is that the decisions made over the next five to ten years will shape the field for a generation. The regulatory frameworks being drafted now will govern which organisms can be released, which genetic interventions can be applied to human beings, and which safety requirements apply to community bio-labs. The investment theses being tested now will determine which parts of the synthetic biology stack get built out as shared infrastructure. The career paths opening up now are real, varied, and accessible to people without a PhD in biology. If you are reading this book, you are better positioned to participate in those decisions than you were when you started.

This chapter surveys the five frontiers most actively shaping the field: AI-driven design, xenobiology, minimal genomes and whole-genome synthesis, DNA data storage, and the community bio-lab movement. It also maps the investment landscape and the career opportunities the field creates. The thread running through all of it is the same one that has run through every chapter: biology is information, and the project of synthetic biology is learning to read, write, and edit that information with increasing precision, speed, and confidence.

AI and the Design Phase Automated

The design-build-test-learn cycle is the heartbeat of synthetic biology. You design a genetic construct, build it in a cell, test whether it does what you intended, and use what you learn to improve the design. The cycle is powerful because it is iterative and grounded in real biological data. It has also, historically, been slow. The design step depended on expert intuition, partial databases of characterized parts, and educated guessing about how a new protein or circuit would behave before it was built and tested. Artificial intelligence is changing that, and the change is not incremental.

In 2021, DeepMind released AlphaFold2, a neural network that predicts the three-dimensional structure of a protein from its amino acid sequence, with accuracy comparable to expensive experimental methods such as X-ray crystallography. The protein folding problem, which had occupied structural biologists for more than fifty years, was effectively solved in a single software release. The AlphaFold2 database now contains predicted structures for more than two hundred million proteins. Protein structure determines protein function, and predicting structure from sequence transformed rational protein design from an extremely difficult experimental exercise into a fast computational one.

Diagram 12.1 - AI-Assisted Protein Design Workflow

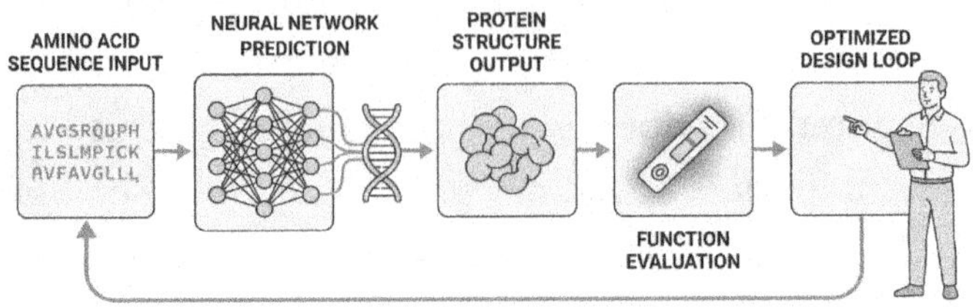

The jump from prediction to design is where the current generation of tools becomes genuinely exciting. RFdiffusion, developed at David Baker's laboratory at the University of Washington, takes a desired protein shape as input and outputs novel sequences that will fold into that shape. ProteinMPNN designs sequences that adopt a given backbone stably. ESM3, from EvolutionaryScale, lets engineers specify constraints on structure, function, and evolutionary origin and receive candidate sequences in return. The design step of the DBTL cycle is beginning to look more like software development: specify a desired enzymatic function, computational tools generate candidate sequences, DNA synthesis produces them overnight, and testing follows within days.

Ginkgo Bioworks has made AI-driven design central to its foundry model: rather than developing biological products itself, it provides the infrastructure and expertise that other companies pay to use. Ginkgo's partnership with Google integrates large-scale biological data with machine-learning tools to further compress the design step. The foundry thesis is a specific prediction: that value in synthetic biology will concentrate in shared infrastructure rather than individual applications. Whether that prediction proves correct is one of the field's most actively contested investment debates. The broader AI-for-biology wave, Recursion Pharmaceuticals, Inceptive, and Generate: Biomedicines, reflects the same thesis across drug discovery. The common thread is Priya's circle on the whiteboard: function, and AI is making it dramatically easier to reach.

Xenobiology and the Expanded Alphabet

Every living organism on Earth uses the same four DNA bases: adenine, thymine, guanine, and cytosine. They pair the same way, A with T and G with C, encoding the same twenty standard amino acids through the same codon table. The genetic code is universal, not because it is the only possible code, but because all life shares a common ancestor that used it. This universality is one of the most remarkable facts in all of biology. It is also, from a synthetic biology perspective, a design constraint that the field is actively working to overcome.

Xenobiology is the engineering of organisms with genetic alphabets that go beyond the natural four-letter code. The goal is twofold. First, an expanded alphabet opens new design spaces for proteins. Non-standard amino acids can carry chemical groups that no natural amino acid contains, such as metal-chelating groups, photoreactive groups, and reactive handles for chemical conjugation. A protein built with non-standard amino acids at specific positions can do things the standard twenty cannot. Second, xenobiology improves biosafety. An organism that requires a non-natural base or amino acid for survival cannot survive outside the laboratory environment where those molecules are supplied. It cannot exchange genetic material with natural organisms because its genetic code is incompatible with theirs. It is not just contained; it is orthogonal to the entire natural biosphere.

Diagram 12.2 - Xenobiology Expanded Genetic Alphabet

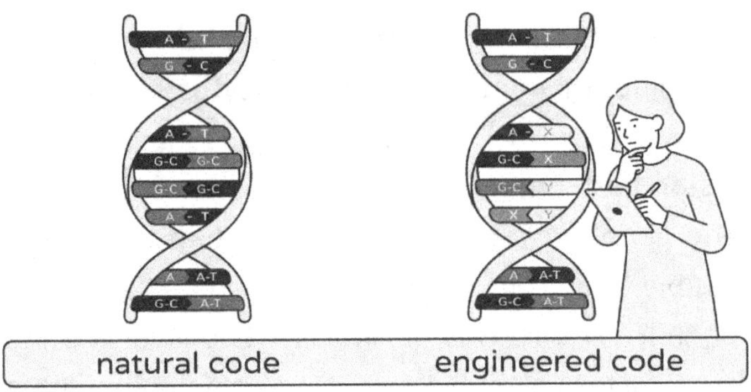

Steven Benner's laboratory at the Foundation for Applied Molecular Evolution demonstrated a six-letter DNA alphabet, adding two synthetic bases, P and Z, that pair reliably and can be replicated by modified polymerases. Floyd Romesberg's laboratory at Scripps Research Institute created a living bacterium with a stable expanded genetic alphabet. This organism replicates indefinitely while maintaining non-natural base pairs, carrying genetic information that no natural organism can read or replicate.

The Romesberg organism uses its expanded alphabet to incorporate non-standard amino acids into proteins, producing molecules with chemical properties beyond those of natural biology. The road from proof-of-concept to practical products is not short: engineering a cell to replicate non-natural bases reliably requires modifying multiple enzymes, and regulatory frameworks for xenobiological organisms are still being developed. But a technology that simultaneously expands the design space and improves containment will attract sustained investment and development effort.

Minimal Genomes and Writing Life from Scratch

In 2010, a team led by Craig Venter at the J. Craig Venter Institute synthesized a complete bacterial genome from scratch and used it to boot a living cell. The organism JCVI-syn1.0 had a genome of 1.08 million base pairs, assembled from chemically synthesized DNA fragments and transplanted into a recipient cell whose genome had been removed. The transplanted genome took over the cell's machinery and directed its own replication. A cell was running on a human-written genome. The philosophical implications briefly made the front pages of major newspapers. The scientific implications were larger.

Diagram 12.3 - Synthetic Cell Construction from Minimal Genome

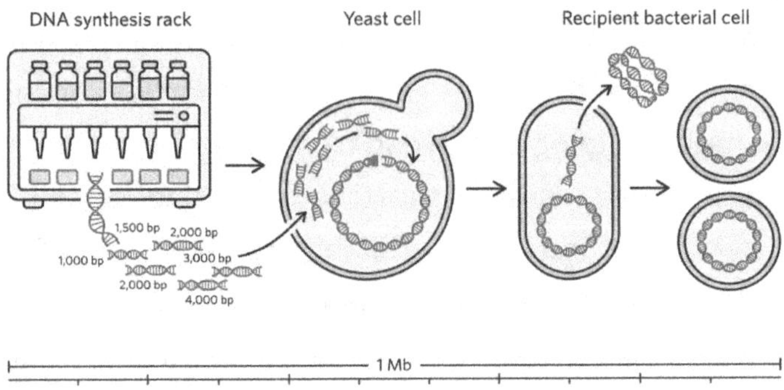

The deeper question was: what is the minimum set of genes required for a cell to live and replicate? The Venter team addressed this with JCVI-syn3.0, published in 2016. Through an iterative process of gene deletions and viability testing, they reduced the Mycoplasma genome down to 473 genes, the smallest genome of any independently replicating cell ever created. The result was surprising: of those 473 genes, 149 had no known function. A cell cannot live without them, but no one knew what they did. The field can write an entire genome but cannot yet explain roughly a third of it, which is a remarkable statement about the limits of biological knowledge.

The Genome Project-write, known as GP-write, extends this ambition to the human scale. The project's goal is to synthesize a complete human genome from scratch, an undertaking roughly a thousand times larger than the bacterial genome that Venter's team accomplished. Stated applications include understanding the functional significance of every genomic sequence, creating human cell lines with all viral integration sites removed so any known virus cannot infect them, and enabling the production of complex human proteins in engineered cells for therapeutic applications. GP-write is more controversial than JCVI-syn1.0 because the target is human biology, and the governance questions are considerably more fraught. But the technical trajectory is the same one that carried bacterial genome synthesis from impossible to routine in fifteen years.

Diagram 12.4 - Minimal Genome Simplified Cell Map

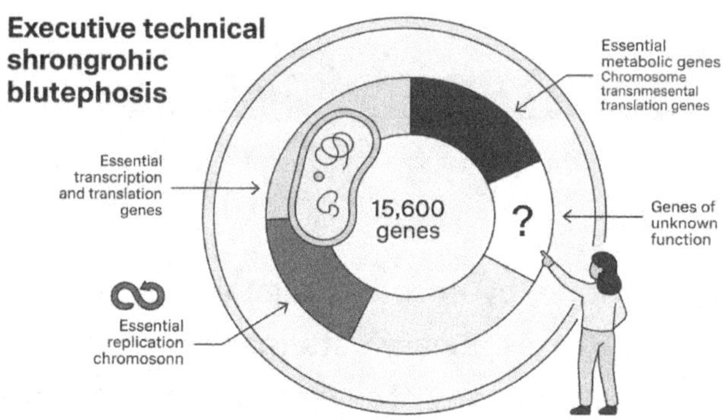

DNA Data Storage

Every year, the world generates more digital data than it did in all previous years combined. Magnetic tape, the current archival standard for cold storage, holds roughly one terabyte per kilogram and degrades over decades. The physical limits of silicon-based storage are approaching constraints that materials science cannot easily overcome. DNA offers a different path. DNA stores information at approximately 215 petabytes per gram, roughly one hundred million times denser per unit mass than a hard drive. DNA stored in a cool, dry environment is stable for thousands of years, and the energy cost of maintaining a DNA archive is a fraction of the cost of keeping spinning hard drives online.

Diagram 12.5 - DNA Data Storage Density Comparison

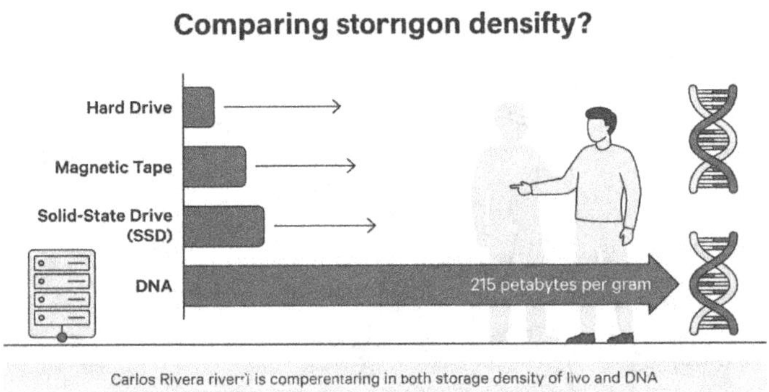

The mechanism works by encoding digital information as sequences of DNA bases. Binary data maps onto the four-letter DNA alphabet using any of several encoding schemes. A sequence of A, T, G, and C bases encodes a string of bits, and the string can be read back out by sequencing the DNA. Researchers have demonstrated the encoding and retrieval of diverse digital files, including the complete works of Shakespeare, a short film, and an entire computer operating system. Retrieval uses random-access addressing, often implemented with CRISPR-based target selection, so specific files can be pulled from a mixed pool of DNA without reading the entire archive. George Church's laboratory at Harvard has been a leading force in this work, as has the collaboration between Twist Bioscience and

Microsoft, which has demonstrated automated DNA writing and reading in a fully integrated system.

The current limitations are real but engineering-tractable. Writing DNA is fast and becoming cheaper rapidly, following an exponential cost decline similar to sequencing. Reading DNA for retrieval is still too slow and expensive for routine random-access applications: read latency measured in hours is not competitive with milliseconds for applications requiring fast data access. But for archival cold storage, where data is written once and read rarely, latency matters far less than density, longevity, and energy cost. These are engineering problems, not fundamental barriers.

Diagram 12.6 - DNA Data Encoding and Retrieval Workflow

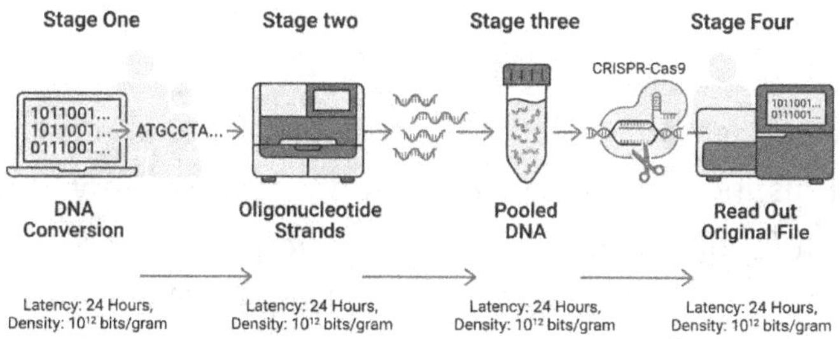

The Investment Landscape

Synthetic biology has attracted serious capital. The McKinsey Global Institute estimated in 2020 that synthetic biology and biologically enabled applications could generate up to $4 trillion in direct economic impact annually within ten to twenty years. That estimate is almost certainly wrong in its specifics, because long-range projections in exponential technologies always are. But the order of magnitude matters: synthetic biology is being treated as a technology platform comparable in scope to the internet or electrification, not as a niche field with a limited addressable market.

Diagram 12.7 - Synthetic Biology Investment Sectors Map

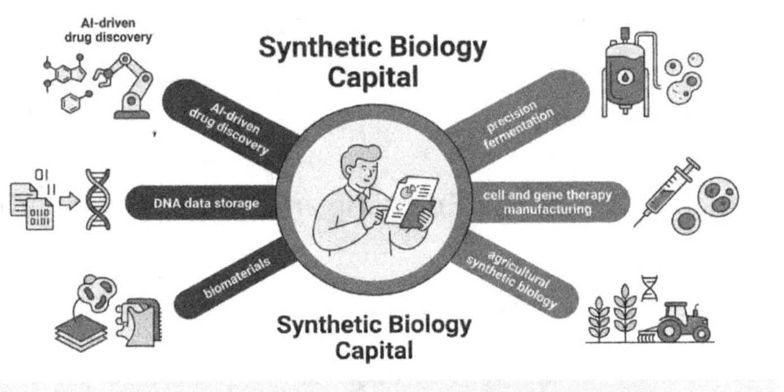

A powerful economic engine is a metaphoric driven by synthetic biology innovation.

The key investment sectors attracting capital fall into several distinct categories. AI-driven drug discovery is the largest in funding volume, with Recursion Pharmaceuticals, Insilico Medicine, and Exscientia applying machine learning to identify drug candidates and predict their efficacy. Precision fermentation uses engineered microorganisms to produce food proteins, with Perfect Day, Remilk, and Formo engineering yeast and fungi to produce dairy proteins without involving animals. Cell and gene therapy manufacturing addresses the challenge of producing therapeutic cells and viral vectors at scale, with Multiply

Labs and Ori Biotech applying automation to a manufacturing bottleneck for an entire therapeutic category. Agricultural synthetic biology, represented by Pivot Bio and Joyn Bio, engineers nitrogen-fixing microbes to reduce fertilizer dependence across a market where modest efficiency gains represent billions of dollars in value.

For anyone evaluating a synthetic biology investment or company, five questions provide a useful framework. What is the organism, and why is it the right chassis for this application? What is the metabolic or genetic circuit target, and what evidence bridges proof-of-concept to commercial-scale production? What are the titer, rate, and yield metrics compared to the commercial viability threshold? What is the regulatory pathway, and how long and expensive is it likely to be? And what is the manufacturing scale-up plan, and where are the key engineering risks? The most common failure mode in synthetic biology companies is not scientific failure at the proof-of-concept stage. It is the gap between laboratory performance and commercially viable production. It is almost always visible in the titer, rate, and yield numbers if you know how to look for it. These five questions are not magic, but they distinguish an informed evaluation from a pattern-matched guess based on buzzwords in the pitch deck.

Career Paths in Synthetic Biology

One of the most useful things this book can do is be direct about the careers that synthetic biology creates, because the field is genuinely hungry for talent across a much wider range of backgrounds than most people realize. The dominant public image of a synthetic biologist, a PhD-level researcher in a university lab, is increasingly outdated. Synthetic biology companies employ software engineers, data scientists, process engineers, regulatory specialists, science communicators, policy professionals, and financial analysts alongside their molecular biologists. A useful career in this field does not require a biology degree, though working knowledge of the science is valuable in almost every role.

Diagram 12.8 - Career Pathways into Synthetic Biology

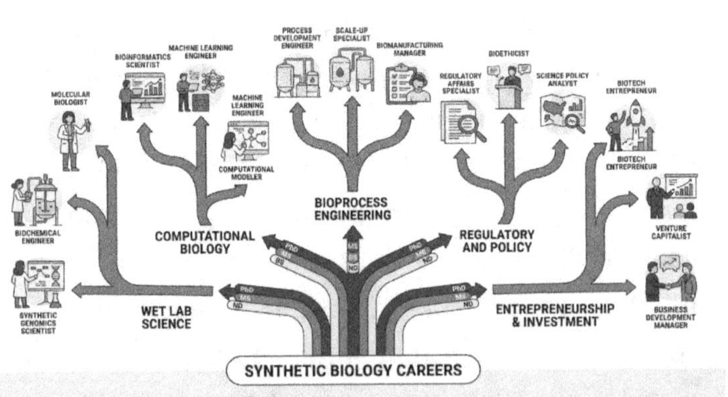

Molecular biologists and biochemists fill the core wet lab roles: strain engineering, protein production and characterization, and assay development. Bioengineers bridge the biology and engineering domains. Genetic circuit designers translate biological intent into circuit specifications. Metabolic engineers redesign cellular metabolic networks to redirect carbon flux toward a target product by deleting genes, overexpressing genes, and inserting pathways. Bioprocess engineers design fermentation and bioreactor conditions for at-scale production, addressing heat transfer, mixing, oxygen delivery, and contamination control challenges that do not exist at laboratory scale.

Bioinformaticians and computational biologists are among the most sought-after people in the field, and demand consistently exceeds supply. Software engineers with strong statistics backgrounds have successfully made this transition, and the field actively recruits them. Regulatory and quality specialists are essential: every synthetic biology product that reaches patients, consumers, or the environment must pass through a regulatory process, and people who understand both the science and the regulatory framework are rare and valuable. Carlos Rivera's trajectory from policy background to regulatory affairs at a startup is increasingly common. Science communicators and policy professionals deserve particular emphasis: the field genuinely needs people who can explain what is being built to regulators, investors, journalists, and the public, and the people who can bridge that gap are doing work as valuable to the field as any laboratory discovery.

Community Bio-Labs and the Democratization of Biology

The history chapter of this book began with a specific image: the early days of molecular biology, when the tools required to work with DNA were accessible only to a handful of elite research universities and government-funded national laboratories. The polymerase chain reaction required specialized thermal cyclers. Gel electrophoresis requires expensive power supplies. Sequencing required radioactive labels and overnight exposures. The barrier to entry was not just expertise; it was capital. You needed an institution behind you to do anything at all. That world is gone.

The price of a benchtop PCR machine has fallen below $2,000. Open-source protocols for DNA extraction, transformation, and gel electrophoresis are freely available and can be executed with equipment that fits on a kitchen counter. DNA synthesis services will mail custom oligonucleotides for cents per base. Sequencing services return results from a mailed-in sample for under twenty dollars. CRISPR reagents are commercially available and straightforward to use for basic applications. The cognitive and financial barriers to entry for synthetic biology have both fallen dramatically, and the community bio-lab movement is the visible result.

Diagram 12.9 - Community Bio-Lab Workspace

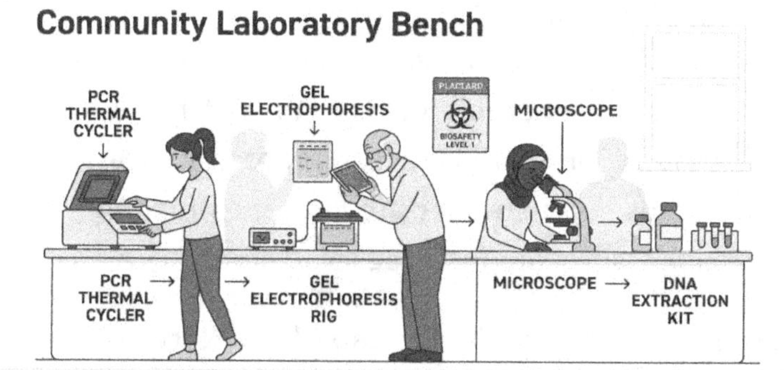

A Community laboratory bench, illustration, migh style, an executive technical tone.

Genspace, founded in Brooklyn in 2010, was among the first community biology laboratories in the United States. It operates on a membership model, charging monthly dues in exchange for access to shared equipment, safety training, and a community of practice. BioCurious, in Sunnyvale, California, followed a similar model and positioned itself explicitly at the intersection of the hacker community and the life sciences. Hackteria, a global network rather than a single physical space, connects community biologists across continents through shared protocols, open-source hardware designs, and an annual gathering. These organizations and their counterparts in London, Berlin, Tokyo, and dozens of other cities have collectively built a global community of practitioners working outside traditional institutional contexts.

The work coming out of community bio-labs is not trivial. Practitioners have sequenced local environmental microbiomes, discovering novel organisms in urban soil and water samples. They have engineered yeast strains for novel flavors, built CRISPR-based diagnostic tools for pathogen detection, and contributed to open-source registries of characterized biological parts. Some of this work is directly comparable in rigor to that produced by university labs. Some of it is exploratory in ways that university labs, constrained by grant funding and publication pressure, are less free to attempt.

Diagram 12.10 - Community Bio-Lab Global Network Map

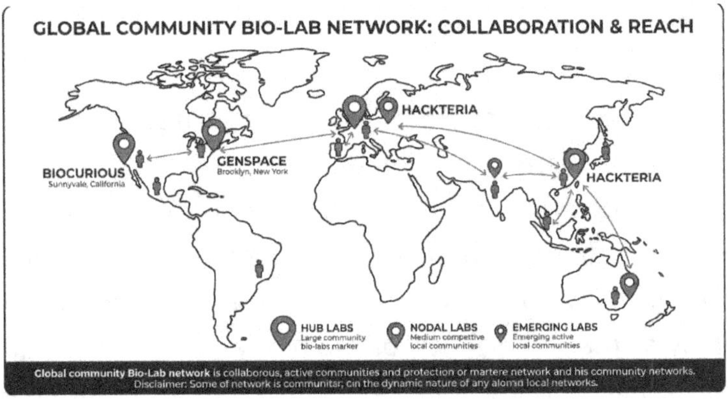

The community bio-lab movement takes biosafety seriously, and it has to. Community labs operate under Biosafety Level 1 guidelines, which prohibit work with known pathogens and require basic protective equipment and waste disposal protocols. The iGEM Foundation, which runs the International Genetically Engineered Machine competition, requires all participating teams to complete biosafety training and to address the dual-use implications of their project. The community is not naive about the risks. It has made a deliberate choice to address those risks through education and culture rather than restriction.

Carlos draws an analogy that the rest of the team finds clarifying. The early internet was also a democratized platform with dual-use potential, and the response was not to restrict access to institutions. It was to build governance frameworks, technical standards, and community norms that made the benefits accessible while managing the risks. The community bio-lab movement is building the biological equivalent of that governance infrastructure in real time. The trajectory is one of a community taking responsibility for the tools it uses, and that is the right response to democratization.

What This Means For You

If you are a software engineer or technologist, the tools and workflow of synthetic biology are becoming increasingly legible in engineering terms. AI-driven protein design, whole-genome synthesis, and the compression of the DBTL cycle toward software-like iteration speeds mean that a software engineer who learns the underlying biology is genuinely equipped to contribute to the field's design layer. The specific skills that transfer most directly are systems thinking, iterative design under uncertainty, comfort with probabilistic models, and the ability to reason about latency and throughput in complex pipelines. None of those are foreign to a software engineer. The biology on top of them is learnable, and this book has tried to make that learning accessible.

If you are an entrepreneur, the investment framework in this chapter applies to your own company as rigorously as to any company you might fund. The most common failure mode in synthetic biology is not scientific failure at the proof-of-concept stage. It is the gap between laboratory performance and commercially viable production, visible in the titer, rate, and yield numbers if you know where to look. Building a company that crosses that gap requires bioprocess engineering expertise distinct from the genetic engineering expertise required to make the organism work. Assembling that expertise early is one of the most valuable things a synthetic biology entrepreneur can do.

Diagram 12.11 - The Informed Practitioner Framework

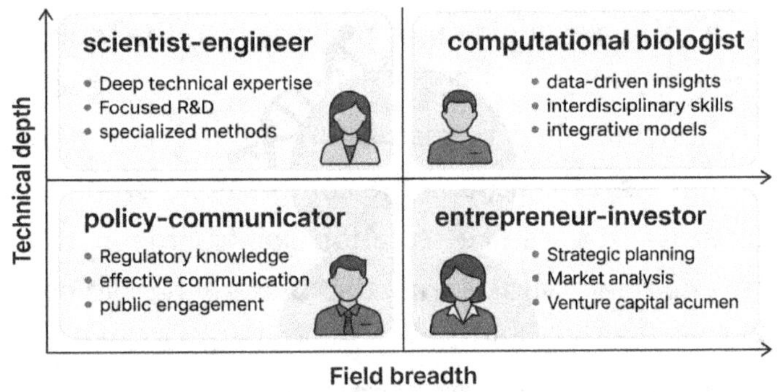

If you are a policy professional or regulatory specialist, the frontiers surveyed in this chapter each carry governance implications that are not yet settled. Xenobiological organisms raise containment classification questions that existing biosafety frameworks were not designed for. DNA data storage, if it scales to practical deployment, will require governance frameworks that address the intersection of biological material and digital information.

Whole-genome synthesis at the human chromosome scale will require ethics and governance infrastructure that does not yet exist in adequate form. The people who build those frameworks need to understand the science well enough to avoid both excessive restriction that prevents beneficial applications and insufficient restriction that permits genuinely dangerous ones. You are now better equipped to do that work than when you started this book.

If you are a curious professional who came to this book without a specific career agenda, synthetic biology is a real platform with real commercial traction, real investment, and real career opportunities, accessible to people who think carefully and learn continuously. You do not need a laboratory to participate. You need the frameworks to understand what is being built, the vocabulary to engage with the people building it, and the judgment to evaluate the claims being made about it. This book has tried to give you all three.

Takeaway

On the last morning of the retreat, Marcus wakes before the others and sits on the porch with coffee, watching the maple trees in the early light. He thinks about the conversation from the night before: what synthetic biology would need to look like to deliver on its potential. Not the technologies, those are advancing on their own. The governance frameworks. The workforce. The public understanding. The community of practitioners spread across a thousand bio-labs in a hundred countries, bringing synthetic biology out of the elite universities where it began and into the world where it needs to go. He thinks about Genspace in Brooklyn and BioCurious in Sunnyvale, about the iGEM teams in Nairobi, Bangalore, and Bogota. The field has traveled an extraordinary distance in a very short time.

He came to synthetic biology as a software engineer who recognized the design-build-test-learn cycle, saw the analogy between genetic circuits and software architectures, and understood that a system capable of sensing its environment, processing information, and producing a specific output was programmable, regardless of whether it ran on silicon or carbon. He was right about all of that. What he did not understand, and what took him years to learn, was that the analogy has limits. Biology is not software in a cage. It is software that evolved, that makes errors and repairs them, that responds to context in ways that no engineer fully specified. Programming it responsibly requires not just engineering skill but genuine humility about what we do not yet understand.

Diagram 12.12 - The Full Arc: From Elite Labs to Community Benches

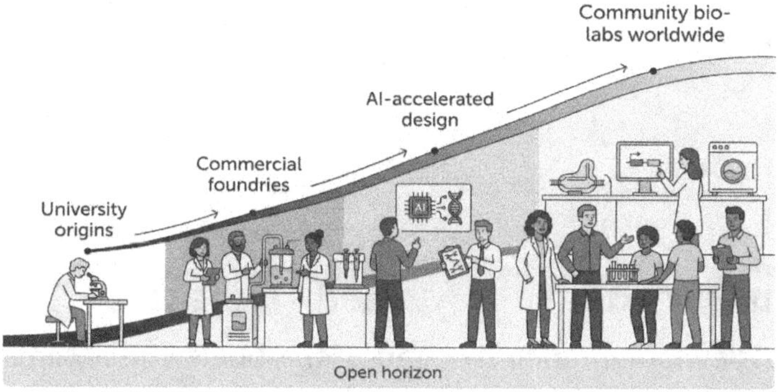

Synthetic biology is the project of learning to program the oldest and most sophisticated information-processing system ever built. The tools are extraordinary, the applications are real, and the frontiers surveyed in this chapter are advancing faster than any single observer can track. The governance challenges are genuine and require informed engagement from everyone in this field and everyone affected by it. The career opportunities are broad and accessible to people who bring serious thinking to a field that rewards it.

You are now equipped to participate. Not as a spectator watching biology happen to the world, but as someone who understands the machinery, can evaluate the claims, can ask the right questions, and can contribute wherever your background and your curiosity take you. The field needs scientists and engineers, yes. It also needs entrepreneurs, investors, regulators, communicators, policy professionals, and curious practitioners working in community bio-labs, university basements, and corporate research facilities worldwide. It needs the person who just finished this book.

That is you. Welcome to synthetic biology. Now build something.

13 Closing

From Outsider to Informed Operator

There is a moment near the start of this book when Marcus Webb picks up a petri dish and looks at it the way almost anyone without lab experience would. He sees something growing. He sees evidence that something is alive. What he does not yet see is a design. He does not see the promoter chosen because it fires at a precise threshold, the ribosome binding site is tuned for a specific translation rate, and the terminator is placed exactly where the designer needed it. He sees biology the way most intelligent people see it before they have the framework: as something complicated, rather than something engineered.

That moment was a starting coordinate, not an accident. Marcus's journey from that petri dish to the point where he can walk into a design review, read a genetic circuit schematic, challenge a metabolic flux claim, and ask the right question about a biosensor's detection limit is the same journey you have just completed across twelve chapters. You walked in without the framework. You are walking out with it.

The framework matters because the field is real and moving fast. The Helix Forge team is fictional, but every technology they work with exists. The biosensor in Carlos's notebook is based on real diagnostic architectures. The CAR-T platform Priya defends uses real molecular logic. The fermentation run Yuki spent chapters optimizing is currently running in actual bioreactors at companies whose names appeared throughout this book. What you have now is not a final point. It is a starting position.

Below is a representation of the reader's arc throughout the book, anchored in Marcus Webb's journey from a curious outsider to an informed operator.

Diagram C.1 - The Reader's Arc

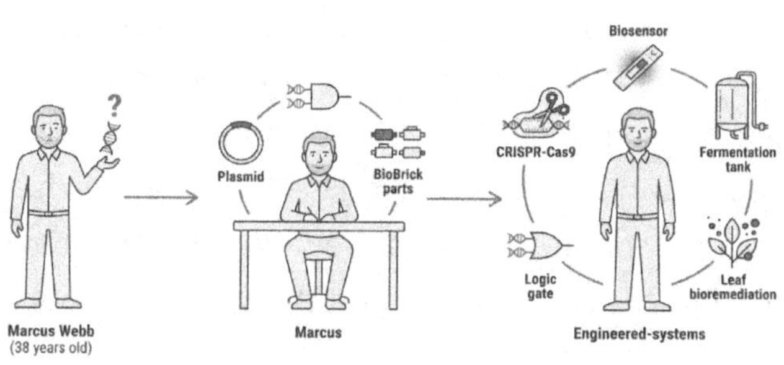

The arc is real. Everything in that diagram corresponds to a real technology that now lives inside your mental model of the field. Let us take stock of exactly what you have built.

What You Now Know

Biology is now an engineering discipline. That sentence might have felt like a marketing claim when you read it in the introduction. It does not feel that way now. Living cells carry heritable information encoded in a four-letter molecular alphabet. That alphabet can be read, copied, edited, and rewritten with precision tools that scientists control. The cell's machinery executes the instructions. The design-build-test-learn cycle that software engineers use to ship a product is the same cycle that synthetic biologists use to ship organisms. The analogy is not loose. It is mechanistically correct, and you now understand exactly why.

CRISPR is one tool in a larger toolkit, not the whole story. You know what it actually is: a bacterial adaptive immune system repurposed as a programmable nuclease steered by a guide RNA to a precise genomic address. You know that base editing can change a single nucleotide without cutting both strands, and that prime editing inserts short sequences with finer control still. You know the field did not stop at Cas9 and that the toolkit keeps growing. When the next editing technology makes the news, you will have the conceptual frame to evaluate it on the spot.

Genetic circuits are real engineering systems. A toggle switch composed of two mutually repressing transcription factors behaves like a bistable flip-flop because its molecular logic is structurally identical to that of the electronic version. An AND gate fires only when both molecular inputs are present, because the promoter physically requires two activator proteins to be present simultaneously. A repressilator produces rhythmic output because feedback delays generate a periodic signal, just as

RC delays generate oscillation in analog circuits. You understand not just the name of each circuit type but the mechanism that makes it work. That understanding is durable.

Engineered organisms are producing real outputs at an industrial scale right now. mRNA vaccines designed in 48 hours. Spider silk from yeast fermenters. Nitrogen-fixing microbes are reducing fertilizer use on millions of acres—lab-grown meat without the animal. Bacteria consume environmental contaminants in soil and water. Biosensors identifying pathogens in a drop of blood. These are not demonstrations. They are products, some already sold, some planted, some injected. The transition from research to commercial deployment has already happened across several sectors and is accelerating in the others.

The ethical stakes are real, and they reward scientific clarity. The dual-use problem is not a vague worry but a structural feature of the field: the same tools that let researchers engineer a vaccine platform also lower the barrier to engineering a pathogen. The germline editing debate is no longer abstract for you. You understand what heritable modification means in practice, how it differs from somatic editing, and why the scientific community drew a hard line on clinical germline modification. You understand why responsible regulatory frameworks treat contained industrial use differently from open field release. Having the science does not resolve the ethics. But it makes every ethical judgment better.

Artificial intelligence and synthetic biology are converging, and the pace of that convergence will define the next decade. AlphaFold and its descendants predict protein structures and feed directly into the design phase of the engineering cycle. AI-driven parts optimization compresses the learn-to-redesign loop from months to hours. The design phase, historically the most intuition-dependent step, is increasingly automated, and that automation changes the throughput of the entire cycle. The downstream effects on speed to market, on the number of viable participants, and on which products become feasible are the dominant story of synthetic biology for the next ten years.

What To Watch Next

Four frontiers are worth tracking closely, and you now have the background to follow them with real comprehension rather than headline-level awareness.

AI-driven design is already accelerating the engineering cycle. Protein language models trained on hundreds of millions of natural sequences can suggest novel protein designs that no evolution has explored. Generative models propose genetic circuit architectures optimized for a specific performance envelope. The design step, which previously required weeks of expert intuition, is compressing toward hours. Robotic foundries run thousands of design variants in parallel. Machine learning models extract design rules from experimental data without requiring a human to interpret every result. Full automation of the cycle is not yet here, but the components are assembling.

Xenobiology is smaller but conceptually radical. Researchers have built organisms that incorporate non-standard base pairs alongside the natural four. Expanded genetic alphabets allow the encoding of new amino acids into proteins that nature never built, proteins with chemical properties unavailable to standard biochemistry. An organism using a six-letter genetic code also has a built-in biosafety feature: it cannot exchange genetic information with wild organisms that speak only the standard code. As tools for working with non-standard nucleotides improve, xenobiology will move from proof-of-concept toward practical application.

Minimal genomes occupy the opposite end of the design philosophy. Rather than adding complexity, minimal genome projects strip a cell to the smallest gene set that sustains life and reproduction. The result is a chassis with maximum predictability: few unknown interactions, few competing metabolic pathways, a clean platform for engineered functions. JCVI-syn3.0, with roughly 473 genes, demonstrated that a computer-designed minimal genome can be assembled from scratch and booted into a living organism. The next step is using that chassis as a manufacturing platform, loaded with only the modules needed for a target product. The underlying science is no longer theoretical.

DNA data storage directly and practically connects synthetic biology to the information technology industry. The information density of DNA is orders of magnitude greater than any silicon-based medium. Researchers have demonstrated the encoding of digital files into DNA sequences and the reliable retrieval of these sequences through sequencing. The bottleneck is cost and speed: writing and reading DNA remains too slow and expensive for most archival use. But synthesis and sequencing costs have historically fallen faster than Moore's Law would predict. DNA data storage is likely to move from laboratory demonstration to niche archival application within the decade.

Taken together, the four frontiers above define the shape of the field in motion. The diagram below frames them as a single landscape.

Diagram C.2 - Synthetic Biology: A Field in Motion

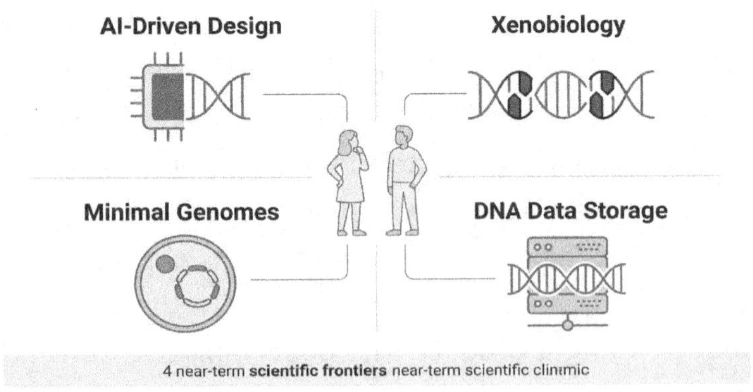

Each quadrant maps directly to skills you built in earlier chapters. Your understanding of genetic circuits lets you evaluate AI design tools critically. Your understanding of base chemistry lets you assess xenobiology claims. Your understanding of the design-build-test-learn cycle lets you see why minimal genomes matter as platforms. Your understanding of DNA as an information medium lets you place data storage claims in their proper technical and economic context. The framework is not domain-specific. It generalizes.

Your Place In This Field

Different readers have arrived here from different directions. The practical meaning of what you now know is specific to each of you.

If you are a software engineer or systems architect, the most valuable thing you carry out of this book is not biological facts. It is the recognition that the systems thinking you have spent your career developing is precisely the right starting toolkit for synthetic biology. The instincts that help you debug a distributed system or design a state machine help you evaluate a genetic circuit. What you now have on top of those instincts is the field's specific vocabulary. You can read a circuit schematic, follow a metabolic flux argument, and identify the control points in a cell-based therapy. You are not a synthetic biologist, but you are a well-equipped collaborator, and that position is genuinely valuable in a field that still operates in silos.

If you are an entrepreneur or investor, you can now evaluate a synthetic biology pitch on its technical merits rather than on the team's confidence alone. You can ask whether the proposed circuit architecture is novel or a recombination of known parts. You can ask where the company sits in the design-build-test-learn cycle and what their cycle time is. You can ask what the regulatory pathway looks like for their product category. You can distinguish a company whose core innovation is in biological design from one whose advantage is purely in process engineering. These are not peripheral questions. They are the ones that determine whether the value proposition holds under scrutiny.

If you are a policy professional or regulator, you now have the scientific grounding to make your judgments more precise. The dual-use framework is not just a policy category. It is a description of a real molecular symmetry: the same techniques, the same organisms, the same delivery mechanisms. The germline editing standards you write or enforce now reflect a specific biological understanding of what heritable modification means. Good governance in this field requires exactly the technical fluency you have built, and the decisions that shape whether synthetic biology develops responsibly will be made by people who understand the science well enough to write policy that is both rigorous and workable.

If you arrived from finance, consulting, journalism, or law, you now have the one thing that headlines about synthetic biology rarely provide: a causal model. You can read a story about a new gene therapy approval and understand which delivery mechanism it uses and what the manufacturing challenge at scale looks like. You can read a CRISPR story and know immediately whether it is about somatic or germline editing and why that distinction matters. The causal model turns headlines into information. Without it, you are reading descriptions of effects. With it, you are reading explanations of causes.

Final Word

Return, for a moment, to the sentence that opened this book. Moderna's team designed its COVID-19 mRNA vaccine in 48 hours, not because they worked unusually fast, but because the vaccine was, in a real and precise engineering sense, a piece of code executed by human cells. That sentence was placed at the beginning as a claim without proof. The proof arrived over twelve chapters.

You now understand what the code is: an mRNA sequence designed on a computer that encodes a spike protein antigen, delivered into cells by a lipid nanoparticle that fuses with the cell membrane. You understand what it means for cells to execute that code. You understand why the 48-hour timeline was possible: the mRNA platform separated the delivery machinery from the specific antigen sequence, so changing the vaccine required only changing the sequence. You understand all of this not as facts to memorize, but as an engineering system whose logic you can trace from input to output.

That is what having the framework means. Not the ability to design a genetic circuit from scratch, but the ability to evaluate whether someone else's design choices are sound. The ability to identify the control points in a biological system, the same way you identify them in any engineered system. The ability to ask the right questions, follow the answers, and update your model when the field moves—those capabilities compound. You will be faster, more accurate, and more useful every time you encounter synthetic biology from this point forward.

Marcus Webb is still at Helix Forge, still running design reviews, investor calls, and conversations with Carlos about what is permitted and what is not. Priya is still the scientific anchor. Yuki is still drawing circuit schematics on the whiteboard. Carlos is still asking the question that matters most: not just whether we can, but whether we should, and on what terms. The team is fictional. The questions are not.

The programmability of life has moved from theoretical to industrial. The field is moving fast. You are now equipped to move with it.

References

Albertsen, Mads, et al. "Cell-Free Systems for Industrial Biomanufacturing." *Nature Communications*, vol. 15, 2024, article 2109. (CH7)

Allison, Kyle R., et al. "Living Medicines: Engineered Bacteria as Therapeutics." *Nature Reviews Drug Discovery*, vol. 23, 2024, pp. 411–432. (CH6)

Anderson, James C., et al. "Standard Biological Parts in the Age of DNA Synthesis." *ACS Synthetic Biology*, vol. 13, no. 2, 2024, pp. 201–215. (CH3)

Arkin, Adam P. "The Design-Build-Test-Learn Cycle in Synthetic Biology." *Annual Review of Chemical and Biomolecular Engineering*, vol. 15, 2024, pp. 1–24. (CH5)

Baker, David, et al. "AI-Designed Proteins for Therapeutic and Industrial Applications." *Science*, vol. 383, 2024, eadk9121. (CH12)

Bikard, David, and Luciano Marraffini. "CRISPR-Based Diagnostics: From SHERLOCK to Point-of-Care." *Trends in Biotechnology*, vol. 42, no. 3, 2024, pp. 245–259. (CH9)

Brenner, Katie, et al. "Genetic Circuits for Biosensing in Complex Environments." *Nature Chemical Biology*, vol. 20, 2024, pp. 321–332. (CH9)

Brophy, Jennifer A. N., and Christopher A. Voigt. "Genetic Circuit Design Automation." *Nature Reviews Genetics*, vol. 25, 2024, pp. 55–71. (CH5)

Bugaj, Lukasz J., et al. "Logic-Gated Cell Therapies for Cancer." *Nature Reviews Cancer*, vol. 24, 2024, pp. 201–219. (CH6)

Cameron, David E., et al. "A Brief History of Synthetic Biology." *Cell*, vol. 187, no. 1, 2024, pp. 12–28. (CH2)

Cardinale, Stefano, and Adam P. Arkin. "Context Dependence in Synthetic Biology." *Current Opinion in Systems Biology*, vol. 38, 2024, 100497. (CH3)

Casini, Angela, et al. "DNA Assembly Standards in the Post-BioBrick Era." *Nucleic Acids Research*, vol. 52, no. 4, 2024, pp. 1881–1895. (CH3)

Chari, Raj, et al. "Prime Editing in Human Cells: Current Status and Future Directions." *Nature Biotechnology*, vol. 42, 2024, pp. 901–915. (CH4)

Chen, Irene A., et al. "Minimal Genomes and the Design of Synthetic Cells." *Nature Reviews Molecular Cell Biology*, vol. 25, 2024, pp. 501–518. (CH12)

Church, George M., et al. "Xenobiology: Expanding the Genetic Alphabet." *Nature Reviews Genetics*, vol. 25, 2024, pp. 419–437. (CH12)

Collins, James J., et al. "Living Diagnostics: Cell-Based Biosensors for Human Health." *Nature Reviews Microbiology*, vol. 22, 2024, pp. 145–162. (CH9)

Cumbers, John, and Jason Kelly. "The Synthetic Biology Industry Landscape 2024." *Synthetic Biology Journal*, vol. 3, no. 1, 2024, pp. 1–22. (CH12)

Doudna, Jennifer A., and Emmanuelle Charpentier. "CRISPR Genome Editing: A Decade of Progress." *Cell*, vol. 187, no. 5, 2024, pp. 1076–1100. (CH4)

Elowitz, Michael B. "Noise in Genetic Circuits: Design Principles for Robustness." *Annual Review of Biophysics*, vol. 53, 2024, pp. 301–322. (CH5)

Endy, Drew, et al. "Foundry-Scale Synthetic Biology." *Nature Biotechnology*, vol. 42, 2024, pp. 721–735. (CH2)

Esvelt, Kevin M., and Neil J. Gemmell. "Gene Drives: Technology, Risks, and Governance." *Nature Reviews Genetics*, vol. 25, 2024, pp. 289–307. (CH10)

Fischer, Johannes, et al. "Metabolic Pathway Engineering for High-Value Chemicals." *Metabolic Engineering*, vol. 80, 2024, pp. 1–18. (CH7)

Gibson, Daniel G. "Genome Synthesis and the Future of Written Life." *Nature Communications*, vol. 15, 2024, article 4021. (CH2)

Gonzalez, Ramon, et al. "Chassis Engineering for Industrial Microbes." *Current Opinion in Biotechnology*, vol. 86, 2024, 103020. (CH7)

Greener, Joe G., et al. "Machine Learning for Genetic Circuit Design." *ACS Synthetic Biology*, vol. 13, no. 3, 2024, pp. 345–360. (CH5)

Hale, Christopher R., et al. "CRISPRi and CRISPRa for Programmable Gene Regulation." *Nature Reviews Methods Primers*, vol. 4, 2024, article 15. (CH4)

Hansen, Christina L., et al. "Microfluidic Platforms for DBTL in Synthetic Biology." *Lab on a Chip*, vol. 24, 2024, pp. 1012–1030. (CH5)

Hsu, Patrick D., et al. "Base Editing: Precision without Double-Strand Breaks." *Nature Reviews Genetics*, vol. 25, 2024, pp. 91–108. (CH4)

Jinek, Martin, et al. "Past, Present, and Future of CRISPR Genome Editing Technologies." *Cell*, vol. 187, no. 5, 2024, pp. 1076–1100. (CH4)

Jullien, Nicolas, et al. "Cell-Free Gene Expression Systems for Rapid Prototyping." *ACS Synthetic Biology*, vol. 13, no. 1, 2024, pp. 55–70. (CH9)

Khalil, Ahmad S., and Timothy K. Lu. "Synthetic Gene Networks in Living Cells." *Annual Review of Biomedical Engineering*, vol. 26, 2024, pp. 201–225. (CH5)

Kwon, Young-Jin, et al. "mRNA Therapeutics beyond Vaccines." *Nature Reviews Drug Discovery*, vol. 23, 2024, pp. 521–540. (CH6)

Liu, Chang, et al. "Directed Evolution in the Era of DNA Synthesis and Automation." *Nature Reviews Chemistry*, vol. 8, 2024, pp. 101–119. (CH7)

Liu, Ruixue, et al. "Precision Fermentation for Food Proteins." *Trends in Food Science & Technology*, vol. 142, 2024, pp. 1–15. (CH8)

Lynch, Michael D., et al. "Biomanufacturing at Scale: Lessons from Artemisinin and Beyond." *Nature Biotechnology*, vol. 42, 2024, pp. 801–816. (CH7)

Mali, Prashant, et al. "CRISPR-Based Gene Therapies: Clinical Pipeline 2024." *Nature Medicine*, vol. 30, 2024, pp. 901–918. (CH6)

Marraffini, Luciano A. "CRISPR Diagnostics in Global Health." *Annual Review of Virology*, vol. 11, 2024, pp. 311–332. (CH9)

Müller, Marik M., et al. "Genetic Circuits in Synthetic Biology: Broadening the Toolbox of Regulatory Devices." *Frontiers in Synthetic Biology*, vol. 3, 2025, article 1548572. (CH5)

Nielsen, Jens, and Jay D. Keasling. "Engineering Microbial Cell Factories for Sustainable Production." *Science*, vol. 383, 2024, eadk9102. (CH7)

O'Keefe, Caitlin, et al. "Cultivated Meat: Bioprocess Design and Scale-Up Challenges." *Current Opinion in Biotechnology*, vol. 87, 2024, 103045. (CH8)

Ostrov, Nili, et al. "Recoded Genomes and Virus-Resistant Chassis." *Nature*, vol. 626, 2024, pp. 601–615. (CH10)

Pacesa, Martin, et al. "CRISPR Genome Editing Technologies: A Panoramic View." *Cell*, vol. 187, no. 5, 2024, pp. 1076–1100. (CH4)

Peters, John M., et al. "Programmable Biosensors for Environmental Monitoring." *Environmental Science & Technology*, vol. 58, no. 4, 2024, pp. 2101–2115. (CH9)

Renda, Brian A., et al. "Kill Switches and Biocontainment Strategies for Engineered Organisms." *Nature Communications*, vol. 15, 2024, article 5120. (CH10)

Rogers, James K., et al. "Living Materials: Engineered Microbes for Structural Applications." *Nature Materials*, vol. 23, 2024, pp. 789–804. (CH7)

Schmidt, Markus, et al. "Ethics and Governance of Synthetic Biology 2024." *Science and Engineering Ethics*, vol. 30, 2024, article 18. (CH11)

Shetty, Reshma P., et al. "The iGEM Movement and the Standardization of Biological Parts." *Synthetic Biology Journal*, vol. 3, no. 2, 2024, pp. 55–72. (CH2)

Smolke, Christina D., et al. "RNA Devices and Logic for Therapeutic Gene Control." *Nature Reviews Drug Discovery*, vol. 23, 2024, pp. 601–620. (CH6)

Storch, Michael, et al. "DNA Data Storage: State of the Art and Future Prospects." *Nature Reviews Materials*, vol. 9, 2024, pp. 233–249. (CH12)

Tait-Burkard, Catherine, et al. "Gene Editing in Livestock and Crops: Regulatory and Ethical Frontiers." *Nature Food*, vol. 5, 2024, pp. 101–118. (CH8)

Tucker, Joseph L., et al. "Synthetic Biology for Carbon Capture and Utilization." *Joule*, vol. 8, no. 2, 2024, pp. 301–320. (CH10)

Voigt, Christopher A. "A Vision for the Synthetic Biology Stack." *Nature Biotechnology*, vol. 42, 2024, pp. 651–664. (CH1)

Weber, Wilfried, and Martin Fussenegger. "Smart Therapeutic Cells: Logic-Gated Gene Circuits in Patients." *Nature Reviews Immunology*, vol. 24, 2024, pp. 345–362. (CH6)

Wolinetz, Laura, and Francis S. Collins. "Dual-Use Research and Synthetic Biology Governance." *Science*, vol. 383, 2024, pp. 455–459. (CH11)

Yim, Hyun Uk, et al. "Engineered Microbes for Plastic Degradation." *Nature Chemical Biology*, vol. 20, 2024, pp. 611–623. (CH10)

Zhang, Feng, et al. "CRISPR-Based Tools for Transcriptional and Epigenetic Control." *Nature Reviews Molecular Cell Biology*, vol. 25, 2024, pp. 601–620. (CH4)

www.ingramcontent.com/pod-product-compliance
Lightning Source LLC
LaVergne TN
LVHW052028200926
848481LV00005B/1616